Planning a Garden

Planning a Garden

Edited by David Stevens

ORBIS PUBLISHING·LONDON

ACKNOWLEDGEMENTS

A–Z Collection   46–7, 64, 69, 96, 113, 126, 129, 130, 158,
   173, 174
B. Alfieri   173
Heather Angel   130
Brecht Einzig Ltd   27
Pat Brindley   27, 46, 58, 61, 74, 85, 87, 102–3, 112, 128,
   136, 137, 161, 162, 164, 165, 174
R. J. Corbin   47, 58, 124–5, 133
John K. B. Cowley   134
V. Finnis   121, 148
M. Fuller   30, 45, 48, 53
Brian Furner   136
Nancy Mary Goodall   146, 150
J. Hamilton   35, 37, 38, 132
Iris Hardwick Library   136–7, 139, 153
A. G. L. Hellyer   42–3, 44, 50
Institute of Geological Sciences   123, 152
Jarrold & Sons Ltd   40–1
Leslie Johns   58
Tania Midgley   147, 152
Kenneth Scowen   161
Harry Smith   44, 58, 65, 101, 122, 126–7, 128–9, 130, 135,
   136–7, 138, 139, 145, 147, 148, 149, 150, 157, 158, 161,
   162, 165, 168–70
Deborah Smith   160
David Stevens   73, 43, 45
R. Verey   102, 103, 104–5
Michael Warren   104, 107, 108, 109–11, 113, 131, 137,
   138, 139, 143–4, 145, 166

© Orbis Publishing Limited, London 1979
Reprinted in this edition 1982, 1984

Printed in Portugal by Resopal

ISBN: 0-85613-460-0

CONTENTS

INTRODUCTION

The number of books and publications on gardening and horticulture are legion. They deal with crops and cultivation, annuals, biannuals and herbaceous plants, shrubs, trees and lawns, as well as equipment, garden buildings and patios.

There is in fact so much material to read and assimilate that one can become not only bogged down but completely disheartened, and it is easy to see why so many gardens reflect this muddled thinking.

Although the individual subjects within the boundaries are covered in great detail there are very few books that really tell you how to either create a garden from scratch or how to sensibly modify an existing layout to suit very personal requirements.

The whole subject of design and 'designers' is a little taboo to most people; it smacks of fanciful ideas in glossy magazines. But really design is the basis of any layout, inside or outside the home, and can be summed up as the most practical solution to the problem in hand.

Although most people feel relatively happy when planning a kitchen or living-room, their ideas tend to dry up when they move outside. This is partly due to the fact that we tend to think of house and garden as two separate entities, one for living in, the other for everything else. If we think of the garden as an outside room, an extension of the home where each activity can fit into an overall pattern, things would not only work better but they would be more attractive and easier to maintain.

It is fair to say that as homes and gardens increase in number the latter, on average, become smaller. Subsequent demand on use of that space is therefore greater and the need to design it properly even more important. The most difficult thing is knowing where to begin.

We have already seen that danger lies in overcomplication; the golden rule is not to rush out and start right away. Whatever the problems, give them time to get into perspective and as an initial exercise try jotting your ideas down on paper, not as a plan at this stage but rather in the form of check-lists that indicate both what you want and what you have got.

As a general guide, you might include a terrace or patio, lawn, vegetables, shed, greenhouse, fruit, planting, room for swing and slide, room for ball games, a path for easy access and wheeled toys, sandpit, trees, pool, rockery, room for washing-line or rotary drier, dustbin store, solid fuel bunkers or oil tank, incinerator, compost and even hutches for pets. When your ideas dry up you'll probably find you have catered for most eventualities.

Once you know what you want, the next job is to try and incorporate all these ideas into some sort of logical order; but before you start on the design, you need to know something else – what you have in terms of existing features.

Many people, moving into a new house with a virgin plot of ground, would think they have very little, but in every case it will be worth making a scale-drawing of the garden and marking in everything that might affect the future layout. It is worth doing this on a piece of squared or graph paper, using a simple scale of a small square to each foot. Mark in the house and garage in relation to the boundaries, the position of doors and windows, the length of the boundaries themselves, any changes in level, existing shrubs, trees and other features, good views or bad, prevailing winds and, most important of all, the north point, or where the sun is in relation to the house.

Once all this information is to hand you can see not only what you want to put into the garden, you also see that the components themselves fall into two broad categories: the plants, lawn, hedges and trees, which can loosely be termed 'soft landscape', and the paths, paving, fences, walling, steps and other items that form the 'hard landscape'.

As with all living things, the bones or framework come first. These are the basis of the composition and in gardening terms, the designer must start with the hard landscape 'skeleton' and follow on with the softer filling-in of plant material.

It is fair to say that no two gardens are alike, for even if they might be of similar proportions they would have different aspects and be subject to different climatic conditions. Most important of all, they would belong to different people. Neither should a garden be 'copied' from this or any other book. By all means get ideas and see how materials can be used in unusual and interesting ways, but adapt these to your personal requirements and by so doing create something original and unique.

In this book we've taken as a basis the principle of hard and soft landscape. First we consider specific gardens and the materials from which they are built. Our patio garden relies heavily on hard surfacing and we look at its construction step by step. From here we move on to other surfaces, some unusual and some common, but all used sensibly so that both the material and the situation in which it is used is shown off to its best advantage.

Front gardens can be a headache; after all, first impressions count, but we do offer practical guidance. Town gardens, courtyard gardens, odd plots and problem plots, a garden for the disabled, and even roof gardens are covered in detail. And individual components such as gates, walls, fences, paths and screens are described, as is that most difficult but rewarding problem, the sloping site.

Here there is ample room for design. Have you considered, for instance, using railway sleepers or logs bedded into a bank for steps? We have, together with a great deal of other stimulating ideas.

From individual gardens we turn our attention to plants and planting – the soft landscape.

The planning of borders and island beds, together with the correct use of specific plant material is explained so that it can be used in a controlled rather than a haphazard manner, while the basic soil types are outlined, together with the species that thrive upon them. Just as there are rules governing the design and construction of a garden, so too are there guidelines to planting. Not only should plants provide colour and interest throughout the year but they must also act as screens to block bad views, give shelter from prevailing winds and form divisions within the garden itself. The mechanics of planting design are explained so that you can build up a framework of background plants that give stability to the composition and allow a second stage of filling-in with lighter, more colourful material.

Throughout the book, both in the section dealing with design and construction and those on planting, you can see that certain basic rules are underlined again and again. This does not mean that all gardens are similar. As we shall see, they are far from that, but it does mean that a successful garden is based on a well-tried formula that takes every relevant factor into account and moulds them to fit a particular requirement.

It is sensible to use an architectural theme close to the building, so that a brick terrace matches the materials used in the house. Exterior woodwork such as a pergola or overhead beams are painted to link with the colour of existing doors and windows. The layout of a terrace should match the house too and rectangles here, used in interesting interlocking patterns, will be far more successful than at a point farther down the garden. In fact the farther away from the house we get, the softer and looser the composition should become, thus providing a feeling of space and movement that diverts attention from rectangular boundaries and makes the garden appear larger than it really is.

Planting too can reflect this theme and strongly formed shapes such as yuccas, acanthus, euphorbias and phormium will reinforce a crisp architectural setting while softer, looser species create a feeling of depth and tranquility. Certain plants, such as conifers on a small scale and Lombardy poplars in the larger landscape, may act as punctuation marks and should be used carefully to highlight a carefully chosen position. Colour too, both in planting and individual features such as pots or seats, is important. A barrel full of brilliant flowers is fine close to the house but when placed at the bottom of the garden will draw the eye and foreshorten the space.

Not only should colour schemes be intelligently deployed but you also have to remember that flowering times vary. Soil types and the availability of sun and shade will determine what species can be grown.

This book is not a guide to a single subject or situation, but an introduction to the whole art of using the garden as an extension of the home. A garden can offer as much hard work and maintenance as you are prepared to put into it. It can be a full-time concern for the keen gardener or a place for recreation that all the family can use, with minimum upkeep. It can be a dining-room and playground, allotment and flower garden.

Most importantly the garden should serve you and not the reverse. This book helps you to do just that: once the rules are understood and the problem assessed, a most exciting project can be embarked upon.

David Stevens

DESIGN AND CONSTRUCTION

THE PATIO GARDEN

How would you like to transform an old back yard into a decorative patio garden? This scheme has been devised for those of you who feel the urge to 'do it yourself'. By following our instructions you will soon be able to enjoy your own handiwork.

Moving into a new home, especially in towns or cities, many people find themselves in possession of only a tiny garden, hardly big enough to encompass a patch of lawn or a flower bed, let alone a greenhouse, vegetable garden, or swimming pool. Such a garden is often called a patio. The word comes from Spain, where it means an inner courtyard, open to the sky, and conjures up visions of pools, fountains, and cool green ferns giving relief from the heat of the day.

In reality you are more likely to have inherited a grey concrete desert without even a flower tub in sight.

As awareness of the importance of outdoor living has increased, so has the potential of 'back yards', and the art of patio gardening has developed these concrete deserts into an extension of the home. We believe that no plot is too small, dark or dingy to be declared a hopeless case. With careful planning the most unpromising site can be turned into anything from a miniature jungle to a spacious outdoor room for all the family.

Our first patio design introduces you to some of the basic principles of successful patio gardening. We have taken an area measuring some 7 metres (23 feet) square and built a patio on two levels which not only adds visual interest but also provides built-in seating, and allows plenty of room for sunbathing and outdoor eating as well. We have introduced an interesting combination of textures and a wide variety of plants. The flooring, a mixture of bricks, wooden deck planks and paving stones, is hard-wearing and easy to clean, while most of the plants are conveniently planned for decorative containers.

The idea behind using containers is that they need not be permanently positioned, but can be moved around according to the season and which plants are looking their best. You can have shrubs, annuals alternating with seasonal bulbs, and anything else that happens to take your fancy.

We have added height to the whole design by means of a pergola. Covered with a quick-growing creeper, it provides privacy with its rooftop greenery, and underneath it there is a mini-woodland of shade-loving plants. The pergola itself is strong enough to support a child's swing. A weatherproof blackboard fixed to the wall also helps to keep the children entertained, while a chequerboard painted onto the paving will keep games-lovers amused.

Creating a feeling of light and spaciousness makes the patio seem much larger than its actual size. Clever use of mirrors, combined with a light-coloured paint on two or more walls, and 'false perspective' trellis work all help to achieve this effect.

As with any major undertaking, to create this patio requires careful initial planning and some hard work, but thereafter it is easy to care for and provides a welcoming environment for all members of the family. It is also a very flexible design, easy to adapt to suit your own particular needs.

To give you an idea of the correct sequence of work involved we have broken down the schedule into seven stages, but within this order you will, of course, undertake the work in your own time and at your own pace. It is not a rushed job to get behind you in a few weekends but a professionally-designed patio of which you and your family will be proud for years to come.

PATIO GROUND PLAN

1 brick-paving
2 timber-decking
3 pergola
4 mirrors
5 raised stone-paving

6 blackboard
7 planted area
8 two steps down
9 French windows
10 trellised wall

7 metres (23 feet) square

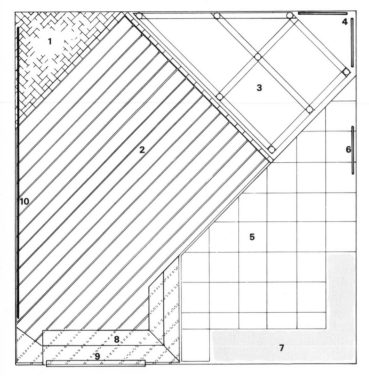

Main materials
(approximate quantities)
4 cu m (5 cu yd) of 20mm
($\frac{3}{4}$ in) all-in ballast, *for all
foundation concrete and base
for paving stones.*
1·5 cu m (2 cu yd) building sand,
*for brickwork and brick-paved
area base.*
twenty-four 50kg (1 cwt) bags
cement, *for concrete mortar mix.*
37 paving stones, 600mm sq
(2 ft sq).
1400 bricks, *for general brickwork and brick-paved area.*
5 circular slabs *for pergola area.*
100m (110 yd) planed timber
(preferably in 3m (10 ft) lengths,
250 × 25mm (10 × 1 in), *for
decking and steps.*
55m (60 yd) sawn timber, 75 ×
50mm (3 × 2 in), *for joists.*
8 lengths salt-glazed pipe,
600mm × 100mm dia (2 ft × 4 in
dia), *for pergola sockets.*

Additional items
plasticizer *for mortar mix.*
hard core.
50mm (2 in) × No. 10 brass
counter-sunk wood screws, *for
decking and steps.*
150mm (6 in) nails, *for pergola.*
8 rustic poles, 2·8m × approx.
100mm dia (9 ft × 4 in dia), *for
pergola uprights.*

6 pergola horizontal members,
approx. 100mm (4 in dia), as:
one 1·8m (6 ft); two 2·6 m (8 ft
6 in); one 2·8m (9 ft); one 3·4m
(11 ft); one 4m (13 ft)
one 2100 × 900mm (7 × 3 ft)
sheet of 12mm ($\frac{1}{2}$ in) marine
plywood, *for perspective trellis.*
8 sq m (9$\frac{1}{2}$ sq yd) trellis.
paint and/or wood preservative,
for trellis work.
2 mirrors, 1m sq (3 ft sq)
blackboard, 1m sq (3 ft sq)
wall fixing screws, wall plugs
and washers, *for mirrors and
blackboard.*

General tools
spade; fork: shovel; pick-axe;
heavy rake; wheelbarrow;
thumper; club hammer; brick
chisel; spirit level; two saw-
horses; timber staight-edge;
twenty 50mm (2 in) square
timber pegs; shuttering timber
(scaffold boards).

For bricklaying
trowel; brick line and pegs;
pointing tool; plywood (or
chipboard) spot board 600mm
sq (24 in sq); soft brush.

For woodworking
saw; hammer; chisel; screw-
driver; plane; drill and jig saw.

SCHEDULE OF WORK

Stage 1 SITE clearing of; topsoil to pergola area; repointing/repainting ext. walls; establishing datum level with pegs. MAIN RETAINING WALL marking out, excavating and laying foundations.
Stage 2 MAIN RETAINING WALL mixing mortar; bricklaying; building and pointing; drainage weep-holes.
Stage 3 SITE further levelling; TIMBER-DECKED AREA concrete raft: erecting timber shuttering; drainage holes, laying concrete; building retaining wall for decking.
Stage 4 SITE final levelling; backfilling planted area.
BRICK-PAVED AREA levelling site.
PERGOLA AREA sinking upright sockets; site preparation.
STONE-PAVED AREA site preparation; laying and cutting stones; pointing.
Stage 5 BRICK-PAVED AREA laying bricks.
TIMBER-DECKED AREA measuring; damp proof course; building sleeper wall.
Stage 6 TIMBER-DECKED AREA laying DPC, joists and decking; timber steps.
PERGOLA AREA erecting timbers.
Stage 7 Make PERSPECTIVE TRELLIS.
Fix MIRRORS, BLACKBOARD
Paint CHEQUERBOARD.

Planning
Although the constructional details we will be giving apply to this specific patio, the techniques involved can easily be adapted to suit different circumstances and a whole range of sites.

Our Patio Garden is designed around a natural slope in the ground, and the differing levels are arranged so as to minimize excavation work and avoid having to carry the excavated soil through the house. One important point to bear in mind early in the planning stage is the level of the house damp proof course (DPC). It is vital that any paved or planted areas are kept at least 15cm (6 in) below the DPC level.

Costing
Before starting, work out the quantities of materials you need so that you can estimate the total cost.

At this stage it is also as well to make a list of the various tools you will need to carry out all of the construction work so that everything is to hand and you aren't held up for a vital piece of equipment. A complete set of tools is essential if the work is to flow smoothly; you can rent some of the specialist ones from your local tool hire firm.

Material quantities
Calculating quantities and ordering of most materials, such as timber, paving stones and slabs and similar items, is quite straightforward, the measurements being taken direct from a scale drawing. Estimating quantities of ballast, sand, cement and bricks, however, can prove a little difficult for anyone unfamiliar with the measures and methods of calculation used in the trade. Estimates, in any case, are only approximate, and it is best to err on the generous side in order to avoid running out.

Ballast and sand are normally supplied by the cubic metre or yard so here you must estimate the total volume required for the different jobs involved. Take your measurements direct from the scale drawing.

Cement is supplied in 50kg (1 cwt) bags and you need approximately six bags per cubic metre of ballast for a foundation concrete mix, and about 12 bags per cubic metre of sand for mortar mixes.

Bricks are normally supplied in multiples of 100, with approximately 120 required per square metre of double skin brickwork, and 60 for single skin work.

Ordering and delivery of materials must tie in with the progress of the work.

BACKDROP TO THE PATIO

If the patio is very much an extension of the home, then the house can also be viewed as an extension of the patio. So it is worth making the house wall look as attractive as possible. Slapping on a cover-up coat of paint is not the answer, however, and this is where our do-it-yourself project starts: giving you the necessary detailed information to make a really good job of your exterior walls. Here and on page 16 we tell you how to complete Stage 1 of the work.

Before you start painting an exterior wall, make sure that it is clean and in good condition, or the new paint will flake off. It makes sense, in any case, to keep your house wall in good repair and weatherproof, because small cracks rapidly become large holes and damp will then find its way indoors with disastrous results.

The following list outlines items that should be attended to before you paint.

View of the patio house wall, showing the planted area in the raised paving

Efflorescence

This shows as powdery white patches on brickwork or plastered walls. It forms when water-soluble salts in the bricks permeate through to the surface and crystallize, and mostly occurs in new buildings that are still drying out. It may also be a sign of dampness, so check for possible causes before treating your wall.

Efflorescence should be removed before painting the wall. You can brush the patches with a stiff (not wire) brush, but for a more effective treatment paint on a fluid such as Efforless, that penetrates the bricks and neutralizes the salts.

Lime-leaching

Lime which has leached into the bricks from the mortar can look very similar to efflorescence. Remove these white stains with a proprietary solution such as Gostan.

Fungus and lichens

Green stains on the brickwork may be a sign of dampness and you should investigate the cause before treating the symptoms. Then clean the wall with a stiff-bristled brush, and apply a proprietary fungicide. If possible, treat the entire wall, as fungus spores could easily be concealed all over it.

Repointing

'Pointing' refers to the mortar between the bricks. If it is crumbling you must replace it or rain will penetrate the brickwork. Chip away the damaged mortar thoroughly, brush the wall to remove dust and loose particles and then apply the new mortar. On the next page you will find full details of how to go about this important job.

If only a small area is to be repaired, you may find it more convenient to buy a bag of ready-mixed mortar.

Broken or chipped bricks

Bricks may be damaged by external causes or may crumble from within. This can happen when water that has been absorbed by the porous brickwork freezes and then expands, causing the bricks to crack.

Remove the broken bricks and insert the replacements with fresh mortar. If

possible, match the new bricks to the existing brickwork. You can sometimes obtain old, weathered bricks from builders' merchants.

You can waterproof brick walls by treating them with a water-repellent to prevent the bricks freezing and cracking.

Damaged rendering

Rendered walls are coated with cement plaster. 'Roughcast' is a rendering in which small stones are mixed into the mortar. Rendering which has cracked or crumbled away to expose the brickwork can allow dampness to set in. Cover hairline cracks with a special masonry paint; open out larger cracks with a hammer and chisel so that you can spread new mortar in under the old rendering, and chip away crumbling edges of larger damaged patches. Bricks made visible by the damage may prove to have broken pointing, in which case you must repoint before repairing the rendering.

If the brickwork is very smooth, brush on a PVA bonding agent before applying new rendering. Mix your mortar as 1 part (by volume) cement, 3 parts sharp sand and 3 parts soft sand, 1 part hydrated lime or proprietary plasticizer. Apply this to the wall with a steel float in a layer about 13mm ($\frac{1}{2}$ in) thick. If the surface

lies below that of the surrounding rendering, score the new mortar deeply with a nail to provide a 'grip' for a second layer, and leave to dry for 24 hours. Once the second layer has been applied, the new patch should be slightly thicker than the old rendering. To achieve a smooth, flush finish draw a flat piece of wood across the patch to scrape off excess mortar.

Patching pebble-dash

This is a finish achieved by embedding small stones in rendering when it is still wet. To repair a 'bald' patch, renew the rendering and then throw pebbles against the fresh mortar with a small trowel. Place a piece of sacking under the working area to catch the pebbles that fall. Press the pebbles firmly into place with a length of flat board or a wooden float. If you are able to mix in some old pebbles that have fallen off the wall, they will help to disguise the repair.

Settlement and shrinkage cracks

Long, wide cracks in the walls are usually caused by movement of the ground beneath the house. You should obtain an expert opinion as to the extent of the problem before attempting any repairs. Only after that should you replace and

repair any damaged bricks and pointing, before embarking on other constructional work. Most new buildings are liable to some shrinkage, and zig-zag cracks may appear in a year or so, when they should be repaired.

Safety precautions

If using a lean-to ladder, tie the base firmly to a long peg hammered into the ground. If the ladder is resting on concrete, place something really heavy in front of the legs to prevent it slipping. The upper end must also be made secure by tying firmly to a good anchor point. If there is no safe point of attachment, then a screw-eye should be fixed to the wall, and the ladder attached to that. The eye can be left in position for future occasions. Be careful not to lean the ladder against a window or plastic guttering.

If much work is to be done above standing height, then a platform composed of a plank laid between a step-ladder and a hop-up is the safest and most time-saving way to work. For very tall jobs, two step-ladders with a plank between them may be needed.

Protect your eyes from flying chips of mortar by wearing goggles, and be sure that both your eyes and your skin are well protected when applying fungicides.

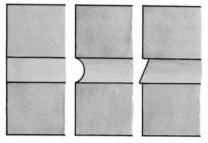

1 *Choose the type of pointing to give the best effect to your brickwork. Left: for flush pointing, surfaces of the joints are level with the bricks. Centre: for keyed pointing, surfaces of the joints are pressed in to give a slightly concave finish. Right: for weathered pointing, sloped surface allows rainwater to run off*

5 *Weathered pointing: for vertical joint press in 3mm ($\frac{1}{8}$ in) at left side of joint, slope mortar up to right, finishing flush with right-hand brick. For horizontal joint press mortar in 3mm ($\frac{1}{8}$ in) at top edge and slope out till flush with lower brick. Hold straight-edge parallel to joint and trim mortar neatly with a frenchman*

2 *Rake out damaged mortar with chisel and hammer. Brush away loose mortar and dust. Dampen bricks*

6 *Flush pointing: when the mortar is nearly dry, rub joints with a piece of clean sacking until almost smooth*

3 *Fill vertical joints with mortar, then press it well in with trowel. Catch excess mortar on your hawk (board)*

7 *Flush pointing: when mortar is completely dry, scrape over surface of joints with piece of wood until smooth*

4 *For keyed pointing, run curved side of bent pipe along joint for indented finish. Trim off excess mortar. Smooth with piece of wood to make watertight*

8 *After repointing is completed, brush over all joints with soft hand brush when mortar has hardened, to give a clean-looking surface*

REPOINTING

If your exterior walls have gaps between the bricks where mortar used to be, then it is time you repointed them. Dampness and worse, such as bugs, soon find their way into damaged brickwork.

General points

Start each stage of the job at the top of the wall and work downwards.

Chip away all damaged pointing to a depth of about 13mm ($\frac{1}{2}$ in) and brush the wall free of dust and chippings.

If repointing a large area, complete about 1 sq m (1 sq yd) at a time.

Do the vertical joints first and then the horizontal ones.

Be sure to match the new pointing to the style of the original joints.

The life of mortar is only about two hours, so mix in small quantities.

Always dampen any surface to which mortar is to be applied.

To avoid splashes of mortar, cover as much of the ground and wall as possible with polythene sheeting propped against the wall with wooden battens. When dry, scrape off any mortar splashes on bricks with a clean trowel.

Making the mortar

The mortar used consists of 1 part cement, 6 parts soft sand and 1 part hydrated lime or plasticizer. For mending small patches, use cup measure rather than buckets. The lime or plasticizer helps to make the mortar more workable and minimizes shrinking or cracking.

Mix the dry ingredients thoroughly on a piece of board. Add water, a very little at a time, turning the mix constantly.

Tools for repointing

You will need a pointed cold chisel and a club hammer; a pointing trowel and a hawk; a stiff-bristled brush for pre-cleaning and a soft brush for finishing; and a frenchman and a straight-edge for trimming off surplus mortar.

The straight-edge is a piece of wood with a square of wood or hardboard attached to each end to hold it slightly away from the wall and allow excess mortar to fall cleanly. You can make up a frenchman from an old table knife by bending about 2·5cm (1 in) of the tip of the blade at right-angles to the main blade.

To give flush pointing a good finish, you will need an old piece of sacking and a small, flat piece of wood. For keyed pointing you will also need a curved piece of metal such as a bent strip of narrow piping (see far left).

PAINTING

Painting, or repainting, outside walls is often thought of as a job for experts. But by making careful preparations, choosing the right tools and buying paint suitable for exterior work, the job can be straight-forward and the results rewarding.

General points

Paint will not stay on loose, dusty or dirty surfaces, so you must first give the wall a thorough brushing to ensure a solid, clean surface.

Where the surface is generally crumbly you should apply a purpose-made primer/sealer as an undercoat.

If lichen, moss or other plant growth is present then the area must be treated with a suitable fungicide before painting. So paint when the air (and the wall) is warm and dry, and, ideally, when rain is not expected for a few days.

Always start painting at the top of the wall and work downwards.

When working from a ladder, have the paint in a paint-kettle, which can then be hung safely from the ladder by an S-hook. Never put a paint pot or a roller tray on a gutter or windowsill. Secure the top of the ladder to the wall with a strong hook and tie.

Protect the ground and all projecting surfaces with polythene sheeting.

Tools for painting

It pays to buy good quality brushes as they last longer, hold more paint and shed fewer bristles. New brushes always shed some bristles, so break them in on undercoats. You will need a fairly large brush: a good size is 100mm (4 in). Also useful are a cutting-in brush (for straight-edge work) and a crevice brush with a flexible metal handle (for painting behind pipes). Where a rendered or reasonably flat wall surface is to be painted then you can use a roller; a sheepskin one is best.

Cleaning painting tools

First lay the brushes on several layers of newspaper, and with the back of a knife scrape off as much paint as possible from all four sides.

Oil-based paints should be cleaned off with white spirit and brushes washed in warm, soapy water and rinsed. For storing overnight, suspend brushes in water and then dry with paper or rags before using again.

Emulsion paint should be washed off in cold water before it hardens.

Rollers and roller trays should be cleaned with white spirit or warm soapy water, according to paint type.

1 Paint rollers should be well soaked in paint but not dripping with it
2 Hang your paint-kettle from an S-hook
3 General-purpose 100mm (4 in) brush, cutting-in, and crevice, brushes
4 Scrape paint off before washing brush

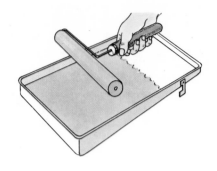

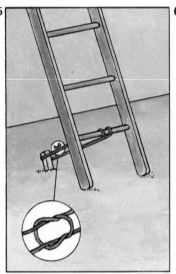

5 Anchor ladder safely at base, using a reef knot on rope ties
6 Pad ladder tops with rags to stop them marking new paintwork, and tie to a hook below the guttering if possible
7 To store oil-based paint brushes over-night, push a nail or stick through a hole drilled in the brush handle and suspend in a jar of water. Brush must not touch bottom of jar
8 A simple platform for working just above head-height is made by laying a plank between step-ladder and hop-up

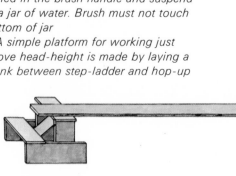

LAYING PATIO FOUNDATIONS: MIXING MORTAR AND BRICKLAYING

After getting the house brickwork and boundary walls in good shape it is time to start preparing the foundations for the raised, paved area.

Although the instructions apply specifically to our patio design, you can easily adapt them to suit your own circumstances. In this Patio Garden we will repeat the essential diagrams so that you can work at your own pace from the seven stages as set out in our Schedule of Work on page 11 without having to turn back for reference.

If you don't feel able to tackle all the work involved yourself, ask a more experienced friend to come and help you with the job.

Farther on we continue with Stages 3 and 4 of the Schedule of Work—preparing for the timber decking and laying the paving stones.

When carrying out work of this type it is essential to undertake the various jobs involved in an organized way so as to avoid unnecessary shifting of materials and to allow the work to proceed smoothly.

SCHEDULE OF WORK Stage 1

After you have completed any necessary repointing of the brickwork and painting of the exterior walls, you must clear the site of all unwanted vegetation and roughly level it. Remove the topsoil from the areas to be excavated and deposit it in the pergola area, for re-use in the plantings there. This not only saves having to import topsoil at a later date and carry it through the house, but also uses up the unwanted soil from the other areas.

Before any excavation work is started you must establish a 'datum' to which all other levels can be quickly related. Normally for this type of work the datum should be located at the highest level and in the case of our Patio Garden this would be at the finished level of the paved area adjacent to the house. Any paved or planted areas must be kept at least 15cm (6 in) below the house damp proof course (DPC) level.

To establish the datum, first excavate a small area adjacent to the house wall and with a base about 40cm (15 in) below the house DPC level. Now hammer a wooden peg into the ground so that the top is 15cm (6 in) lower than the DPC (see raised area diagram).

Main retaining wall

Using timber pegs and the brick line of the house wall, mark the boundary of the raised, paved area. A brick retaining wall must be built at this line in order to support the paving slabs and to retain safely the trapped earth (see the section plan diagram). A wall of this type is normally reckoned to retain a height of roughly three times its thickness. So for the wall specified, a 22·5cm (9 in) thickness, i.e. two bricks, is necessary. To be stable the wall must sit on a firm concrete foundation as illustrated in the section plan and raised area diagrams.

Retaining wall foundation

To establish the depth of the foundation trench, dig away some earth immediately below the marked border line. Using the original datum peg as a reference for the level, hammer a second peg about 60cm

Ground plan, drawn to scale, is an essential reference while you work on the patio site

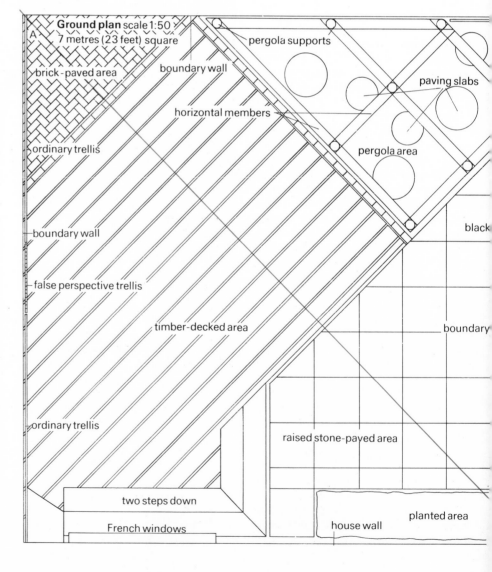

Ground plan scale 1:50
7 metres (23 feet) square
brick-paved area
boundary wall
pergola supports
paving slabs
horizontal members
ordinary trellis
pergola area
boundary wall
black
false perspective trellis
timber-decked area
boundary
ordinary trellis
raised stone-paved area
two steps down
planted area
French windows
house wall

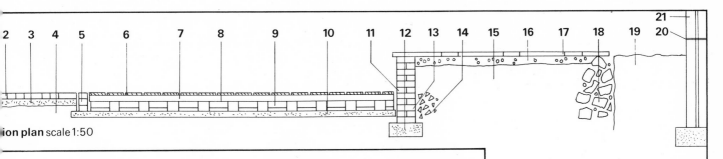

ion plan scale 1:50

(24 in) inside the paved area confine and level off, using the timber straight-edge and spirit level (as shown in the raised area diagram).

With the straight-edge laid on top of the two pegs, some measure can be gained of the excavation necessary to complete the wall foundation trench.

Next dig the trench and hammer in pegs to the finished concrete level (raised area diagram). Pile up the subsoil as you remove it ready for back-filling after the wall has been completed. With the trench neatly finished pour in concrete and level it to the tops of the wooden pegs.

Concrete mix

A suitable mix for this purpose is 1 part cement to 4·5 parts 20mm ($\frac{3}{4}$ in) all-in ballast. Mix dry ingredients first on a clean surface and then add sufficient water to produce a stiff mix. This must be poured into the foundation trench and carefully tamped level with the peg tops. Take care at this stage to produce a neat, flat surface as this will do much to simplify subsequent bricklaying.

SCHEDULE OF WORK Stage 2

For a wall that is subject to virtually constant dampness from the retained earth, a hard type of brick will prove more durable than a soft or 'common' type. Similarly, hard bricks will also be required for the brick-paved corner in the patio. It is worth spending some time finding the best type of brick available.

Mortar for bricklaying

Bricks are laid using a mortar mix of 3 parts soft sand to 1 part cement. Adding a plasticizer will make the mix more workable as well as minimizing subsequent shrinkage or cracking.

Mix the dry ingredients first on a clean surface and then add the water and plasticizer to produce a fairly stiff, but workable, mix. Transfer 2–3 shovels of mortar to your spot board which should be positioned near the work.

Building the main retaining wall

The art of bricklaying is something that can only be acquired with practice, but a relatively low wall of this type should be within the scope of most people provided the work is tackled in the order shown. Be sure to use the spirit level constantly to check that you are building the wall absolutely vertical.

Using the timber straight-edge as a guide, lay a line of bricks along the complete length of the wall. Next build up the ends and then the angled corner. Use a length of timber, marked with the brick courses and mortar joints, as a gauge to ensure that the building of the three columns proceeds accurately.

Key
1 boundary wall 2 brick paving
3 sand/cement base 4 subsoil/hardcore
5 retaining wall 6 timber decking
7 75mm x 50mm (3in x 2in) joist
8 DPC between bricks and timber
9 brick sleeper wall 10 concrete raft
11 main retaining wall
12 concrete foundation
13 drainage weep-holes 14 hardcore infill
15 subsoil/hardcore 16 ballast infill
17 paving stones 18 loose-laid rubble wall
19 topsoil (planted area) 20 DPC 21 house wall

Once this part of the work has been completed, 'filling in' is simply a matter of stretching the brick line to the courses of bricks and progressively building upward, one course at a time. The mortar joints, or pointing, should be finished as described on page 14.

Drainage weep-holes

To prevent a possible build-up of water behind the retaining wall, leave weep-holes in the course of bricks immediately above the concrete raft level for the timber decking (see section plan). To do this, simply omit the vertical mortar joint at about 70cm (27 in) intervals as the bricks are laid.

Raised area diagram reference for Stage 1

HARDCORE AND BALLAST

Hardcore consists of broken-up pieces of brick and other building materials. Quality and size of particles varies, but it is essential to get hardcore that is composed mainly of solid material, otherwise it will gradually break down and be detrimental to the foundations.

Ideally you should obtain brick hardcore that is free from foreign matter. You can buy it from builders or break up bricks yourself.

Ballast (or aggregate) adds bulk and strength to concrete. It consists of fine and coarse sand and small pebbles in different sizes, according to the job requirement.

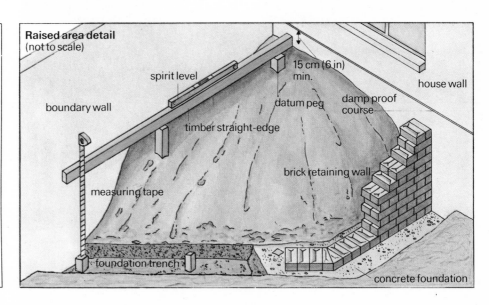

Raised area detail (not to scale)

spirit level
15 cm (6 in) min.
house wall
boundary wall
datum peg
damp proof course
timber straight-edge
brick retaining wall
measuring tape
foundation trench
concrete foundation

MIXING MORTAR

To mix by hand: if necessary, measure out cement in a bucket, shaking it well down and scraping it off level. Thoroughly mix cement with sand, make a well in the middle of the heap and pour in water (and plasticizer if used), until the mix is fairly stiff but still workable (right).

Shovel the dry ingredients into the centre to absorb the water and turn the heap to obtain an even, moist mixture. Add more water if required, but don't over-do it and take care not to let the walls fall in.

Then test by ridging with a shovel to leave clear cut marks (far right, above). Too much, or too little, water will not leave distinct ridges, so correct the water quantity now.

Cut off a slice of mortar with your trowel, and shape the back to a curve, using a sawing action (right), before picking it up. To lift a full load of mortar at a time, sweep your trowel underneath the slice, from the back, to give a good, sausage-like portion (far right).

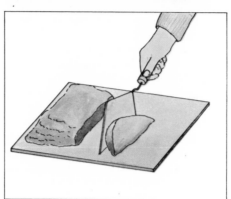
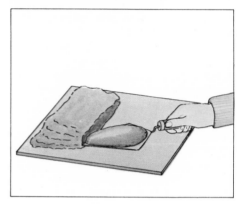

BRICKLAYING

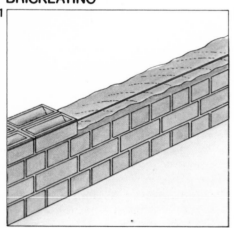

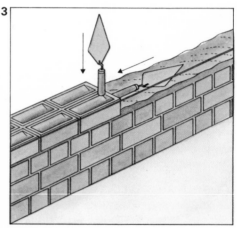

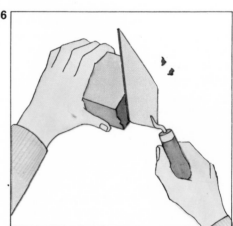

Transfer a few shovels of mortar to a spot board. Roll off a sausage of mortar mix onto the row of bricks in one smooth action by pulling the trowel back towards you. **1** Then smooth this mortar layer with the point of the trowel to form a bed of about 10mm ($\frac{3}{8}$ in) deep.

2 Before laying a brick 'butter' the end forming an upright joint with a sausage of mortar.

3 Tap brick into position horizontally and vertically with the trowel handle.

4 Check horizontal and vertical levels with a spirit level.

5 Cut bricks by marking a line then, on a firm surface, hold a chisel in position and strike a hard blow with a club hammer.

6 Clean rough edges with edge of trowel.

DECKING AND PAVING THE PATIO

You are now in the thick of making your own patio and for Stages 3 and 4 of the Schedule of Work you must check with the ground plan illustrated to scale on page 16.

SCHEDULE OF WORK Stage 3

With the main wall completed, you can proceed with further levelling and re-shaping of the site by piling the surplus subsoil from the lower level into the higher level. Take care to see that no pressure is applied to this main retaining wall until the mortar has set solidly. Now you should be ready to prepare the timber-decked area.

The ground plan and general detail diagram illustrate the layout of the timber decking. For this you must make a concrete raft foundation to which the timber structure will be laid.

Preparing for the raft foundation

The first stage of the work involves re-moving the topsoil to the pergola area. Once this has been accomplished, and fairly firm subsoil exposed, you can begin work adjusting the whole area to the necessary level. Lay straight-edge across the two previously positioned high-level datum pegs so that it overhangs the re-taining wall. Now measure vertically down to the lower level, using the spirit level as a guide, as shown in the raised area diagram (see page 17). Hammer in a supplementary datum peg to the fin-ished top level of the concrete raft. You can then carry out further levelling using the straight-edge and spirit level for a regular surface over all the raft site.

Where the excavation work has ex-posed reasonably firm subsoil, then the concrete may be laid directly onto this. However, where topsoil removal has re-duced the level below that required, the difference must be made up with clean, broken brick, stones or similar 'hard-core' material.

The concrete raft must be approxi-mately 30cm (12 in) oversize to the timber decking along the pergola and brick-paved edges. This is to provide a foundation for the retaining walls that are necessary to cope with the difference

Use a scaffolding board, first across, then along the raft concrete, on the top surface of the shuttering timbers

in levels at these junctions (see general detail diagram).

Laying the shuttering

Concrete shuttering, or formwork, con-sists of planks of timber laid to the edges of the area to be concreted. This forms an edge to which the top of the concrete can easily be levelled and also contains, and provides, a clean edge to the work in hand.

Timber for shuttering must be solid: scaffolding boards are ideal. With the aid of the spirit level and straight-edge, lay the top edge of the boards flush to the top of the supplementary datum peg. Hammer supporting timber pegs into the outside edge of the shuttering so that it does not move under the pressure of the poured concrete.

Drainage holes

The raft foundation will be surrounded by walls when the work is completed and for this reason drainage holes must be left through the concrete at about 1m (3 ft 3 in) centres. To do this, lay blocks of wood in the area prior to pouring the concrete, and then remove them before the concrete finally sets.

Where the subsoil consists of heavy clay and is not self-draining, it may be necessary to excavate a soakaway pit to ensure adequate drainage.

This would normally mean digging a 60cm (24 in) cube-shaped hole and filling it with hardcore under one main drain-age hole. It would also be necessary to slope the concrete surface slightly to-wards the drainage point.

Pouring the raft concrete

A suitable mix for the raft concrete is 1 part cement to 4·5 parts 20mm ($\frac{3}{4}$ in) all-in ballast. Mix the dry ingredients first on a clean surface and then add sufficient water to produce a stiff mix. After pour-ing, tamp and level the concrete ready for the next stage of the work. Tamping and levelling can be carried out with a scaffolding board used on edge along the top surface of the shuttering (see below).

Decked area retaining walls

Next build brick retaining walls to the edge of the concrete raft (see the section plan and general detail diagram). As the height of this wall is only 22·5cm (9 in), a single skin wall will prove adequate.

Do the bricklaying by the same method described for the main retaining wall for the raised area on page 17, the only difference being in the bond used, which you can see illustrated in the general detail diagram.

SCHEDULE OF WORK Stage 4

With all the retaining walls built and dry, you can proceed with the final back-filling and levelling work. Some broken brick or other hardcore must be laid at the inside base of the main retaining wall (see section plan), to allow free drainage through the weep-holes. Then use well-compacted hardcore and excavated sub-soil to fill the main raised area. The division between paved and planted area is built up as necessary, using loosely-laid brick or stone as back-filling proceeds. The planted area should also be back-filled with topsoil.

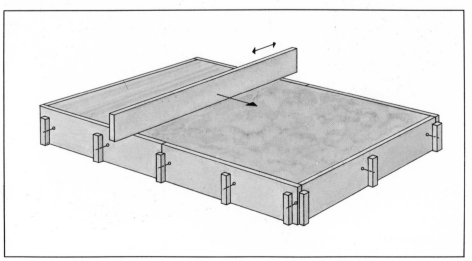

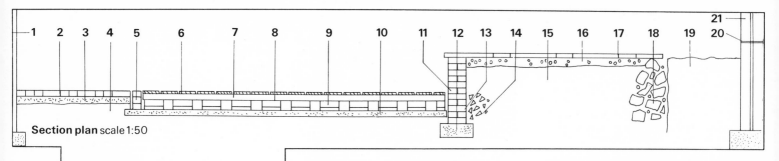

Section plan scale 1:50

Key
1 boundary wall **2** brick paving
3 sand/cement base **4** subsoil/hardcore
5 retaining wall **6** timber decking
7 75mm x 50mm (3in x 2in) joist
8 DPC between bricks and timber
9 brick sleeper wall **10** concrete raft
11 main retaining wall
12 concrete foundation
13 drainage weep-holes **14** hardcore infill
15 subsoil/hardcore **16** ballast infill
17 paving stones **18** loose-laid rubble wall
19 topsoil (planted area) **20** DPC **21** house wall

Levelling the brick-paved area
This area must be levelled in a similar way, with hardcore and subsoil being well compacted as a foundation for paving. Be sure to include pockets of subsoil as work proceeds, ready for subsequent planting of trees and shrubs. We have allowed for a *Magnolia grandiflora* to grow out of such a pocket against the trellised wall. Otherwise you must confine your plantings to tubs.

Preparing for the pergola
The first task here is to provide sockets for the rustic timber uprights. For this you should use 600mm (24 in) lengths of 100mm (4 in) diameter salt-glazed soil pipe. Position these in the ground (as shown in the general detail diagram); set them upright, using a post and the spirit level as a guide.

The main pergola area consists of topsoil that will support the woodland and other shade-loving plants to be planted here. Circular paving slabs give easy access, and to make a foundation for these, lay subsoil and ballast in the appropriate spots as you carry out the back-filling with topsoil.

Laying the raised area paving
As with bricklaying, the skill of laying paving stones can only be finally achieved through practice. However, by taking extra care and frequently using the spirit level and string guide, the beginner can produce a neat job.

Prepare the ground (see next page),

noting that the finished level of the ballast must be flush with the top of the main retaining wall (see general detail diagram).

Before starting to lay the paving stones, carefully set out the pattern to which the stones will be laid so as to avoid the use of small pieces of cut stone. The ground plan illustrates this point, where the cut stones along the retaining wall edge are all kept to a reasonable size.

Using the brick line and pegs, establish a line at right-angles to the planted area edge and as parallel as possible to the adjoining boundary wall. The line must be one paving stone width plus 2·5cm (1 in) maximum from the wall and positioned to represent the finished paving level, which should of course be flush with the top of the original datum peg.

Lay the first line of stones to the string line and then work backwards over the whole area until all the whole stones have been laid checking levels as you go.

Refer to the general detail diagram (below) and section plan (above) at all stages

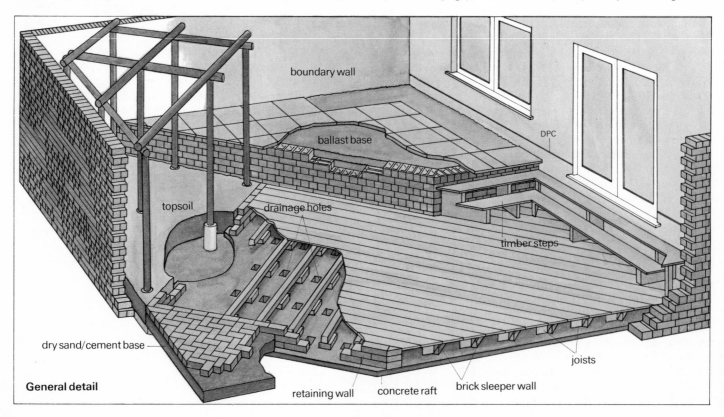

General detail

LAYING PAVING STONES

Having chosen your type of paving, estimated the quantity of stones needed and arranged for them to be delivered, it is time to prepare the ground.

If necessary, remove soil to a depth of 7–10cm (3–4 in) below the final required level. Then roll or tamp in a 5cm (2 in) layer of ballast. On springy or spongy soil use a 5cm layer of hardcore topped with sand. Check with a spirit level to ensure that the finished surface of your foundation is flat and accurate in all directions. Extra care taken at this stage will do much to simplify subsequent paving work.

You will need to mark out the area for paving with string, and then set out the pattern of your stones in such a way as to avoid having to use small, cut pieces. The stone supplier may be able to supply stones according to your specifications. Sizes and shapes for the cut stones should be taken direct from the plan of your paved area. To cut the stones yourself, follow the instructions below and practise on a spare bit of paving.

1 Mark out the edge of the first row with a string line. Each paving stone is then set on five blobs of a stiff 3 to 1 sand/cement mortar mix (that is, four blobs set just in from each corner and one in the centre).

2 To allow 9mm ($\frac{3}{8}$ in) gap between

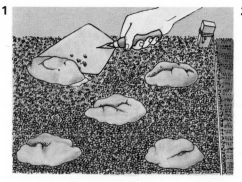
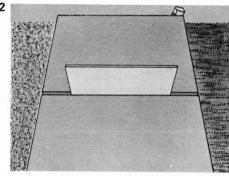
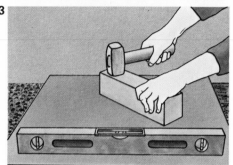
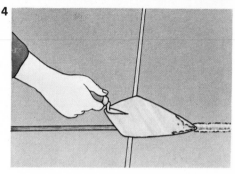

stones for final pointing, you need to use pieces of chipboard or plywood as temporary spacers.

3 Then tap each stone level, using a club hammer over a block of wood, until it lies level with its neighbours and no longer rocks on the foundation. With a trowel, cut away any surplus cement that may be squeezed out.

Always work backwards from your

first row of paving, and refer frequently to your spirit level and string guide during laying so as to maintain a flat and even surface.

4 About a week after laying the paving you will need to point the spaces between the stones. For this, use the same 3 to 1 part sand/cement mortar mix and pack it into the joints, smoothing it with a trowel to slightly below level of stones.

CUTTING PAVING STONES

While it is possible to cut the stones by using a club hammer and bolster (or brick chisel), a far more satisfactory method is to hire a purpose-made power cutter from a tool hire firm. However, if you decide to do-it-yourself, it is worth taking your time to achieve a neat job.

1 Mark your cutting line, with a chalk or even a soft pencil, across both faces and edges of the stone.

Place the stone to be cut on a bed of soft soil and press it firmly down so that it will remain steady while you are chiselling.

2 Using a club hammer and bolster, cut a shallow scratch, about 2mm ($\frac{1}{16}$ in) deep, as evenly and straight as possible. At the end of your cutting line, chisel across the thickness of the stone. Then turn the stone over carefully and chisel across the second face.

3 Place a block of wood at one end of the scratch and strike it firmly with the club hammer. Repeat the process along the length of the scratch. You should hear the ringing tone turn to a dull thud.

4 Clean off any uneven edges with the bolster to obtain a neat join.

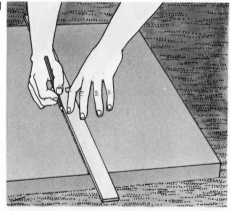
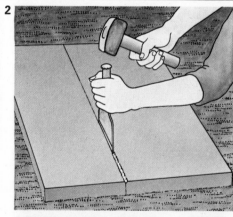
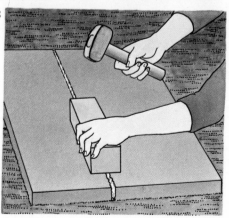
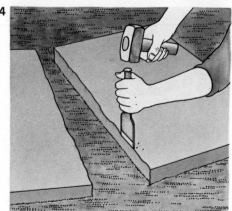

FINAL STAGES IN THE PATIO GARDEN

Following our Patio Garden design you will have learned how to do many things yourself – from preparing foundations, laying a damp proof course and building brick walls, to the surface work of laying stone or brick paving and timber decking, as well as repointing and painting old brickwork.

After the building work comes the pleasure of choosing what plants to grow where, the right containers for them, and how to plant the deep bed in the raised, paved area. These details are given along with other garden designs later in the book.

SCHEDULE OF WORK Stage 5

When you have successfully completed the first four stages of work you will be ready to lay the decorative brick paving in the far left corner, opposite the French windows.

Laying the brick-paved area

For this brick paving a slightly different laying technique is employed from that for the stone-paved area we described earlier.

Here you should lay a 5cm (2 in) thick bed of a very stiff 5 to 1 sand/cement mix and carefully level it so that when the bricks are laid in position and gently tapped, the surface will become flush to the adjacent 11–12cm (4½ in) thick retaining wall.

You can obtain the right stiff mix by adding just sufficient water to produce a crumbly texture. Use a string line in conjunction with the spirit level to help you make a neat job of it. The dry sand/cement bed should be lightly dampened as work proceeds, using a watering can with a sprinkler rose.

Leave a 9mm (⅜ in) pointing gap between all the bricks and fill this with a 3 to 1 mortar mix after you have completed all the paving. Lay all the full-sized bricks first, before you insert any necessary cut pieces. You can cut the bricks to the required size with a club hammer and brick chisel. (You can follow the same laying technique if you wish to use a broken stone paving.)

Timber for decking and joists

An ideal timber for this purpose is Western red cedar, but if this type is too costly or not readily available, you should consult your local timber merchant as to the best alternative available. With some types of timber the supplier may suggest pre-impregnation with a preservative.

The 250×25mm (10×1 in) decking is fitted to 75×50mm (3×2 in) joists, which

Fix trellis either side of your false perspective arched pathway, and paint to choice, or protect with preservative

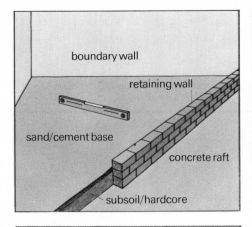

For brick paving: (top) level the sand/ cement base; (top right) keep the bed lightly dampened as you lay the bricks;

(above left) if gently tapped, the laid bricks become flush to retaining wall; (above) point the gaps between bricks

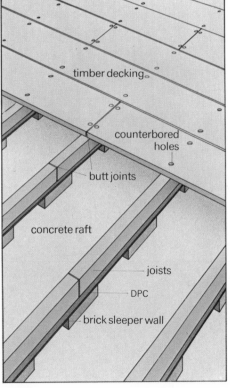

For timber decking: fit timber to joists supported on brick sleeper wall, with DPC between timber and bricks. Fill counter-sunk screw-holes with plugs

in turn are supported on a brick 'sleeper' wall with a damp proof course between brick and timber. The joists must be set at 40cm (16 in) centres and the planks of the decking laid with 9mm ($\frac{3}{8}$ in) gaps between each to allow surface water to run through (see ground and section plans and general detail diagram). Take care with all the timber work to ensure that the timber never comes into direct contact with any concrete or masonry.

Building the sleeper wall

Set one brick in a corner accurately to the sleeper wall height and then use this as a datum to transfer the levels, through the straight-edge and spirit level, to a second brick positioned at the far end of this first sleeper wall. You can then stretch a string line to the bricks to lay the remainder of the wall accurately. The space between bricks should be about 15cm (6 in); see section plan. Build the balance of sleeper walls the same way.

Note For Patio ground plan, see page 16, for section plan, pages 17 and 20, and general detail diagram, page 20.

SCHEDULE OF WORK Stage 6

Having fitted the decking to the joists, now follow the correct sequence of work.

Laying the decking

After the mortar has set, lay a strip of DPC material on top of the wall before laying the joists in position. Then fix the decking to the joists, using rust-proofed screws (ideally brass ones), counter-sunk below the surface. Fill the holes with a matching timber plug.

Timber for steps

To give access from the house down to the timber decking and also up to the raised paved area, you will need steps. Build these up from timber left over from decking (see general detail diagram).

Erecting the pergola

Cut the vertical rustic poles, all about 100mm (4 in) in diameter, to a 2·8m length (9 ft) and then drop them into the previously prepared sockets (see Stage 4 on page 20). Cut the three horizontal under members to length and fit them to the tops of the vertical members by nailing through. Then fix the second horizontal layer (see general detail diagram).

SCHEDULE OF WORK Stage 7

No matter how small a patio, a trellis like this one, designed to give the illusion of depth, looks effective. We fitted ours to the left-hand boundary wall.

False perspective trellis work

This is quite simple to carry out if you follow our grid pattern. First of all, lightly pencil 10cm (4 in) squares onto a sheet of 12mm (½ in) thick marine plywood. You can then 'transfer' the design to the plywood panel by reference to the grid pattern. Cutting is best carried out using either a self-powered or drill jig saw attachment. After cutting, smooth all edges by sanding before painting with one coat of primer, two undercoats and one top coat of oil paint.

This false perspective trellis is flanked on both sides by the more conventional rectangular trellis which you buy ready-made. You can paint this any colour to suit your scheme, or leave it natural and protect it with wood preservative.

To fix all the trellis work to the brick walls, use conventional plastic wall plugs and screws. In order to prevent contact between the trellis timber and wall brickwork (as this provides a point where early rotting and staining may occur) use 100mm (4 in) long fixing screws with 35mm (1½ in) long plastic tube spacers fitted over the screw shank between the trellis and wall.

Fixing the mirrors and blackboard

Reflections from the two square mirrors fitted to the boundary walls under the pergola (see ground plan) add an air of mystery to the patio. Be sure to get the waterproof-backed type and fit them to the walls with standard-type plastic wall fixing plugs and brass screws through holes pre-drilled in the mirrors. The holes for the screws must be loosely-sized and a thick rubber washer fitted to the screw shank between mirror and wall to allow for expansion and contraction of the glass during extremes of temperature.

For the children's benefit it is well worth making an outdoor blackboard. Cut this yourself from a sheet of waterproof plywood and treat it with a special blackboard paint (and renew this as necessary). Fix it to the wall near to the main paved area (see ground plan) in the same way as the mirrors.

Painting the chequerboard

You can paint any pattern you like on the raised paving, but we thought a simple chequerboard was useful for the games enthusiasts and decorative in its own right. The area must be completely dust-free and lightly dampened before you start applying an emulsion paint.

Use grid to transfer your perspective pattern to marine plywood. You can add mirror glass panels here to good effect

False perspective trellis

12mm (½ in) marine plywood

210cm (7 ft)

10cm (4 in) squares

90cm (3 ft)

GRAVEL SURFACING

Gravel can be used anywhere, but looks best when close to buildings; less formal than paving, though more severe than grass, it acts as a visual link between the two. It is useful around plantings and the base of trees as it allows the roots to breathe and absorb water.

When laying gravel, the various stages of preparation are very important, especially in driveways where heavy traffic can quickly cause havoc with a badly-executed job.

Preparation and laying
For the best results, really thorough consolidation is necessary at each juncture and, where space permits, you can hire a mechanical 'vibrating' roller and this will give ideal results in the minimum time. In cramped areas, or paths, a 500–750kg (10–15 cwt) hand roller may be all that is practical. Therefore it makes sense to facilitate rolling by keeping the shapes of gravel areas simple.

If you are thinking of using gravel for a drive, you will find that a 'sub base' is normally needed. This will have been carried out by a combination of the builders and traffic over the years on a developed site. When you are operating on virgin ground, it would be wise to call in a contractor to do at least the basic soil-shifting and levelling.

Assuming that the sub base is sound, continue with the main stages of construction. First of all, clean the surface thoroughly, grubbing out all vegetation, moss and weeds, and filling any pot-holes with rammed hardcore.

Lay a base of hardcore, crushed stone

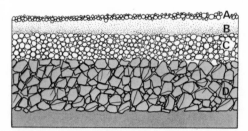

*Cross-section of gravel **A**, laid on 2·5cm (1 in) layer of hoggin **B**, and 5cm (2 in) layer of coarse gravel **C**, over hardcore **D***

or clinker, and roll it to a finished thickness of 10cm (4 in). Then put down a layer of coarse gravel, small enough to pass through a 5cm (2 in) screen, and roll it to a finished thickness of 5cm (2 in). Roll on a 2·5cm (1 in) covering of fine gravel mixed with hoggin as a binder. 'Hoggin' is a technical term used by contractors and is simply a clay, usually from the same pit as the gravel, that seals

and binds the surface together. Wet it just enough to achieve an even spread; if too wet, it will clog rollers and tools, sticking to everything except the surface of the drive itself.

On top, to finish with, spread and roll 13mm ($\frac{1}{2}$ in) washed 'pea' shingle. The surface should now be firm; there is nothing worse than a treadmill effect on your way to the front door.

Drainage
It is especially important to provide drainage with gravel and if, after digging a trial hole, you find the water-table to be within 60cm (2 ft) of the surface, lay a simple drain on one or both sides of the drive. (See bottom diagram).

Retaining edges
The gravel may well be retained by a building or some kind of paving but, where it meets a soft surface such as plantings or grass, you may need a definite edge. You can obtain a neat and

attractive finish by laying bricks on edge, but make sure that these are a hard, well-fired variety that will resist frost. Set the bricks in concrete and bring the gravel within 13mm ($\frac{1}{2}$ in) of the top. If the area abuts a lawn, the grass should, in turn, be 13mm ($\frac{1}{2}$ in) above the brick, allowing the mower to run easily along the top.

Plants for use with gravel
Architectural foliage blends well with gravel and enhances the composition by highlighting and ornamenting its edge. The large strongly-veined leaves of *Hosta sieboldiana*, a blue-leaved plantain lily, contrast effectively with the tall spiky uprights of *Yucca flaccida* (Adam's needle). *Fatsia japonica* (Japanese aralia or figleaf palm), hellebores, bergenia (pig squeak) and sinarundinaria – better known as bamboo – can also be included. These will mature to form a dramatic and virtually maintenance-free composition. Avoid 'spotty' effects of single specimens by planting in small groups.

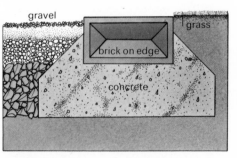

Above: cross-section showing edging brick set in concrete with gravel below on one side and grass above on the other

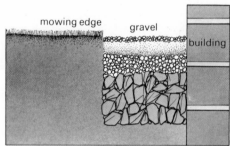

Above: cross-section of gravel abutting a lawn and laid against a building that acts as a retaining edge

Below: cross-section of a 10cm (4in) land drain installed on one side of the gravel area; graded porous fill allows seepage, making a new water-table

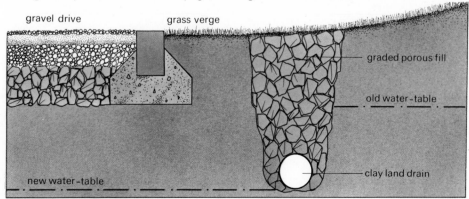

COBBLES

Smooth surfaces, such as concrete, paving slabs and tarmac, invite pedestrian traffic. A surface area of small, uneven 'modules', such as a pebble path, has the opposite effect, while cobbles are a positive deterrent.

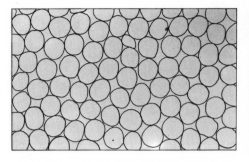 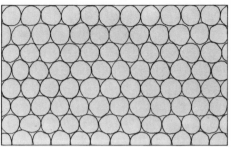

Above: plans of how to lay cobbles in a random pattern (left), and in courses (right)
Below: a more ambitious design, showing how to lay cobbles in a radius pattern

Cobbles are useful as they prevent people from cutting corners, protect beds by the front door from the delivery men, and generally direct the necessary tread of feet along the right paths.

They are round or oval stones, often flint, and similar to those found on the beach. Cobbles come in graded sizes up to 10cm (4 in) in diameter and can be laid in a variety of patterns, ranging from sophisticated formal designs, utilizing stones of different size, to loosely-arranged piles.

It is important to lay cobbles (or any small module) correctly, remembering that it's the material itself that counts, and not the background. The 'currant

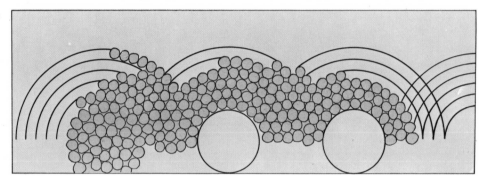

*Cross section of cobbles **A**, laid on 5cm (2 in) layer of concrete **B**, and 5cm (2 in) layer of sand **C**, over a hardcore base **D***

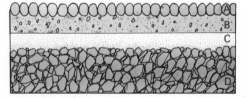

Below: cross-section showing combination of paving with informal planting, cobbles and larger boulders that will serve to deter people from cutting corners and so keep them on the path you would like them to use

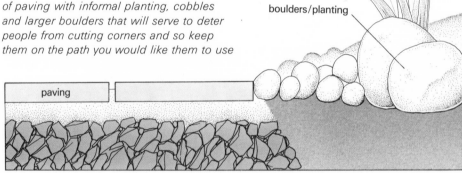

boulders/planting

paving

bun' effect, where a few cobbles are dotted at random in a sea of concrete, is to be avoided. The overall impression should be one of 'eggs in a crate', with little or no mortar showing between tightly-packed stones.

Where you intend cobbles to withstand cars (as an oil-drip), or pedestrians, a well-consolidated base of hardcore or crushed stone will be necessary. Put a layer of sand on top of this and roll it to a finished thickness of 5cm (2 in). Next, spread concrete (2 parts cement to 6 parts sand and gravel mixture) 5cm (2 in) thick and press the cobbles into this by hand. Use a straight-edge to ensure that the finished surface is flat and tamp any high stones down to the level of the rest.

An alternative, often used in Europe, is to lay the cobbles on a dry mortar or a concrete mix and then wet the mix from a watering can (with the rose on), thus preventing any of the cobbles becoming marked with cement which would be virtually impossible to remove.

Below: use of paving, loose cobbles and brick edging as part of overall design scheme

LAYING BRICK PATHS

Brick paving is like a good wine – it needs to be carefully laid down, is rich in flavour and improves with age.

As with all surfacing materials, brick has a character of its own, and because of its size, tends to be used where detail and intimacy are important. The incongruity of having vast areas of brick paving around some of the newer public buildings is immediately apparent because, besides being prohibitively expensive, it can be desperately monotonous.

It is, then, a surface to be used carefully, taking into consideration the immediate surroundings and any other relevant parts of the design.

Although bricks are available in a standard size of $225 \times 113 \times 75$mm ($9 \times 4\frac{1}{2} \times 3$ in), the range of textures and finishes is enormous. The density or hardness can also vary from a virtually indestructible 'engineering' brick to a much softer stock.

Taking these differences into account, it is quite obvious that while a perfectly uniform engineering brick could look superb in an austere modern composition, it would look out of place in a cottage garden.

The method of laying bricks also alters their character; open joints emphasize each module, while flush pointing provides a more uniform surface.

Remember, too, that bricks can be laid either flat or on edge and that this, as well as the type and direction of the bond, will affect the finished composition.

Assuming these factors have been taken into account during the design stage we can now start to look at the various methods of laying brick paving.

Laying a path

Ideally, the foundation for a path should consist of 8cm (3 in) of well-consolidated hardcore. If surface drainage is likely to

Above: Alchemilla mollis *spilling onto brick path laid in a stretcher bond*
Below: warm clay texture of this path leads eye and foot gently to conservatory

Herringbone
Square to path (on edge)

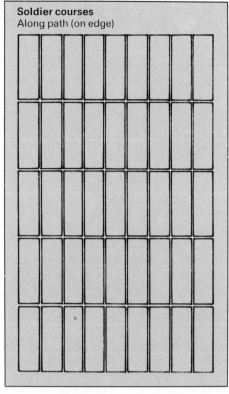

Soldier courses
Along path (on edge)

weave – although there are modifications to these that will extend the range.

Stretcher bond This is exactly what it says, with the bricks laid end to end, as in a wall. The pattern can either be across or down the length of the path. This obviously has an effect on the overall design of the garden. If the line is down the path, the length and direction of the feature will be emphasized; bricks laid across a path give it a feeling of greater width. Stretcher bond also allows a camber to be easily incorporated and so will drain quickly after rain.

Herringbone You can see fine examples of this traditional paving pattern in its original form at many historic buildings. As with stretcher bond, the bricks can be laid flat or on edge, and either parallel or diagonally across the line of the path.

This is an intrinsically complicated design, and looks it. It is therefore better to use it in an intricate, detailed situation – too much of it could become fussy and oppressive to the eye. A camber is difficult to lay and the pattern should be worked to a straight cross fall.

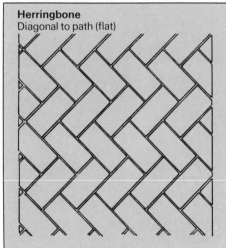

Herringbone
Diagonal to path (flat)

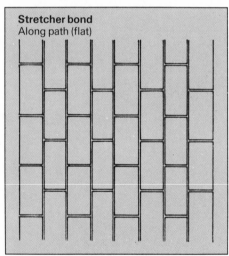

Stretcher bond
Along path (flat)

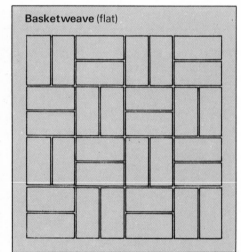

Basketweave (flat)

be a problem, roughly shape the hardcore to a slight camber or cross fall.

The usual method of laying brick paving on the prepared hardcore foundation is as follows: bed the bricks on a 5cm (2 in) thick, dry layer of sand and cement (using – by volume – 1 part sand to 4 parts cement). When you have finished the path, or section of path, wet the surface with water from a can (keeping the rose on) and then brush the same mix into the open joints. When the joints have almost set you can rub them back to accentuate individual bricks and emphasize the pattern as a whole.

A choice of patterns
Bricks can be laid in three basic patterns – stretcher bond, herringbone and basket-

Stretcher bond
Across path (on edge)

Above: illustrations of brick paving laid in three different patterns – herringbone, stretcher bond (soldier coursing is a variant of this, without the staggering) and basketweave

Basketweave Again, this pattern is a traditional one. Bricks can be laid flat in pairs, or on edge in threes. The effect is more static, as bolder squares give stability to the overall design

If the path is on a slope and you don't need steps, it is possible to 'haunch', or lay the bricks at a slight angle, to obtain a better foothold. This is really only practical with a simple pattern, as in the stretcher bond, laid across the path.

Finally, it is essential to be neat in your work. Bricks are a small module and there are a lot of joints in relation to the total surface area. The beauty of a brick path lies in its precise pattern and texture; to spoil this with unsightly splashes of mortar or loose jointing is a sure sign of poor workmanship.

PRE-CAST CONCRETE PATHS

Paths are not only an essential part of any garden but also an important design element, leading the eye as well as the feet. In this section we show how the various materials differ in character.

Pre-cast concrete slabs are probably the most widely-used material for paving. They come in many different shapes, sizes and colours from a standard grey laid in conventional pattern to interesting hexagonal and interlocking designs. Their relatively low price makes them more competitive than natural stone. As well as being durable, various textures are available, the non-slip varieties being particularly useful in the garden.

For medium-to-heavy traffic Lay a base of rammed hardcore 15cm (6 in) thick. Bed slabs on a 5cm (2 in) layer of mortar, leaving 6mm ($\frac{1}{4}$ in) gaps for pointing.

For light traffic Lay each slab on five spots of mortar, in centre and at corners.

For stepping stones in a lawn Remove a section of turf and simply place slab in position, making sure that the hard surface is 13mm ($\frac{1}{2}$ in) below the lawn, to avoid damaging a mower.

For aggregate slabs With a surface of small stones or pebbles (exposed by brushing before concrete finally hardens)

these non-slip slabs should be laid to a slight 'fall' to avoid water standing in the rougher texture and freezing in winter.

FOR CURVED PATHS

Straight paths, using rectangular or square slabs, are relatively simple to lay but curves are more involved. Here you must peg out the line in advance, marking this with a sharpened stick or 'scribe' that is swung on the end of a cord secured to the appropriate radius. When the slabs are laid to this line a wedge-shaped joint ensues (see diagram). This can either be left open and planted with low-growing aromatic herbs or, if traffic is heavy, be carefully filled with small cobbles bedded in mortar.

HEXAGONAL OR INTERLOCKING

Six-sided slabs form attractive paths but the key to success here is to lay a random pattern that echoes the irregular shape of the module itself. This is particularly effective crossing a planted area, the hard and soft materials overlapping so that it is difficult to define a precise boundary between the two.

Interlocking concrete shapes, rather like pieces of jig-saw puzzle, should be treated in the same way as hexagonal paths, as a rigid edge looks clumsy.

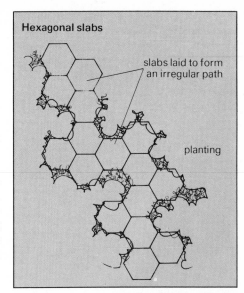

Hexagonal slabs

slabs laid to form an irregular path

planting

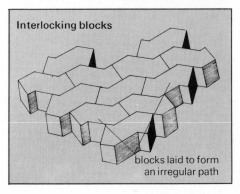

Interlocking blocks

blocks laid to form an irregular path

Hexagonal slabs or interlocking blocks both look better in irregular patterns, while with a curved path (left) you must work out your line in advance from radius points

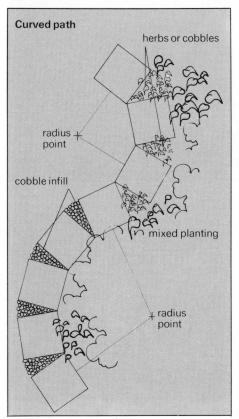

Curved path

herbs or cobbles

radius point

cobble infill

mixed planting

radius point

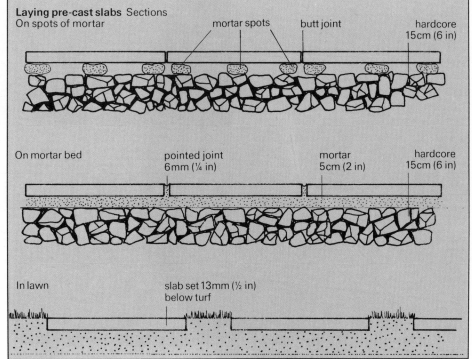

Laying pre-cast slabs Sections

On spots of mortar — mortar spots — butt joint — hardcore 15cm (6 in)

On mortar bed — pointed joint 6mm (¼ in) — mortar 5cm (2 in) — hardcore 15cm (6 in)

In lawn — slab set 13mm (½ in) below turf

BUILDING A RAMP

On previous pages we have described the different forms of surfacing a garden. Here we look at a further alternative – ramps – and give practical advice on how to build them.

Steps, circular or otherwise, are not always practical on a slope requiring wheeled access. Here a different solution is needed to cater for bicycles, wheelbarrows, prams or wheelchairs. A ramp is the obvious answer and the ways in which this can be constructed are as numerous as steps.

As a general rule the gradient should remain constant, both from a visual and a practical point of view. Steep ramps are tiring and if the slope is too great to tackle in one run, you should incorporate a 'hairpin' so that you go up in two evenly-graded sections.

Concrete for ramps

Concrete is the obvious material for this purpose. Laid on a suitably-compacted layer of hardcore, a final level is achieved by using wooden shutters, held in place by pegs. The finish with concrete can be varied, the easiest way being simply to tamp the top, between the shutters, with a long straight-edge. This will produce a ribbed effect, giving better traction for wheels and feet alike.

Brushed concrete (see page 86) can look effective and there is a wheeled tool available with an embossed face that you run over the concrete when partially dry to achieve the dimpled effect often seen in driveways and pavement edges laid by the local authorities. An important point to remember is to keep the concrete mix fairly 'dry'. As work progresses you will find that the tamping and trowelling will bring ample moisture to the surface. Too much moisture weakens the mix.

Brick, stone, cobbles or setts

Ramps can be made from brick, stone, or cobbles. Granite setts are also suitable and you can sometimes obtain old ones from city streets being demolished.

Setts are either full-sized (about the size of a thick brick), or half-sized (virtually square). The advantage this type of module has over concrete or tarmac is that it can be 'haunched' up at an angle, each course being tilted to obtain a better foothold on the slope.

When laying any small-scale material make sure you keep the surface clear from mortar; there is nothing worse than seeing the finished job spoilt in this way – it is also the trademark of a poor workman.

A ramp, with steps alongside to provide extra safety for pedestrians

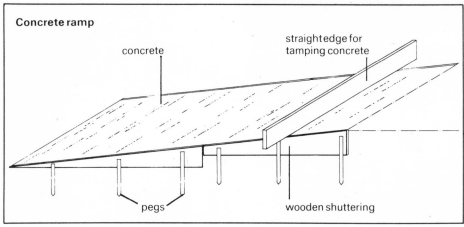

Concrete ramp

concrete

straight edge for tamping concrete

pegs

wooden shuttering

Left: tamp concrete for a non-slip surface
Below: angled granite setts make a good alternative to a ramp-type driveway

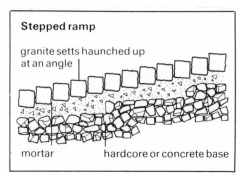

Stepped ramp

granite setts haunched up at an angle

mortar   hardcore or concrete base

FENCES AND SCREENS

Screening around or within the garden can be natural – in the form of a hedge or other planting – or prefabricated. While the former takes time to establish and needs a certain amount of maintenance, the latter is visually 'stiffer' and requires less upkeep – although it does involve a greater outlay of capital.
Here we describe and illustrate a varied selection of fences and screens, including the ubiquitous ranch fence, and the pastoral ha-ha – in effect, a dry moat, conceived to prevent stray cattle wandering into the garden.

Most people look at a fence, *call* it a fence, and leave it at that, when in fact the possibilities are endless. Fences are generally considered as a background, the usual approach being to hide them as soon as possible. While this is logical up to a point, might it not also be feasible to use at least part of this expensive item as a positive feature?

With the passing of hand craftwork and the inevitable change to mass production, a great deal of individuality has been sacrificed. Fences are no exception: time was when you could cross Britain and see a wide range of local designs, but this is virtually impossible today.

Fence of battened slats complements the angle of the terrace design

Battened slats
A number of interesting vertical screens can be made with 150×19mm ($6 \times \frac{3}{4}$ in) slats, these being battened from behind so that the fixings are virtually invisible. Stain the wood with brown Cuprinol (not creosote, as this is toxic to plants), and use the composition in an architectural setting, close to the house and perhaps as a foil to the horizontal lines of white overhead beams. Slats could alternatively be set at an angle of 45 degrees (see illustration below).

Ranch fence
This type often fails to fulfill its real potential. It is an architectural feature, and can be used to great advantage on a sloping site, emphasizing a pattern of steps or terraced lawns. Use colour sensibly – why should such a fence, if painted, inevitably be white? Congo brown (BS 3–038) is a splendid landscape colour, and if your house is a certain colour don't be afraid to continue this for a distance in the garden.

Interwoven panels
Most people will be familiar with interwoven-panel fencing, and it is invariably erected with the weave running horizontally. Try turning the panels to a vertical position, either the whole run or in groups of two or three. The complete character of the fence is altered and it becomes far more attractive. Link the

ensuing pattern with boldly-planted beds for optimum effect.

Timber in all its guises has infinite permutations, but as the cost continues to rise and rise it is best to try to save money wherever possible. Rough-sawn timber is markedly cheaper than boards that are planed all round (PAR).

Scaffold poles
Everyone has seen scaffold poles but how many people have considered using them as a screen? Get them cut to the length you want (adding 45cm/18 in for the distance below ground), and concrete them into prepared holes, varying the distance between each pole for greater or lesser visibility. They are particularly effective for dividing areas of the garden, a partial view through the fence adding to the attraction. Climbing plants will quickly ramble up the poles, and remember that painting it white makes an open screen harder to see past than if you use darker colours.

Wattle hurdles
There are still one or two attractive local fencing materials available, the best and probably most widespread being wattle hurdles. These are woven by craftsmen from hazel branches and were originally used for penning sheep, each shepherd carrying four hurdles on his back and erecting a screen wherever necessary. Today they are becoming increasingly

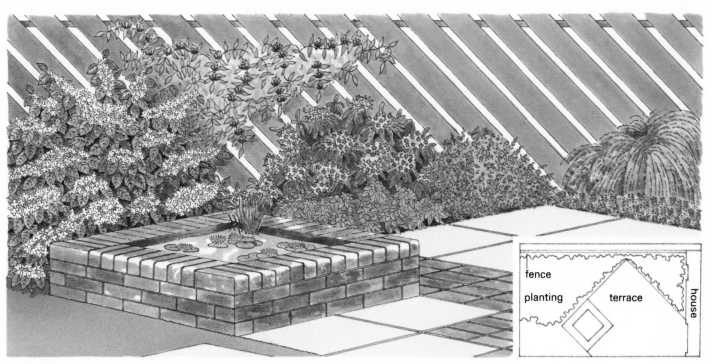

fence

planting   terrace

house

popular for garden use. They are cheaper than most mass-produced fencing, and although they have a life of only about 6–8 years, they blend well with virtually any background and make a superb foil for plants.

Ha-ha or post-and-rail?

In a rural situation, if you want a fence at all, you will probably want it to be inconspicuous. The traditional method of merging a garden and landscape was the ha-ha, a ditch stone-faced on one side, that allowed the view to run out without letting the cattle in. Today few people have the money or space to build this sort of feature, and a simple post-and-rail often looks the best. If you worry about dogs or small children, attach a section of sheep netting from ground level up to the first rail: this will be virtually invisible

*Interwoven fencing (top right) with
alternately-arranged panels
Wattle hurdles (above right) blend well
with almost any background planting
Ranch fences (right and bottom) are
particularly suited to sloping sites
Below: use scaffold poles for climbers*

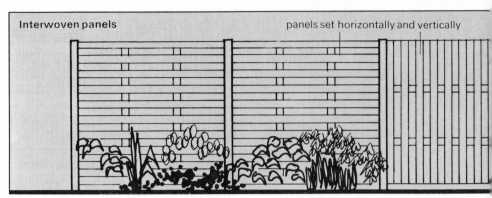

Interwoven panels — panels set horizontally and vertically

Wattle hurdles

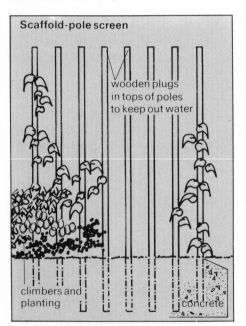

Scaffold-pole screen

wooden plugs in tops of poles to keep out water

climbers and planting

concrete

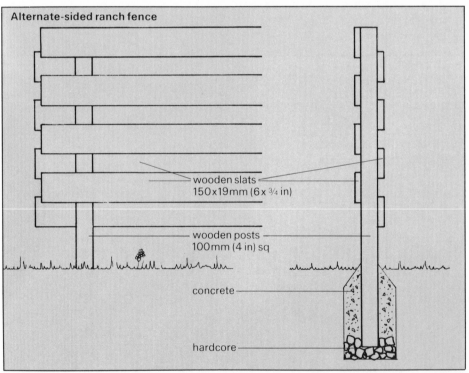

Alternate-sided ranch fence

wooden slats 150x19mm (6 x ¾ in)

wooden posts 100mm (4 in) sq

concrete

hardcore

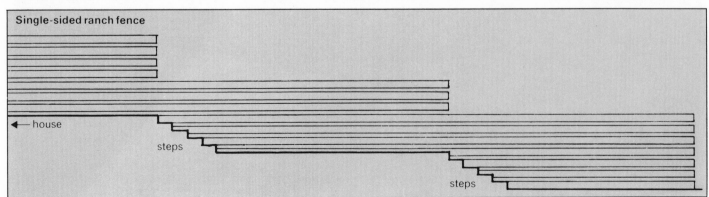

Single-sided ranch fence

← house

steps

steps

but still provide an effective barrier.

Iron park fences can sometimes be picked up at farm and estate sales, and look marvellous in the right setting.

Fences are thus barriers, but remember that part of the art of garden design is to use them to the best advantage. Sympathy is the key, making a strongly-composed slatted fence link dramatically with a town house, while as little as two or three strands of wire can be equally as effective in the country, bringing the landscape right in to blend with a rolling lawn.

Palisade fence

concrete

hardcore

wooden slats
75 x 19mm (3 x ¾ in)

wooden posts
75mm (3 in) sq

battens
50 x 25mm (2 x 1 in)

Post-and-rail fence

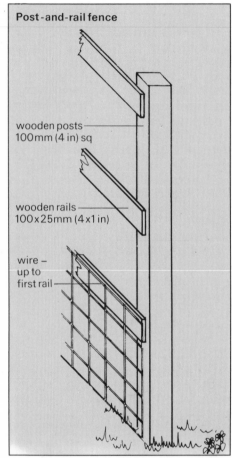

wooden posts
100mm (4 in) sq

wooden rails
100 x 25mm (4 x 1 in)

wire –
up to
first rail

Palisade fence (above) has slats nailed or screwed to horizontal battens
Post-and-rail (right) includes section of sheep netting between ground and first rail to keep small children and pets within the garden
Rural ha-ha (below) allows clear view of surrounding countryside

Ha-ha

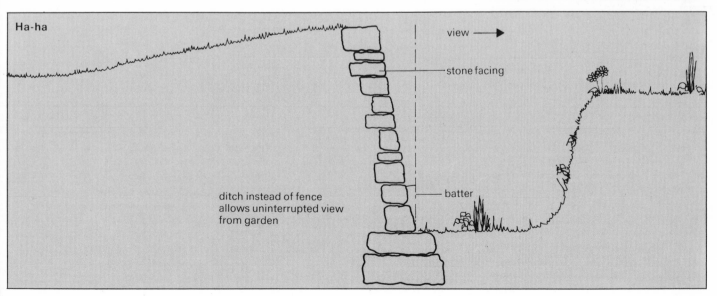

view →

stone facing

batter

ditch instead of fence
allows uninterrupted view
from garden

MAKING FEDGES

Another device useful for dividing a garden merits close attention.

A fedge is exactly what it sounds – a cross between a fence and a hedge. This is not as extraordinary as it seems, for a fedge is a useful device with a positive role to play in the garden.

Basically, a fedge consists of climbing plants covering a prefabricated framework; this might be an old wall, fence or purpose-built wire screen. Once the plants are established, the framework becomes incidental and completely obscured.

Such a feature opens up interesting design possibilities and combines an architectural form with the softer, sprawling nature of the climbers used, providing a useful link between house and garden.

By its nature a fedge is most effective up to a maximum height of 2m (6½ ft). Beyond this many climbers tend to get a little straggly and the bottom growth becomes sparse and untidy. For this reason fedges are not really suited for use on a boundary where screening is important but are better adapted to the garden's own internal divisions – perhaps between a lawn and a vegetable plot, or for marking off a play area.

Constructing a fedge

The traditional method of constructing a fedge is to use chestnut fencing, allowing the climber simply to ramble up and over it. Although cheap and flexible, it is likely to decay fairly quickly. A sturdier method, and one that can give rise to a wide range of architectural patterns, involves using a combination of 10mm ($\frac{3}{8}$ in) mild steel rods of the type used in reinforced concrete, in combination with a plastic mesh such as Netlon.

First, decide on the height and length of the fedge, remembering that it need not be a straight or a necessarily continuous run; if you are in doubt about the final result in relation to the rest of the garden, work out the pattern to scale on graph paper. Next, select the finished shape you want; this can be rectangular, hooped or wedge shaped. Each shape, being more or less formal, will have its own characteristic.

The reinforcing rods are then carefully bent in a vice to the shape of a simple template (a pattern used as a guide in cutting) made from plywood or hardboard, thus ensuring that each hoop matches the next.

The hoops in a fedge 1·5m (5 ft) high should be under a metre (or yard) apart.

An effective method of anchoring them is to slide each section into a length of scaffold pole set into the ground. The plastic mesh is then stretched over the finished line of hoops and neatly fixed by plastic-coated wire.

While this technique is suitable for fedges of considerable length and scale in the larger garden, another simple form of fedge can be made from railway sleepers set vertically into the ground 2m (6½ ft) apart. The netting in this case should be nailed to the outside of the sleepers, and climbers planted in the usual way.

Plants for fedges

Of all fedging plants, hedera (ivy) is undoubtedly the best – tough, evergreen, and relatively fast to cover a framework. The large-leaved varieties are the most suitable and *Hedera colchica*, with its bold, heart-shaped green leaves, is ideal. *H. c.* Variegata has the added bonus of really large leaves, the dark centres of which are in striking contrast to the soft, yellow, outer variegations. Hedera is also useful in that it tolerates shade – a point to remember when screening some of those awkward features such as compost heaps and bonfire areas.

Of the other climbers, aristolochia (Dutchman's pipe), lonicera (honeysuckle), passiflora (passion flower) and *Polygonum baldschuanicum* (Russian vine) can all be used, but be sure the lonicera you choose is an evergreen and remember that some climbers, the Russian vine in particular, will need continual pruning to keep them in check.

Maintaining a fedge

Fedge maintenance is normally confined to keeping it neat and tidy, removing dead leaves before they get clogged in the structure and pruning the more prominent climbers to keep them in hand. Pruning need not be too severe; if there is room, the climber can be allowed to run along the ground too, sweeping up and over the fedge in a continuous run.

Once established, the fedge will be a permanent and attractive feature, part of the basic framework forming a background for softer elements in the design.

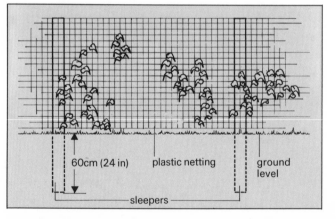

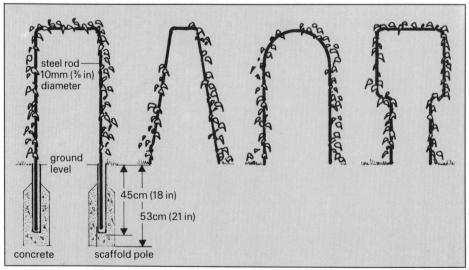

Left: fedge for the larger garden with climbers on plastic netting secured to the outside of railway sleepers
Below: climbers on wire frameworks bent to a variety of interesting shapes

WALLS

Walls can be made from a variety of materials and take on several forms, suiting – where possible – the character of their surroundings. Here we outline some alternatives.

Walls are an integral part of many gardens, providing shelter and division, as well as an interest of their own.

We have already seen when laying the patio foundations (page 16) the constructional techniques involved in using a wide range of materials, but it is worth remembering that the initial choice of what type of wall to use can have an immediate and lasting effect on the design as a whole.

Walls can be broadly classified into functional and decorative, and to get the best out of either type it is wise to follow certain rules that are largely governed by the characteristic qualities of the material that you decide to use.

As with all design, try to be sympathetic to the immediate surroundings. If your house is brick, then use a similar brick in a wall running out from the building; if stone is predominant, follow suit. The incongruity of a Cotswold-stone wall in the middle of a brick-built suburban estate should be obvious!

First, then, you must consider what options are open to you, and how these can be used to the best advantage.

Brick walling
Brick is the most widely-available walling material, the range of finishes and constructional possibilities being vast. As a general rule, 11·5 and 23cm (4½ and 9 in) thicknesses are used for garden walling and, of course, the latter is stronger and more visually correct. An 11·5cm (4½ in) wall is obviously cheaper but will need buttressing every 1·8–3m (6–10 ft), depending on the height, and will look much too flimsy when close to a building. The top, or coping, of such a wall is also a problem. Bricks set on end tend to emphasize the visual instability, and the neatest finish probably consists of bricks cut in half (cut headers), or a neat pre-cast concrete strip.

Right, above: low, double stone wall separating patio from lawn and marking a change of level in the garden; the hollow on top of the wall has been earth-filled and planted with geraniums, forming its own miniature border
Right: see-through, honeycomb brick wall

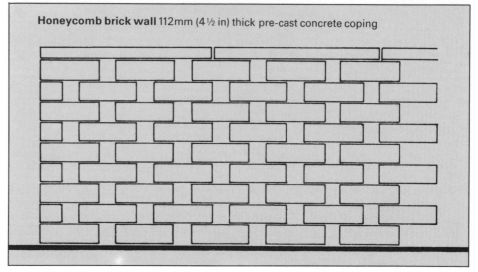

Honeycomb brick wall 112mm (4 ½ in) thick pre-cast concrete coping

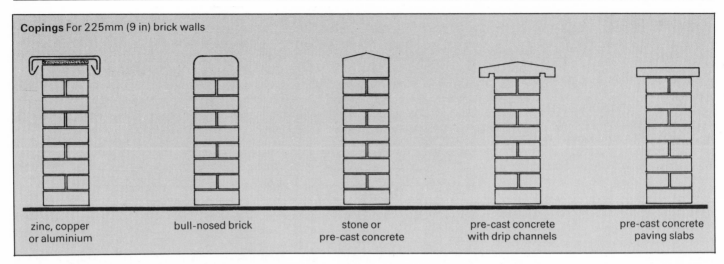

Copings For 225mm (9 in) brick walls

zinc, copper
or aluminium

bull-nosed brick

stone or
pre-cast concrete

pre-cast concrete
with drip channels

pre-cast concrete
paving slabs

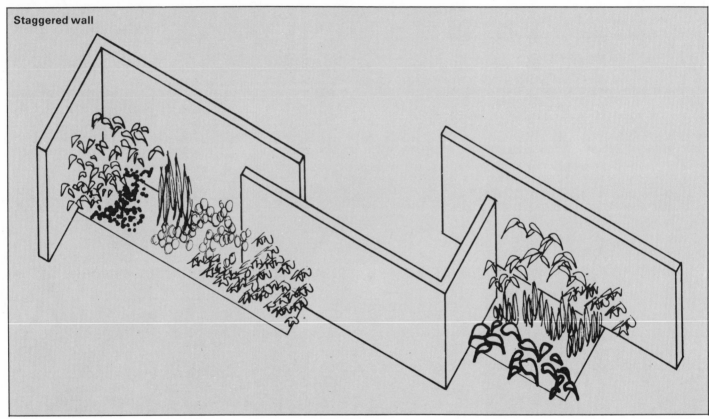

Staggered wall

*Top: alternative copings for brick walls
Above: staggering can be used to break
up a long, monotonous stretch of wall*

A honeycomb, or pierced 11·5cm (4½ in) wall can be most attractive, combining the best of brick and screen blocks. It will still need buttresses, but farther apart as there is less wind resistance.

A 23cm (9 in) wall is best finished with a row of bricks on edge, although once again a wide variety of pre-cast concrete and stone copings are available. These might well be appropriate if you are matching existing walls in the garden or even a particular detail in the house itself.

If you want a particularly long wall, you may have to incorporate expansion joints at regular intervals. These are simply gaps of approximately 13mm (½ in) and will prevent cracks forming due to variations in temperature or possible slight subsidence. An attractive way to handle a long run of garden walling is to use a staggered pattern with sections overlapping one another, and then planting to add interest to the composition.

Stone walling
Stone is a superb walling material but as we have seen it must be carefully used, bearing in mind the overall design and locality. Here again, the thickness of a wall can vary and the coping usually matches traditional patterns. Working in stone is not easy and is a job best left to craftsmen; don't let an odd-job man persuade you otherwise.

Walling with concrete blocks
Many people are shy of using concrete blocks for walling, feeling that they are too utilitarian. Such blocks, available in 115 and 235mm (4½ and 9 in) thicknesses, can be ideal, however, and the hollow pattern, measuring 235 × 235 × 450mm (9 × 9 × 18 in) is perfect for a boundary wall. The surface texture of blocks varies but some of the smooth finishes can look really crisp and architectural, if carefully pointed with a slightly-recessed joint. They readily accept paint and if you extend an interior colour along such a wall, the link between house and garden

Landscape bloc wall

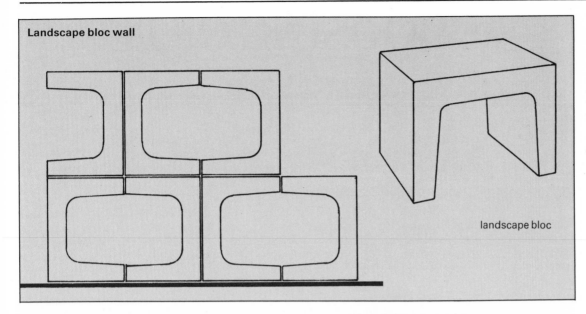

landscape bloc

Left: the landscape bloc is a new and versatile pre-cast concrete unit
Below left: here the landscape bloc doubles up as a seat and a retaining wall
Bottom: screen block wall with fleur-de-lis motif, a popular form in town gardens

Seat and retaining wall
Section

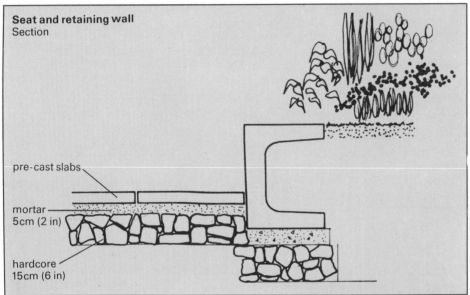

pre-cast slabs

mortar
5cm (2 in)

hardcore
15cm (6 in)

becomes particularly strong. Coping can be made either from brick on edge or a pre-cast concrete strip.

Walling with screen blocks

The ubiquitous screen block, measuring $300 \times 300 \times 115mm$ ($12 \times 12 \times 4\frac{1}{2}$ in), is now one of the more popular materials as it is relatively cheap and decorative. Unfortunately, its very popularity has led to its abuse; it is used in every possible situation often without any real thought. In many cases, a honeycomb brick wall would be more appropriate close to a building, but when you are using screen blocks, try and be sympathetic, picking up any building lines and using lots of climbing plants to soften the outline. They can be painted, but do avoid prettying them; they look 'busy' enough already.

'Landscape bloc' walls

One of the most exciting walling designs in recent years is the 'landscape bloc'. Each bloc measures $560 \times 415 \times 415mm$ ($22 \times 16 \times 16$ in), having a U-shaped section. These blocs can be put together to form endless permutations, not only for making screen walls, but retaining walls, steps and even tables and chairs. They are made of pre-cast concrete and the off-white finish is sufficiently unobtrusive to make them acceptable nearly everywhere. One word of caution though: don't get carried away with any good idea – a surfeit can be very boring.

The building of walls is not therefore an afterthought in the overall garden layout. Careful evaluation of your needs and existing features will be necessary to get the best out of the material you choose. In the final analysis, the old design criterion of 'simplicity is best' works every time.

Throughout the book we are trying to show how a garden can best reflect the needs of its owner. Much of the hard work involved in garden planning is taken for granted by a visitor and it is invariably the finishing touches that catch the eye, making or marring the composition.

Gates are just such details and it is worth considering which will be the most appropriate for your needs.

Front gates

The front gate is usually the most important of the property; first impressions count after all. A large garden may have two or more front gates, one for the drive and one for pedestrians. A smaller garden may only need one, while tiny spaces with just enough room for car-standing and the simplest design may well be more practical with no gate at all.

Pretension should be avoided at all costs – the incongruity of heavily-worked, wrought-iron gates in front of a suburban villa should be self evident! What is really needed is a link between house and garden, achieved by sympathetic use of materials.

Don't forget also that the gate should be in keeping with an adjoining fence, congruent with the latter's height and line as well as style.

Modern gates

If the house is relatively modern, with perhaps part of the exterior, garage and carport in white timber, it would be logical to have a boundary that follows suit. Here, a fence of horizontal slats would be ideal, with the gate or gates continuing in line in a similar construction; hinges and incidental details will be quite sufficient to indicate the entrance. Such a line will also increase the apparent width of the garden, while planting should be used to soften and emphasize the points of entry.

CHOOSING GATES

Front gates, back gates, side gates, farm gates, gates within the garden and gates without – all perform different functions and each should have a character of its own. A careful choice can enhance your garden composition.

Period gates

An older Edwardian or Victorian property has a different character and the gates should follow suit. Wrought iron could be correct here, but is expensive. A better solution would be to use a heavy timber construction, a solid five-bar gate being quite acceptable. If you are really keen on finding a 'period' gate it can be rewarding to keep your eyes open when you are out and about. Old properties undergoing conversion often yield un-expected treasures and the old gate, in need of some repair, is often dumped into a rubbish 'skip' outside the house.

A word about wrought iron here. It can be superb for gates in the right situation – no stately home should be without them for instance – but on a smaller scale you have to be careful. The 'off the peg' gates that are on sale at so many garden centres are at best scaled down versions of something grander, or, instead, poor examples of craftsmanship that really do

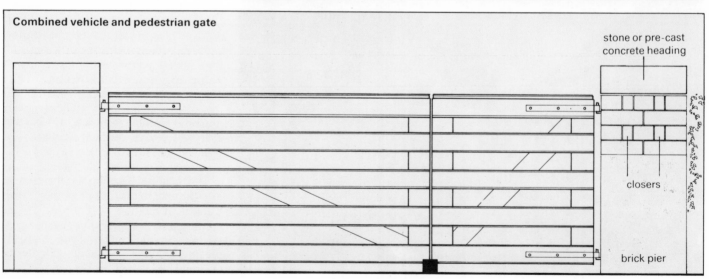

Combined vehicle and pedestrian gate

stone or pre-cast concrete heading

closers

brick pier

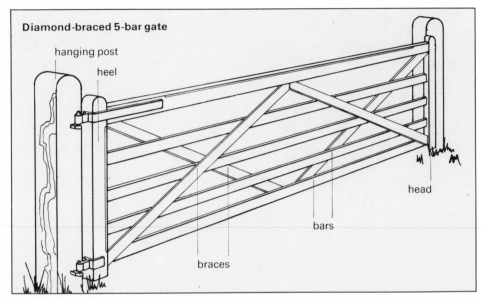

Diamond-braced 5-bar gate

hanging post

heel

head

bars

braces

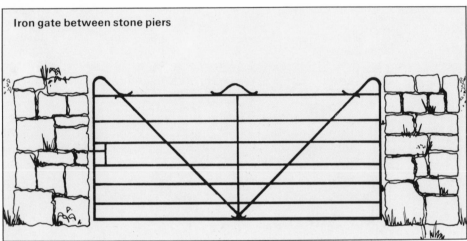

Iron gate between stone piers

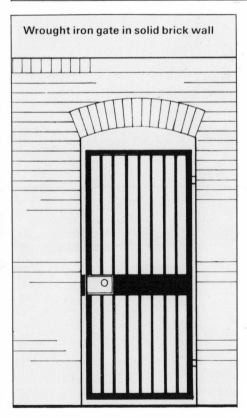

Wrought iron gate in solid brick wall

Many different styles of gate are available to satisfy the functional and aesthetic requirements of the owner. For a design to succeed, the style must be appropriate to the setting. Clockwise from bottom, far left: two-in-one, for pedestrians and vehicles; elaborate formality in wrought iron; traditional country-style 5-bar gate; simplicity in iron and stone; unfussy wrought iron for maximum contrast with brick

little credit to the makers or the garden they grace. As with all design, simplicity is the key; a plain wrought-iron railing and gate, for instance, is the perfect foil for a classical town house.

Gates in the country
Country houses, on the other hand, have completely different requirements. Here the locality is all-important and gates, as with all building materials, should respect both their surroundings and their neighbours.

Here, too, a front gate is often the only gate, serving cars, pedestrians and, if a

farm, machinery as well. Sufficient width is therefore important and the usual opening for a gate of this type is 4·3m (14 ft). A private drive is smaller, 2·4 or 3m (8 or 10 ft) being ideal (the latter size allowing room for the ubiquitous oil tanker), while private footpaths should be 90cm (3 ft) wide.

In the country it can be most effective to contrast the gate with its posts, the solidity of massive piers acting as a superb foil to a simple iron gate. Remember though that the gate must always be visually 'lighter' than the adjoining boundary, a solid gate in a post-and-rail fence looking ludicrous.

Timber gates
Timber is by far the most common material in the country and gates should therefore be as light as possible whilst retaining maximum strength. It is standard practice to design the 'heel' (the upright timber that carries the hinges) and the load-bearing struts in thicker sections than the rest of the gate.

Weights of timber gates will also vary, depending on the wood used. Of the hardwoods, oak and Spanish chestnut are best, being the heaviest and most durable and weighing anything up to 56 kilos (125 lb) for a 3m (10 ft) opening. If wear is likely to be less, pine or spruce should be quite adequate, but remember that these need particularly regular applications of preservative and, of course, should be well seasoned in the first place.

All gates, whether in town or country, should open inwards, for obvious safety reasons.

In view of harmony
Having said so much about main gates, we should also look at others that are more utilitarian but nonetheless important. Back and side gates should blend with their surroundings. Gates in brick walls, where the wall carries over the gate, are usually best close-boarded, although this can be a situation for a well-designed pattern, in wrought iron, particularly if you want a view in or out of the garden.

Colour is also important and should form a positive link with the fence or the adjoining house. The fad for painting garden gates in a garish colour really has no merit. True, it draws the eye, but it detracts from all else and often foreshortens an interesting view.

In the final analysis, a gate should represent the way through a boundary, by using materials that are sympathetic and practical. Avoid anything flashy – this belongs elsewhere – and remember that simplicity is always best.

SLOPING SITE GARDENS

From a design standpoint, a completely flat garden raises problems, for it can so easily become dull and obvious. Slopes are helpful because they give variety and this can be exploited to great advantage. But sloping ground is harder to work than a level site and if terracing is introduced it can also be more costly to lay out. It is, however, extremely useful for breaking up the shape of the slope.

Here we confine ourselves to the methods of terracing. Then we go on to look at other ways of dealing with a sloping site, from paths, planted banks and rock gardening, to a variety of steps that can be adapted to sloping sites.

The first question you have to decide upon is whether to terrace and so convert the slope into a series of levels, or whether to accept it as it is. In a tiny garden it will have to be either one or the other, but where there is more space to play with it may be better to combine the two, contrasting the obvious artificiality of terraces with the more natural appearance of irregularly-contoured land. This can accord well with the common practice of allowing the garden to become progressively less formal the farther it is from the house.

One or two terraces close to the house may serve the dual purpose of providing comfortable outdoor 'rooms' in which chairs and tables can be placed when required, and at the same time providing a firm setting for the building. If a garden slopes uninterruptedly downward from a house, it will inevitably give it a slight appearance of instability, as if the building itself might one day begin to slip down the incline. An upward slope will give an opposite impression of the garden sliding down into the living rooms (and something of the kind does happen occasionally when freak rain storms

The gardens at Bodnant, looking from the croquet terrace to the rose terrace. Steps divide on either side of a fountain and pool, and the wall provides shelter for a wide variety of shrubs

Measuring with boning rods

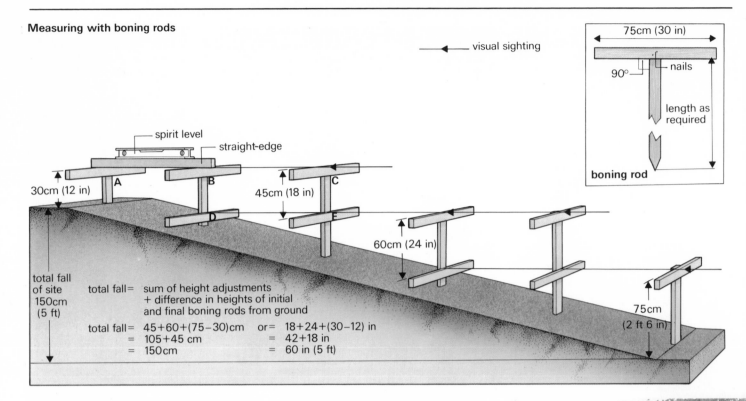

← visual sighting

75cm (30 in)

90° — nails

length as required

boning rod

spirit level

straight-edge

30cm (12 in)

A   B

45cm (18 in)   C

D   E

60cm (24 in)

total fall of site 150cm (5 ft)

75cm (2 ft 6 in)

total fall = sum of height adjustments + difference in heights of initial and final boning rods from ground

total fall = 45+60+(75−30)cm   or = 18+24+(30−12) in
= 105+45 cm   = 42+18 in
= 150cm   = 60 in (5 ft)

occur). Good wide terraces, solidly retained with masonry, can completely correct either impression.

In making good terraces, especially if there are several of them, it is essential that they should all differ in width, depth and treatment. The advantage of this diversity can be seen very clearly in some of Britain's famous gardens; for example, at Bodnant in north Wales, five magnificent terraces overlook the valley of the river Conway, and at Powis Castle, Welshpool, the slope is even steeper and the terraces more architectural. No one would suggest that in small gardens these grandeurs should be imitated, but they do forcefully illustrate the advantages of variety, and that is possible however modest the scale of the operation.

Terracing with boning rods
To begin with, draw a plan of your site to scale on graph paper. You will invariably find that slopes are steeper than they appear and it is absolutely essential to know what the differences in level are before embarking on any scheme of terracing. There is no need to use expensive equipment such as a theodolyte for this preliminary survey. On a small scale it can all be carried out with a straight-edged plank, a spirit level, and some stakes with a short piece of board nailed across the top of each in the form of a letter T. These are known as 'boning rods' and they are very useful for sighting across once a preliminary level, or for that matter any desired angle of slope, has been established (see diagram).

Armed with correct level distances, and the scale plan of the site, you can set about determining how wide each terrace should be, how deep its retaining wall or bank and how much, if any, of the land should be left with its natural slope. If the land falls across the site as well as along its length, it will be necessary for you to take levels in both directions, and then to make the required provisions for soil movement and retention.

To measure slopes for terracing First, drive in a short boning rod (**A**) at the highest point of the slope, and then place one end of the plank on the edge of this and drive in a longer boning rod (**B**) down the slope to support the other end of the plank. Lay the spirit level on the top of the plank and adjust the second stake until the bubble is at dead centre. This means that the tops of the two boning rods will now be level, and by taking a sighting across them you will then be able to drive in a third rod (**C**) farther down the slope, without needing to use the spirit level or plank again.

If the slope is steep, it will quickly become impractical to make boning rods tall enough to maintain the original level, so that instead you measure an identical distance down the last two rods, nail on additional cross pieces at this new lower level, and continue as before. The sum of the height adjustments made in this way, plus the difference in height from soil level to the top of the first boning rod and to the top of the last boning rod, is the difference in level from the top to the bottom of the slope.

Steep banks

Terraces can be retained by steep banks, but they may easily prove a nuisance to maintain. It is difficult to cut steeply sloping banks, and rocky banks take a lot of weeding. Ground cover can be fairly satisfactory, especially if some very soil-binding evergreen is used such as *Hypericum calycinum*, but then you must take care that it does not stray farther than it is required. Some small shrubs also grow well on steep banks, and in warm sunny places, cistus, available in considerable variety, can be very effective. There are also cotoneasters such as *Cotoneaster dammeri*, *C. microphylla*, *C. horizontalis* and *C. salicifolius repens* that thrive on sunny banks and, in the shade, both the

Right: natural approach to a gradient and formal effect (below right) at Dartington Hall in Devon. Below: an effective use of terracing and planting can transform a short, sharp slope into an attractive miniature garden

greater and lesser periwinkles (*Vinca major* and *V. minor*) will grow well.

Retaining walls

You will save labour in the long run by retaining terraces with walls and if they are cleverly designed and well built these also give the best effect. However, walls can be expensive, even when built at home, so it will be wise to check on the quantity of the stone or brick you would require and the probable cost before coming to any decision.

Whatever the material used, walls can be either mortared or unmortared (usually known as 'dry'). Mortared walls are strong and durable, excellent for climbing or trained plants, but useless as a home for plants. For that, dry walls are essential, with plenty of good soil packed between each course and uninterrupted access for roots to the main body of soil behind. In fact well-built dry walls, by simulating more closely the conditions rock plants are accustomed to growing in (often vertical crevices), are better for many of them than rock gardens.

Lewisias, ramondas and haberleas often prove difficult to manage on the flat, but are perfectly at home in the crevices of a good dry wall and this kind of gardening can become an interesting hobby in itself. Alternatively there are easy plants such as arabis, perennial alyssum, aubrietia and

Above: Cytisus × kewensis *on a dry wall*
Left: sloping garden incorporating varying styles, with artificial terraces at the far end and a shrubbery in the foreground

Steps and balustrades

Terraces necessitate steps for access and again these permit considerable diversity in style, material and planting. There is no reason why steps should follow the most obvious straight line. Sometimes a change in direction can produce interesting shapes or contrasts of light and shade. Materials can be varied, too, possibly with panels or surrounds of paving brick to contrast with concrete or stone slabs. But steps should always be set in mortar for they are likely to get a lot of wear, and loose or irregular steps can be dangerous.

When steps require balustrades, these may provide additional scope for training plants, particularly soft-stemmed climbers such as vines or clematis that won't catch in clothing or harm anyone.

Terraces

Because terraces are so clearly artificial it is appropriate that their design and planting should be seen to be man-made. They are the wrong place for rock gardens and cascades and the right place for carefully-proportioned beds, fountains and ornamental plant containers. Garden roses look well on terraces as do other highly-developed flowers such as fuchsias, pelargoniums and many bedding plants. If your fancy runs to topiary, a terrace is as good a place as any on which to display it. Here, too, lavender can be used to form little hedges or the shapes of beds can be more sharply defined with clipped edges

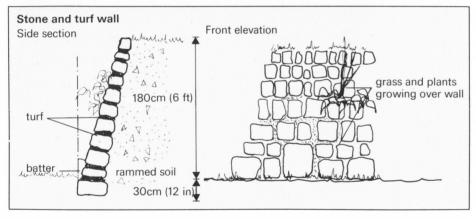

Stone and turf wall
Side section
Front elevation
180cm (6 ft)
turf
grass and plants growing over wall
batter
rammed soil
30cm (12 in)

many trailing campanulas that grow profusely in walls either planted on the face or established on top and allowed to cascade downwards. A dry wall need never be dull.

Building a dry wall

These are built in much the same way as mortared walls with the important difference that soil takes the place of cement. They can be made with dressed or undressed stone, or any of the various building blocks available from merchants. Alternate rows of stone must be staggered to give the wall a bond, just as bricks are bonded in any constructional work. The first row of stones must be well

Above: front elevation and side section showing how to build a dry stone and turf wall using squarish stones bonded with turf that also acts as a planting medium

bedded into the soil and if the wall is over 1 metre (3 ft) high it is usually best to build it with a slight inward slope, or 'batter', for greater stability. Soil should not only be spread fairly thickly between the blocks but also rammed in behind them so that there are no hollow places left. When mortared walls are made, leave holes every few feet to allow water to drain out of the retained soil; this is not necessary with unmortared walls since every crevice acts as a drainage channel.

Above: 'stagger' steps for a soft effect
Right: logs with gravelled treads set
into the slope lend strength and charm
to a woodland garden

of box, thyme or santolina (cotton lavender). In fact it is only when there are differences of level that the old-fashioned formal style of gardening can be fully appreciated, for you need to be able to look down on a pattern of beds or flowers from above to see it at its best.

Topsoil and subsoil

Terracing involves the movement of soil and it is important when doing this not to leave the relatively infertile subsoil on top and bury the good topsoil. To avoid this danger, remove the topsoil to a depth of at least 20cm (8 in) and stack it in some convenient place. Then make the necessary adjustment of level and when this is done replace the topsoil where it belongs, on top, but not under paving or other areas where there will be no plants.

Problems of subsidence

Soil that has been removed takes a considerable time to settle. This can be shortened by treading and ramming as the in-filling proceeds, but even then some subsidence is bound to occur over a period of weeks if not months. So it is unwise to be in too great a hurry to complete such tasks as permanent planting, lawn making and the laying of paths. It is better to make a temporary display with annuals and bedding plants and to cover paths and lawn sites with cheap, quick-growing rye grass, until the site is firm and no further subsidence feared.

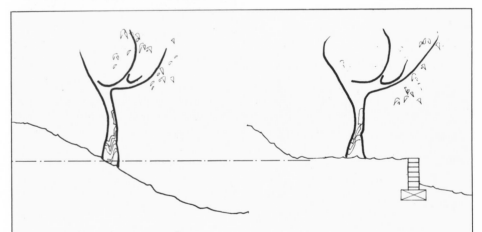

Retaining levels around trees

When terracing a slope, the position of trees is an important factor. Most mature trees are very sensitive to any changes in level around the trunk or bulk of the root system.
To overcome this problem, make a shelf around the tree, using the existing level as its base. The size of this shelf should approximate to that of the canopy or spread of branches overhead and it will need to be retained by a wall where it drops down to meet the natural slope of the ground. The type of wall will depend on the overall design of the area and it can be allowed to blend gradually into the slope on either side.
If you think the wall looks too severe, you can construct a platform using a steep earth bank to regain the lower level. You may need to stabilize this with planting; a rampant ground cover, such as Hypericum calycinum, Vinca minor *or* Hedera colchica *is ideal, as it knits together quickly and prevents long-term soil erosion.*
Young trees being far more adaptable, are less troublesome

PLANTING SLOPES

Having dealt with the methods and merits of terracing, it is time to look at planting schemes that do not involve so much labour in shifting soil and building retaining walls.

One method, similar to terracing, is to turn the slope into a series of banks separated by level paths. If the nature of the site permits it, both banks and paths can be curved to give the effect of an amphitheatre, although this may involve more soil-moving than would be necessary with straight banks and paths.

Grassed banks

It is unwise to put banks, straight or curved, down to grass without very careful consideration of the work this will involve. Grassed banks can look very effective, as many old formal gardens prove, but invariably they are difficult and tiring to mow. Since the introduction of light rotary hover mowers such as the Flymo Domestic, bank cutting is easier than it was, as these mowers can be moved freely in all directions, and be swung like a pendulum from the top of a bank. But it is still a fairly tricky job, for a rotary hover mower out of control can be a menace, since it will slide down any slope, cutting everything that comes into its path.

It is also sensible to make fairly shallow banks that you can tend from the adjacent paths with a minimum need to scramble on them. This applies equally, whether the banks are grassed or planted, for even the densest of ground cover will need some attention.

Planted banks

If you decide upon planting, the possibilities are almost endless, with the one proviso that the plants chosen must be able to withstand the sharp drainage and the occasional dryness of such places.

Small shrubs such as cistus and broom are ideal, as well as many creeping or sprawling rock plants such as helianthemum, aubrietia, arabis, alyssum and numerous campanula and dianthus (pinks).

Many grey or silver-leaved plants such as santolina, artemisia, anaphalis and helichrysum thrive on banks, but very rampant plants like cerastium enjoy the conditions so much that they become weeds.

Some sprawling roses such as Max Graf and *Rosa × paulii* grow well on banks, but their thorny stems make it rather difficult to move amongst them when they need pruning and weeding.

This is a case where shallow banks that can be tended from the level paths are almost a necessity.

Annuals and bedding plants usually thrive on sunny banks as many of them come from countries like South Africa and Australia, or areas of Central and South America that have warm, sunny climates. But most of these plants flower exclusively in summer and will leave the banks bare in winter, unless you include some evergreen shrubs as a permanent framework.

Bank gardening of this kind can produce effects just as formal and dignified as those characteristic of walled terraces, but at a much lower cost of construction, since no expensive walling stone is required. But many people do not like formal gardens or else they may wish for a gradual transition, from formality close to the house, to more natural styles farther away. This approach can offer numerous interesting variations, and sloping sites are just as suited to it as they are to terracing.

Plants for banks: helianthemum Brilliant (below) give a blaze of colour in summer and Artemisia arborescens *with* Senecio greyii *(bottom) give good contrast*

Woodland glade gardening

What is a little misleadingly called 'woodland', or 'woodland glade', gardening can be very satisfactory even on the steepest of slopes. There need be no forest trees in the woodland; indeed, unless the area to be planted is half an acre or more, there almost certainly should be none.

The woodland can be artificially created using small ornamental trees. However, avoid anything larger than a mountain ash or amelanchier (snowy mespilus) and mix in some of the smaller maples and birches, laburnums, ornamental crab apples, Japanese cherries (if the site is not so rural that every bud will be stripped by birds) and magnolias (which never seem to be attacked by anything).

If the soil is lime-free, rhododendrons, azaleas and camellias will thrive under the trees and, whatever its character, it will be possible to grow skimmias and hydrangeas. Below these again, you can grow herbaceous perennials, hostas (green, blue-grey and variegated), foxgloves,

Plants for woodland: Amelanchier canadensis *(left) has a height and spread of 3m (10 ft) when fully grown; woodland hosta (below) likes shade*

cyclamen, polygonatum (Solomon's seal), lilies of the valley, dog's tooth violets, snowdrops and daffodils. Woodland gardens do not produce a lot of weeds because of the tree canopy and so are easy to look after.

Rock gardens

Rock gardens, by contrast, can make a lot of work, for most of the weeding must be done by hand, but a naturally hilly site is ideal for them. It makes construction easy, too, since the rocks can be bedded into the slope to create the effect of a natural outcrop. Stone-chipping paths can be distributed in a natural way through the rocks, providing easy access to the plants. If you desire some more open spaces, they can be created with carpet-forming plants such as *Arenaria balearica*, various acaena and *Cotula squalida*, underplanted with small bulbs such as crocus and narcissus species, chionodoxas, muscari and scillas.

Small shrubs also fit well into the rock garden setting, not simply the dwarf conifers but flowering shrubs such as daphne, cistus, various small brooms, such as *Cytisus kewensis* and *C. beanii*, and shrubs such as *Cotoneaster adpressus* and *C. microphyllus thymifolia*.

AN INTRODUCTION TO STEPS

Most people think of steps situated in the garden as being regularly spaced, rectangular and straight. As a result, the majority of flights are built to a standard pattern, when often a different approach could provide interest and create an attractive feature that can become a permanent part of the 'hard' landscape.

You can construct steps from a wide variety of materials. Cobbles and stone, timber and gravel, concrete and brick are all available to form numerous permutations. The shape of the individual steps can be round or hexagonal and the flights can be staggered or straight. Whatever the composition, it can be softened by planting.

Steps for steep slopes
A steep slope normally requires a sensible, neat flight with a number of closely-spaced treads. You should vary your material to suit the situation: timber is less formal than brick which is not as formal as stone, pre-cast slabs and concrete. With stone or pre-cast slabs, make the tread overhang the riser by about 5cm

(2 in). This will then cast an aesthetically pleasing shadow on the tread below.

Steps for gentle slopes
Gentle slopes give a wider range of choice, but remember that simplicity is the key to all design and in building steps, you are forming a pattern that should not become 'fussy'. If, for example, you are using a combination of brick and pre-cast slabs, be sure to arrange them in sensible proportions. Brick is dominant visually and is therefore particularly suitable at the top and bottom of the flight. Use a well-fired variety, and avoid soft bricks that may shatter in frosty weather. 'Bull-nosed' bricks, with a specially-rounded leading edge, are available for the front of the step.

Irregular steps
Steps that have free or irregular outlines present problems of their own. Slabs, stone and even brick are unsuitable as they have to be cut at the edges. This is a lengthy, laborious and expensive proposition, especially if you have to hire a contractor to carry it out. In this instance, materials such as concrete, tarmac and very small paving modules like cobbles, come into their own as they can all be adapted to a specific shape.

Big steps
Do not be put off by the idea of big steps; they give an impression of space and tranquillity. The infill is of brushed concrete and takes advantage of a technique used all too little in this country. It simply involves laying a normal concrete mix of 1:2:3 – one part cement, two parts sand, three parts aggregate – ensuring that the aggregate is made up from an attractive selection of small rounded pebbles. Once the job starts to harden, or 'go off', brush the surface carefully with a stiff broom. This will expose the aggregate and produce a striking marbled effect when dry. In very hot weather cover the surface with damp sacking to prevent damage. In frosty weather dry sacking will suffice.

Above left: the charm of irregular steps of natural stone, seen at Wisley
Left: construction of overhanging treads, and bull-nosed riser for a bottom step

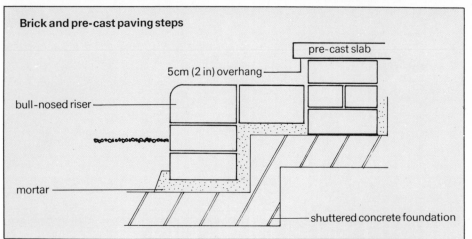

Brick and pre-cast paving steps

pre-cast slab

5cm (2 in) overhang

bull-nosed riser

mortar

shuttered concrete foundation

CANTILEVERED AND HEXAGONAL STEPS

A change of level in your garden gives you an excuse to build an imaginative flight of steps. Having given you ideas for steep and gentle slopes, and told you how to make steps from brick and pre-cast paving, here we suggest more ambitious designs to form focal points in your garden.

Cantilever steps

These are unusual steps and can be built to negotiate the face of a retaining wall. Concrete is best for this operation as you can bed reinforcing rods into the basic structure. You can easily adapt some types of lintel and these can be bought ready-made from a builder's merchant. Natural stone can be used in a similar way. Be sure that at least half the step is bedded into the wall and, as a general rule, try to match the materials so that the flight is compatible with its background.

Above right: set a graceful flight of cantilevered steps into a retaining wall Below: ground plan, showing how steps are set 50 per cent into the wall. Allow 5 cm (2 in) overlap between each step

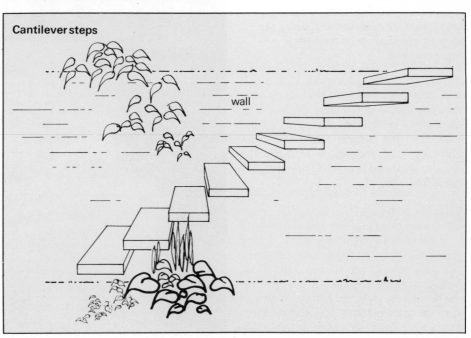

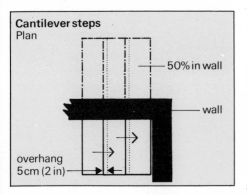

Hexagonal steps

In the ground plan drawing we show a series of interlocking hexagonal steps that would be ideal for linking two levels close to a building; the obvious geometry provides a strong visual link with the house. Each hexagon could be anything from up to 3m (10 ft) across with one step overlapping another to give a feeling of gentle progression. The low retaining walls forming the risers are approximately 15cm (6 in) high and built of brick. With big steps, 23cm (9 in) brickwork looks far better than 11cm (4½ in) and the extra effort is amply repaid by the end result.

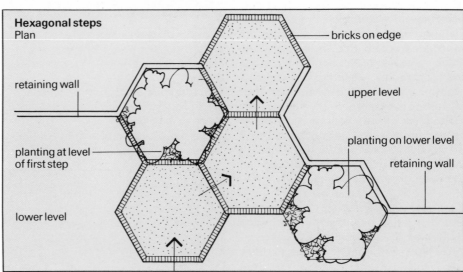

Above: ground plan showing successful use of hexagonal steps to link a relatively large area. Below: section showing foundation details of hexagonal steps

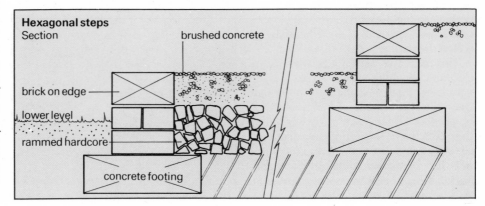

CIRCULAR STEPS

It is surprising how often you need steps in the garden. Now that we have described the art of making hexagonal or cantilevered ones, we look at circular steps and their construction.

As a general rule rectangular shapes link naturally with the house while circular patterns are more suitable for informal situations, woodland and the further reaches of the garden. Such basic rules also apply to individual features and circular steps can be particularly interesting in this context.

Circular steps
These may be of any size and can be built in a number of attractive ways. Where space is unlimited large circular brick retaining walls, up to 3m (10 ft) in diameter can overlap one another to form the risers of a slow, lazy flight. You can vary the sizes of the circle and fill them with a wide range of materials, including grass, concrete, cobbles and even tarmac, the choice depending on the underlying design of the area. The point to remember when dealing with 'free' shapes is that the infill material must be flexible, thus cobbles are fine, while pre-cast concrete slabs or stone would involve a great deal of cutting to conform to the pattern.

A 23cm (9 in) wall is structurally correct for the surround and this will need to stand on a concrete footing 45cm (18 in) wide, the depth being dependent on the conditions of the ground.

Concrete pipes for steps
Another simple and relatively cheap step is formed by using large-diameter concrete pipes. Sewer pipes are ideal, as they are available in a wide range of sizes from 1–3m (3–10 ft). Here you sink most of the pipe in the ground, leaving just enough of one end above the surface to form the riser of the step. Again you can vary sizes within the flight and a staggered pattern looks most attractive, with planting to soften the outline.

This technique need not be confined to dry land, stepping stones across a large pool being made in a similar way. In this case paint the outside of the pipe with a bituminous sealer (such as Synthaprufe) thus effectively disguising the depth of concrete below the surface. Fill the pipes with any of the materials already mentioned. It is, of course, essential to drain the pool while work is in progress.

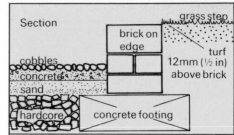

Above: a dramatic effect achieved with the use of granite setts for risers, with half-setts for treads and cobbles as a top surface
Below: plan of another set of steps shows how circle sizes and surface materials can vary
Right: cross-section, with brick surround set below lawn level to facilitate mowing

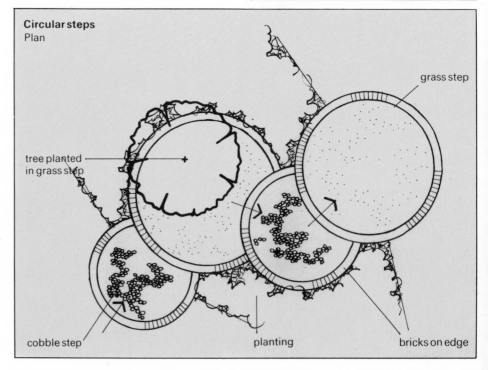

Circular steps
Plan

50

RAILWAY SLEEPERS FOR STEPS

Railway sleepers constitute a versatile material that will blend well into a natural setting. You can give a new lease of life to these solid timbers by using them as steps; they can also be adapted for paving or a retaining wall.

Timber is an essential part of garden design and is used in a wide range of applications from fencing to summerhouses and steps.

Railway sleepers, though often neglected, form an interesting and relatively cheap constructional material and are now becoming readily available as railways switch over to using concrete for track-laying.

Sources of supply vary; they can be obtained either from your local rail depot or from a middle man. In any event, enquire first at the rail depot, where you will normally be referred to the right person.

Sleepers are dark brown or black in colour, measure approximately 2·45m × 20cm × 13cm (8 ft × 8 in × 5 in), and need only two people to lift them with ease. This makes them ideal material for the rapid building of steps, retaining walls and raised beds.

As they have been weather-proofed with tar, you can expect sleepers to last indefinitely, and they can be maintained by a biennial treatment with a non-toxic wood preservative. Although creosote is in common use, remember that it is toxic and needs at least twelve months to become neutral and safe for any plants you want to put in.

Preparation and laying
In aesthetic terms, sleepers blend equally well with an architectural feature or a softly-planted bank, as their long, solid outline provides a feeling of stability and sympathy with the immediate surroundings. This is due largely to the fact that they are man-made from a natural material and so can adapt themselves equally well to fit into a natural or an artificial setting.

When you are considering how sleepers can be used in a particular situation, look at the overall design of the area.

If, for example, you need informal steps, use them in a staggered pattern and soften the outline with planting, adding one or two boulders for sculptural detail. In this instance, they can be laid 'dry' as the bank can be quite simply cut out to accept them and their weight alone will be sufficient to hold them in place.

You can create a more formal effect by building a straight or staggered flight of steps and filling the space between the sleepers with rolled gravel, hoggin (a binding mixture of clay and gravel) or crushed stone. This will give a long easy climb that would be perfect for linking a terrace with a less formal woodland or wild garden.

If the tops of sleepers are going to be exposed, as in the case of steps or paving, they should be laid upside down, to hide the bolt holes.

Below: a natural effect; front view of railway sleepers for steps and slopes, using a staggered pattern and softening the outline with plants and boulders Below right: a side section of the same Right: a formal effect; retaining wall, with sleepers and paving slabs in mortar

Paving slabs and retaining walls
You can achieve a really crisp architectural design by using sleepers in conjunction with pre-cast paving. The slab can either overhang the sleeper, possibly bedded in concrete, or sit flush behind it; the latter method allows the edge of the step to be clearly seen.

When you are building retaining walls and raised beds, work out the design in advance. Cutting sleepers can be hard work with a manual bow saw so try to borrow or hire a chain saw. The sleepers are stretcher-bonded in the same way as brickwork and either laid dry, or bedded on the soil, allowing plants to grow in between the joints.

You do not need complicated foundations for simple structures. Merely sink the first course into the ground so that the tops are flush with the surface. If the ground is heavy or unstable and high retaining walls of over a metre (or yard) are necessary, it may be advisable to bolt the sleepers onto steel angles in the ground before work starts. The wall can also be built to a slight angle, with several joints left open along its length to provide drainage.

A light or open-textured fill behind the wall will help drainage and lengthen the life of the timber.

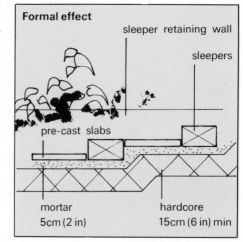

Formal effect

sleeper retaining wall

sleepers

pre-cast slabs

mortar
5cm (2 in)

hardcore
15cm (6 in) min

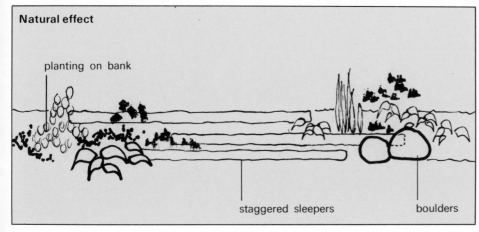

Natural effect

planting on bank

staggered sleepers   boulders

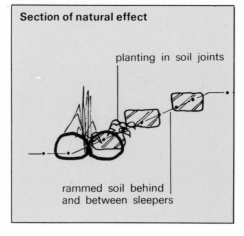

Section of natural effect

planting in soil joints

rammed soil behind
and between sleepers

LOGS FOR STEPS

Log steps should be broad, easy and inviting, a natural material to lead you from lawn to wild garden. We also show logs used as paving, seats and stepping stones.

If you are lucky enough to live in an area where timber is readily available in the form of logs, you will find that you have the basic material for a number of interesting garden projects.

Logs have an informal character and are ideal in a softly-planted woodland or in the farthest reaches of a garden where different features need to blend with one another. They can also be used in more architectural patterns as a link between the obvious, regular geometry around a building and the natural setting of the open areas beyond.

You can use virtually any type of timber; the hardwoods include beech, oak and elm, and last the longest. If you are thinking of using elm, remember that it may have been affected by Dutch Elm disease and still be capable of harbouring infection. It is wise to strip the bark off any elm logs and burn it immediately.

Making steps

Steps can be formed in a number of ways, using long or short lengths. Don't worry if the longer logs are slightly bent or twisted, as this will add to the character of the flight of steps.

You can make wide steps using single tree trunks quite simply by bedding them into the slope and driving wedges into the ground in front of each log to prevent movement. The treads can then be filled with crushed stone, hoggin or rammed soil. The length between each step need not be constant as some variety adds interest to the flight. It's also a good idea to 'stagger' the logs and encourage plant growth at the sides to soften and hide the ends of the timber.

If you can only obtain short logs, say 50cm (20 in) long, you can still make steps out of them. In this instance, drive them vertically into the ground, close together, so that the complete row forms a riser of the desired length.

Retaining walls

You can extend this technique by using longer logs to hold back sections of a slope and create retaining walls. Once again, the pattern can be varied, allowing the height of each platform to be slightly different. If the bank is in an informal part of the garden, the spaces between the log walls can be filled with softly-spreading foliage. If, on the other hand, the area is more formal, it might be better to use loose cobbles in conjunction with boulders and architectural planting.

Paving and stepping stones

Offcuts can be particularly useful in a number of ways, either as paving or as stepping stones. As paving, sections can be bedded into mortar in the usual way, or laid dry, allowing the occasional low plant to grow in soil that has been brushed into the joints.

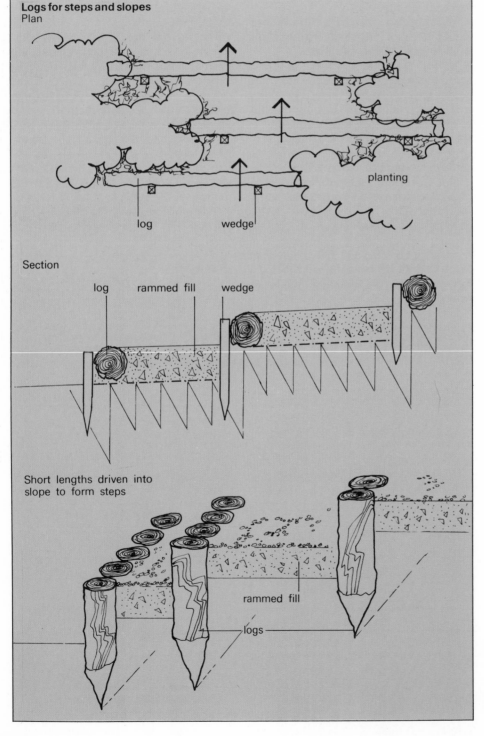

Logs for steps and slopes
Plan

planting

log   wedge

Section

log   rammed fill   wedge

Short lengths driven into slope to form steps

rammed fill

logs

Above left: ground plan (top) and section of single logs laid lengthwise to form shallow steps. The filling can be dispensed with if the ground is firm and the traffic light
Left: short logs, sharpened at one end and driven into the ground, also blend well into a country setting

Stepping stones can be laid dry, but if they are to cross a lawn, make sure that the logs are set just below the surface of the turf so that a mower can run smoothly over the top.

The 'stones' made of wood achieve just the right visual balance through planting and woodland, where real stone or pre-cast slabs might seem out of place.

Right: offcuts used as stepping stones make an effective pathway
Below: plan (top) and sections showing how to arrange logs as a retaining wall

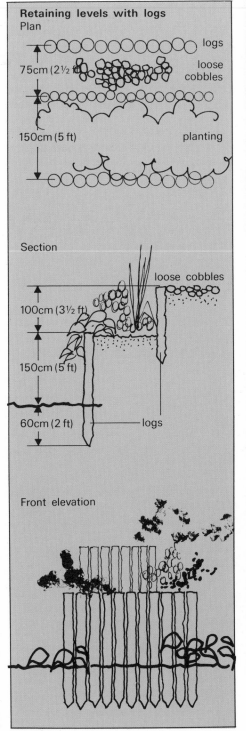

Retaining levels with logs
Plan

logs

loose cobbles

75cm (2½ ft)

150cm (5 ft)   planting

Section

loose cobbles

100cm (3½ ft)

150cm (5 ft)

60cm (2 ft) — logs

Front elevation

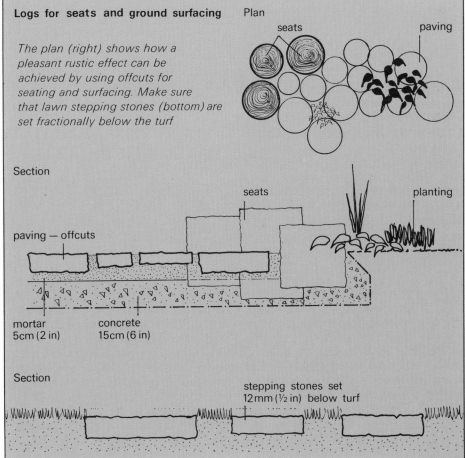

Logs for seats and ground surfacing   Plan

seats   paving

The plan (right) shows how a pleasant rustic effect can be achieved by using offcuts for seating and surfacing. Make sure that lawn stepping stones (bottom) are set fractionally below the turf

Section

seats   planting

paving — offcuts

mortar
5cm (2 in)   concrete
15cm (6 in)

Section

stepping stones set
12mm (½ in) below turf

THE FRONT APPROACH: improving your front garden

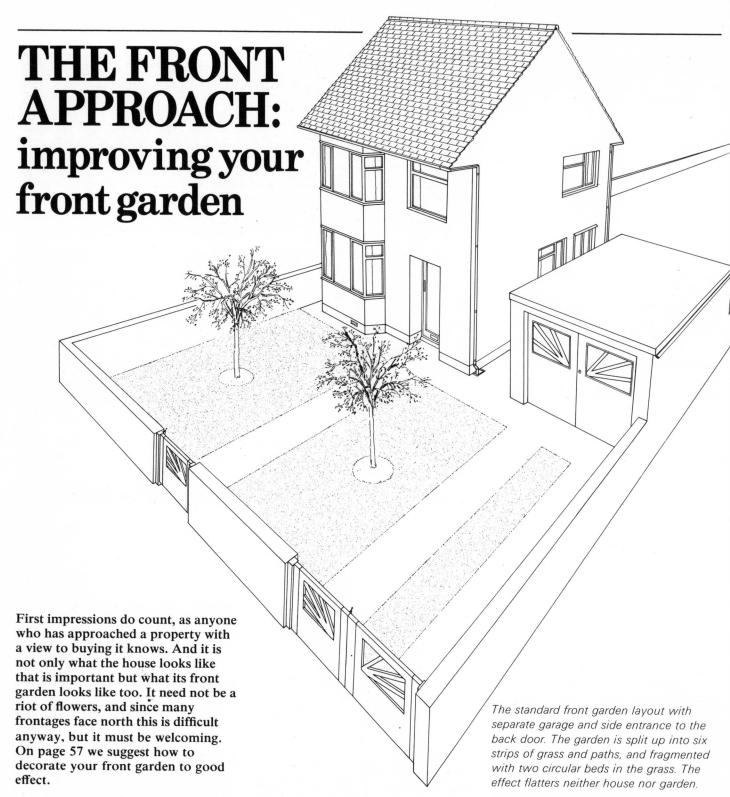

First impressions do count, as anyone who has approached a property with a view to buying it knows. And it is not only what the house looks like that is important but what its front garden looks like too. It need not be a riot of flowers, and since many frontages face north this is difficult anyway, but it must be welcoming. On page 57 we suggest how to decorate your front garden to good effect.

The standard front garden layout with separate garage and side entrance to the back door. The garden is split up into six strips of grass and paths, and fragmented with two circular beds in the grass. The effect flatters neither house nor garden.

Visitors to the home with a front garden area (and that, don't forget, includes the milkman and the dustman), want a hard, dry, easy access, with a minimum of steps or loose slabs, or eye-height hanging baskets. The driver wants room to park, with space for his passenger and himself to get out easily from his car without landing in a rose bed. If oil deliveries are expected, there must be easy access for the storage tank without the feed-pipe having to trail through areas of planting. The dustman wants his bins as close to his cart

as possible, as do you, to cut down on the inevitable trail of rubbish that is left. The postman, if he is allowed, will beat a path to the next house through your hedge unless he is deterred or directed another way. These are aspects of a front area as seen from the visitors' point of view – for them it is more of a place of arrival and departure than a true garden. With the visitors' needs in mind, now consider what are your own. You wish to present a pleasant face to the world and the materials you use to make up that face

should suit the style of house and location. For the front garden is often public and seen as one of many in a street or close, and while having a character of its own, it should not ruin its neighbours' outlook or strike a jarring note.

Types of enclosure
Consider the types available, and indeed whether you want them at all. Some enclosures will, of course, give you some privacy, will possibly keep your children and pets in and other peoples' out, and

Plan A *(right): an improved front
approach with carport extended to form a
covered way, well-planned combination of
paving, concrete and loose gravel surfacing
and a shrub planting area for privacy*

Plan B *(below): an alternative, combining
brick and stone or concrete paving, and
allowing for an open grass frontage (this
is sometimes a local regulation); shrubs
provide a screened area to the left, with
room for a favourite garden ornament*

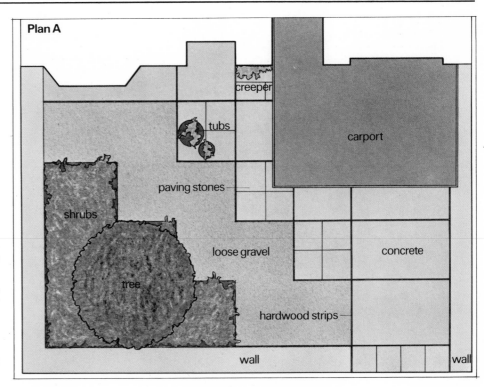

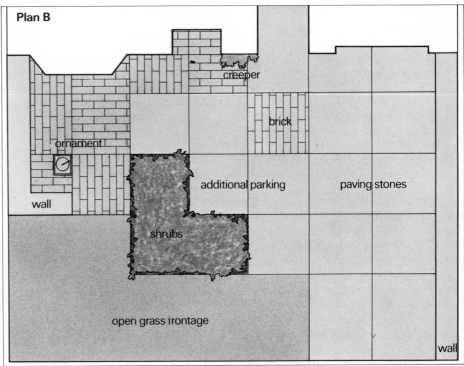

will also help to cut out noise if you are on
a busy road.

Walling This is the most expensive form
of enclosure, and if built in brick or stone
to match your house it looks very smart.
Concrete block, rendered, if you like, with
a brick or slab coping, is a cheaper
version.

Openwork concrete screening You can
soften this form of screening with large-
leaved climbers like vines rambling
through it, but it is too heavy a material to
use in conjunction with a small front area.

Fencing Coming down in scale, there are
dozens of types of fencing available in
timber. You can even try making your
own over a small run. Consider, too, a
combination low wall and timber fence,
which has the advantage of preventing
timber rotting along the bottom.

A more open fencing can be obtained
by using picket fencing or railings.
Fencing is also available in a glass-
reinforced plastic such as Fibreglass, that
needs little maintenance other than the
occasional wash-down.

Hedging If you consider a hedge surround
to your garden, think further than privet,
which needs endless clipping, and *Cup-
ressocyparis leylandii* (cypress), which will
not magically stop growing at the height
you want. They become trees 10m (40 ft)
high in no time at all!

Other than the traditional type of
hedge – beech, hornbeam, thorn or yew –
consider holly, which grows slowly, needs
little clipping and is a good deterrent for
undesirable visiting pets. Or pyracantha,
which with minimal clipping will flower
and have berries. You could use the
upright form of escallonia for a sunny
position and even upright rosemary for a
looser effect.

Planning out your front area

Within your selected enclosure, list the
facilities you require on your site, whether
you are starting from scratch or not –
front access, side access, garage access
and so on. If they can all work as one it
means that the garden will not be cut up
into masses of little areas with irritating

spaces between interlocking paths that
need to be filled with plants.

Do you require room to park a second
car or a caravan or boat? Will these go in
the area at the side of the house, if you
have a space there, and if so can they be
screened in any way? You may need a
washdown area, a hard surface and a tap
for this job and some form of drainage so
that the surplus water does not flow into
the garage. If there is an oil-storage tank
at the side of the house, you must allow
for access to this, and, of course, to the

dustbin area as well.

Now make an accurate plan of the area,
marking in the obvious locations for these
functions, and join them together with
hard surfacing. You should then at least
have a practical layout. When moving
into a house that the developer or
previous owner has already planned, it is
worth going through the same exercise
even if you have to compromise with what
you have inherited and what you really
want. Even if this front area does not
constitute a garden for relaxing in, your

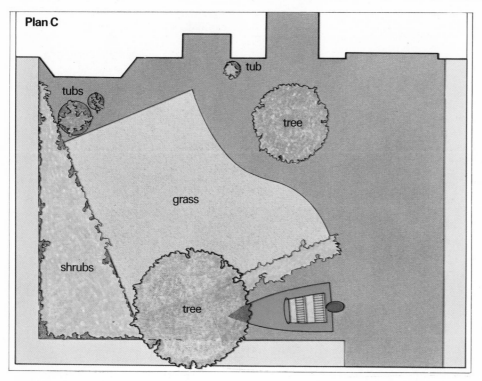

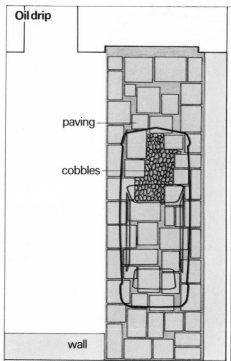

Plan C *(above): a different free-form approach with small, manageable lawn and a tarmac or gravel surface, allowing for room to park a boat conveniently. Above right: a York stone drive-in with decorative cobbled oil-drip area for car*

design should still divide off the more public area from the private.

Types of ground surfacing

Because the front area takes such heavy wear, the materials which you use to build it should be of the best (not necessarily the most expensive) and they should be well laid. Badly-jointed paving – crazy or not – can be lethal when grass comes through the joints, making the surface slippery in rain or with rotting autumn leaves on it. It cannot be over-emphasized that a good surface is the key to a serviceable front area. Stone in a country area and brick in a more sophisticated setting are very handsome as paving materials, parti-cularly if you can use the same as the structure of the house.

Brick For paving, if you buy paviors, (which are slightly larger and thinner than a building brick laid flat and fairly expensive), you need fewer than if you paved with conventional building bricks. It is worth remembering, too, that while the cost of materials like brick, or granite setts, is moderately high, it is the time and labour of laying them that really puts up the price.

Old York stone Where it is available, York stone is ideal paving for a town garden, although it does become stained by oil. To prevent this happening you could insert a cobbled oil-drip area just under where the car usually stands.

Concrete paving stone This now comes in all shapes, sizes and textured finishes. If you are using the straightforward square or rectangular stones, stick to one colour, for it is only a front garden you are laying, not an Italian piazza! New paving stones come textured as granite setts, cobbled, or as stable tiles (rather like slabs of chocolate), and can be attractive in the right setting. The cheaper slabs tend to crack easily and are difficult to cut without breaking. Most of these stones should be laid on concrete if they are to bear the weight of vehicles.

Small interlocking paving stones are available that fit together not unlike a simple jigsaw. They are easy to lay, and being a small irregular element are ideal for a setting that is not totally flat. For a small-scale area, a small paving unit of brick or tile is more attractive than slabs of concrete.

Tarmac On larger areas of frontage you may consider using tarmac, or be talked into re-laying it on an existing drive by door-to-door representatives from small firms offering this service. While some are specialists in this work, many are not. Before parting with any money, obtain a detailed specification of the work they propose to do, ensuring that an adequate base and foundation are laid for the weight of car you put on it. Other possibilities here are coloured tarmac, or rolling a local stone into the surface for a gravelled effect, or just using areas of tarmac within paving. Do not, though, allow a firm to scatter at random the odd white chip in the surface which will end up looking like a piece of candy.

When surfacing with tarmac you will need a curbed edge of brick or concrete, or the surface will break away at the edges because of frost. As you will get a quicker water run-off after rain, you must look to your drainage as well.

Concrete A cheaper broad-scale treat-ment for the drive-in might well be concrete laid *in situ*, and brushed when nearly dry, or 'green' as it is called, to expose the gravel or aggregate in the concrete. It should be laid in squares to allow for expansion, and these can be broken up with brick or any other small element to make an attractive pattern.

Gravel The cheapest large-scale medium is probably gravel. The disadvantage here is that it is picked up easily and gets carried indoors, but if a foot-scraper is provided you should not suffer from this hazard. Be sure to lay the gravel on hardcore and 'binding' gravel. The latter is unwashed and the clay content hardens and binds it together. If you put the finishing gravel layer on too thickly it will bog you down; to consolidate the finished surface, roll and water it. Gravel comes either as a chipping from a local stone quarry (when it is sharp-edged and not too good for children to fall down on) or preferably rounded (washed by water).

After deciding on your ground surface, you can spend many happy hours con-sidering what trees, shrubs and flowers to plant.

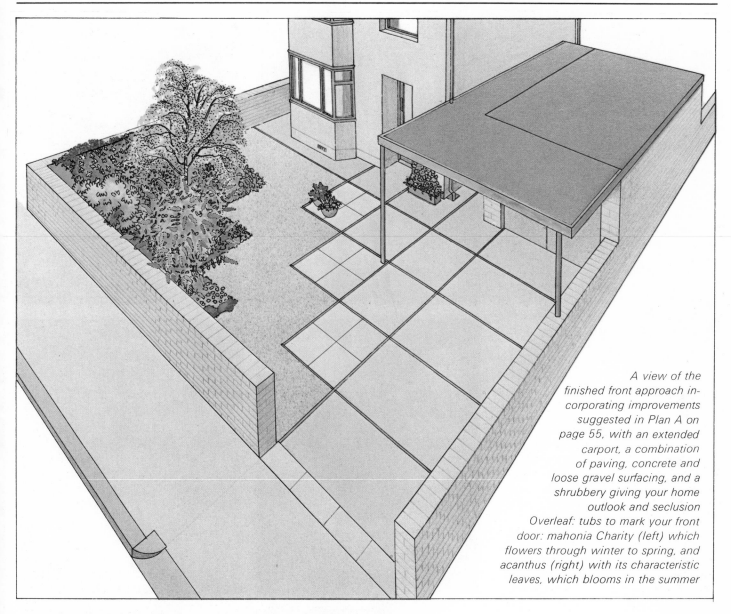

ADDING COLOUR TO THE FRONT GARDEN

We have just looked at types of enclosure and suggested varieties of ground surfacing to guide you in planning and structuring your front garden area. Now we give you a selection of suitable plants and shrubs to help you to determine its final appearance.

The plantings of the leftovers, the bits between the hard surfacing and against the house and garage should be fairly tough, with a good proportion of evergreen for an all-year-round effect. Evergreen conjures up ideas of laurel and privet (which incidentally are both effective when used well), but there are many other suitable plants, such as cotoneasters, certain viburnums, hebes, fatsia, senecio and choisya which are all attractive evergreens that flower, and some have berries too. These can also survive in an area with not too much sun. The ever-popular conifer, however, being by its shape a point-of-emphasis plant, is not suitable for most frontages.

In your layout, try to avoid little pieces of lawn which are tedious to cut, and consider instead areas of low ground cover. Here you will want something flat. Ivy is suitable in this situation, and hypericum (St John's wort or rose of Sharon), or low juniper would be admirable. Plant boldly and simply for the positive effect that is needed.

Before making your final selection of plants, do some homework on their ultimate size. A weeping willow in the middle of the front garden may look charming for a year or two, but very quickly grows to 10m (30 ft) across. And there is no point in planting shrubs on either side of a path if they need cutting back each year to allow you to walk there.

You could choose a particularly handsome sculptural plant adjacent to the front door, marking its importance. Tubs with bay trees have traditionally been used here, or, more recently, conifers again. But what about *Mahonia bealei*, or its near relation *M*. Charity? The leaves are an attractive, waxy evergreen, and the yellow flowers smell delicious in the early spring. Euphorbias (or spurges) make another good sculptural plant, or for a sunny situation try the upright-growing rosemary Miss Jessup. A good herbaceous plant in the sun is the beautiful-leafed acanthus.

Scent on entering a garden is always appreciated. Mahonia again is good, as is the evergreen *Daphne odora marginata*. *Choisya ternata*, the Mexican orange blossom, has scented white flowers and glossy foliage for cutting all year round.

If you are thinking of a climber up the front of the house or on the garage wall, consider a honeysuckle, for its scent. But, whichever climber you settle on, remember that it is the plant you have put there for display, not its means of support. Use simple wires running along the brick courses rather than complicated patterns of trellis that are liable to rot.

For points of coloured emphasis use window boxes, or pots filled with bulbs and annuals.

Highlighting your home

Lastly, if you provide a serviceable and welcoming frontage to your house, do help your visitors to find it. Put a name or number in a position not only visible to pedestrians but also to car drivers. It helps, too, if the lettering is legible and not too much in the mock Tudor rustic style. Let the name and number be illuminated at night, as well as any change of level at the entrance. With luck this may deter the night intruder, as well as guide the more welcome guest.

Top left: evergreen hebe Autumn Glory
Top right: the scented Choisya ternata
Above left: Fatsia japonica *in flower*
Above: Hedera canariensis *on tree stump*
Below: Mahonia bealei, *cultivated in Japan*

A SMALL TOWN GARDEN

Town gardens are often tiny, and here we look at their possibilities and their limitations. On page 62 we give details of construction and planting.

No two garden designs should look exactly the same, with their size, shape and situation all varying to determine an individual composition. Each site has its own difficulties and town gardens present their own quite distinct limitations.

First, space is likely to be limited, walls of surrounding buildings will cast heavy shade and the views will often be dull and oppressive. On the other side of the coin, shelter is excellent and the chances of severe frost are considerably less than in a garden that stands open to the elements.

Because the area is likely to be small, careful planning is obviously important, but it is also true to say that once completed, a town garden can be a real asset, acting as an extension of the house and demanding very little maintenance. However, in such a situation people often refuse to take up the challenge, feeling that the problems are either insurmountable or too small to bother about. They may be quite adept at designing the rooms inside the house, but the outside 'room' – probably much bigger – gets neglected.

When space is limited a simple approach is called for. Grass is often impossible in an urban area, with shade making growth difficult and concentrated activity quickly producing a quagmire. A hard surface, on the other hand, will provide a solid base for a table and chairs, children's bicycles and even an ironing board for those who like to do their household chores outdoors. Hard surfaces also dry quickly after rain and consequently get maximum use throughout the year.

Planting is important to soften the walls and take the edges off the inevitably rectangular boundaries. Some of the beds will be in shade, meaning that the choice of plant species is important. It is also very helpful to raise the planted areas – this not only gives the young shrubs and herbaceous material initial height, but it makes any maintenance considerably easier.

If views of surrounding buildings are gloomy, rather than increase the height of walls and fences in an attempt to blot them out, it is far better to work on the principle of creating a partial screen, utilizing a possible combination of trellis, planting and perhaps a carefully-chosen small tree. Overhead beams, running out from the house, are useful in this respect as well, giving support for climbing plants and giving a feeling of enclosure without being too dominant. As a general rule it is probably best to leave the beams as an open framework – a canopy of perspex or PVC tends to gather leaves and general debris and dirt.

Water is a definite asset in a town garden where hot summer weather can become oppressive. However, a conventional pool takes up valuable space as well as being a hazard for young children so a small raised pool, tucked into a corner, with a lion's head or other decorative spout, is a traditional solution. But several other interesting permutations revolve around the use of boulders, cobbles and even old millstones, water being pumped through and over them to form a delightful feature. By using these techniques you can emphasize an important fact – it is the sound of running water that really counts in providing a cooling influence on the immediate surroundings.

Perhaps the most important factor of all is the planting. It not only has to undergo close scrutiny throughout the year but also withstand the restrictions of shade and a partially-polluted atmosphere. Plants are easily affected by dust and dirt in the air and this can have the effect of blocking the tiny pores or 'stomata' through which they breathe. Some of the felty, grey-leaved species are particularly susceptible, the hairs on the leaves trapping and holding a thick layer of dirt that is difficult to remove.

These, then, are some of the factors and restrictions that govern the creation of a town garden; but they are by no means insuperable. With careful planning it need not be difficult to create a charming composition.

Planning our town garden

The garden shown here is typical of the 'yard' at the back of many older terraced houses, the main area measuring 3.5 × 5m (12 × 16 ft), while a side passage leads to a door out of the dining room. As with all garden design, we first drew up both a list of priorities and a plan of the existing area, marking in the north point, good or bad views, the heights of walls and fences, the position of drains, pipes, manholes, changes of level, doors and windows, as well as any existing vegetation.

If you have just moved in, look out for any seedling trees, particularly sycamore: if they grow to more than, say, 7.5m (25 ft), have them out. There are occasional exceptions when you come across the odd huge tree that, although completely dominant, is the making of a small garden.

The choice of surfacing

Many terraces have no rear or side access, meaning that all materials have to come in and out through the house. This makes careful planning absolutely essential. In our garden the existing surface was an uneven mass of poorly-laid concrete, and under normal circumstances you would think nothing of digging it up and loading it onto a waiting skip or lorry. In a confined space, however, this is a nightmare as every shovel load has to be bagged up and carried through the house. This is where a little forethought is invaluable: raised beds, as we have already mentioned, save maintenance and as the plants will thrive in 45cm (18 in) of topsoil this leaves a considerable height to be made up. Broken concrete makes good hardcore, is sharp-draining and will be an ideal filler for the bottom of those beds.

The raised areas in our design wrap themselves around two sides of the garden, just enough to look after the unwanted material and leave the ground clean. The main part of the 'floor' is given over to paving and measures approximately 3 × 2.5m (10 × 8 ft), the size of a reasonable room inside the house. As the house and the surrounding boundary walls were built of brick it seemed reasonable to incorporate at least some of this material in the 'floor'. A good, well-fired, second-hand stock brick is fine for paving, despite the advice of some architects and surveyors. It has the added advantage of an immediate mellow look. Our pattern of brick was based on the main lines of the building and this allowed for a second 'infill' material.

Light, or lack of it, is often a problem in an urban situation and if you can use a pale, reflective material, so much the better. White paving is probably best avoided as it tends to pick up dirt easily. We chose a pale sandstone-coloured precast slab. This mixture of materials ties the composition together while the water feature is emphasized as a focal point.

Devising a water feature

The uses of water in a small garden are legion and as our ground space was limited we decided to try a somewhat different approach. We placed a polythene water tank in the existing raised bed and neatly fitted into this a drilled slate slab. A length of copper pipe was pushed through the hole in the slab and a submersible pump was fitted and the tank filled loosely with large cobbles. When the tank was filled with water and the pump turned on, a steady flow rose through and over the slab, the pressure being just enough to lift the jet clear of the surface. This looked attractive, was pleasing to the ear and was entirely safe with young children.

Improving the side passage

The side passage was only 1.5m (5 ft) wide, a long narrow space that was difficult to handle. The kitchen window not only looked onto it but was in turn overlooked by the upstairs windows of the house next door. To raise the wall would have cut virtually all the light out and involved considerable cost. An attractive solution was to fit timber beams above the passage; we painted these white to reflect the light and they made an ideal host for climbing plants. The direct view from the neighbouring windows was broken and so was the expanse of

brickwork that formed the house itself. The floor of the passage was shady and as the door from the dining room was only used occasionally, we laid a simple stepping-stone path with pre-cast slabs. The gaps between and around the slabs were planted with two tough ground-covering plants, *Epimedium × warleyense* (barrenwort) and *Vinca minor* (lesser periwinkle).

Built-in cupboard for storage

Storage in a small garden is a problem and there are always things to put away, often in a hurry when unexpected guests

The successful combination of different ingredients is the secret of this pleasant town garden. Brick and pre-cast paving provides an attractive hard surface, while ground cover such as Vinca minor Caeruleo-plena (above right) fills the planting gaps between paving slabs

Small Town Garden
Plan

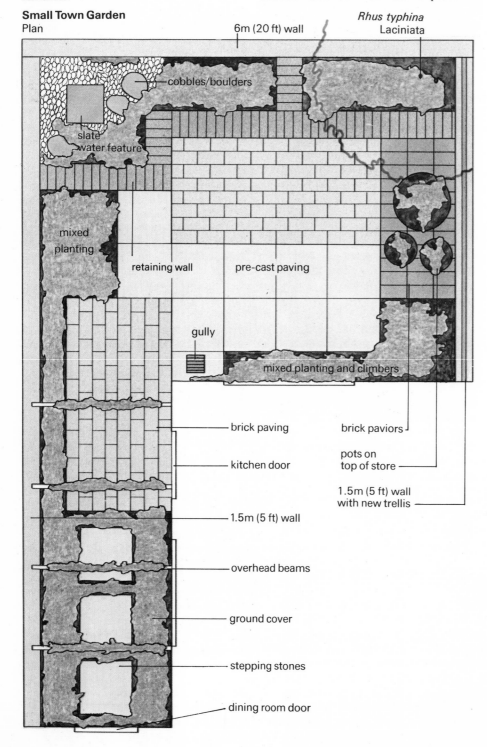

6m (20 ft) wall

Rhus typhina Laciniata

cobbles/boulders

slate water feature

mixed planting

retaining wall

pre-cast paving

gully

mixed planting and climbers

brick paving

kitchen door

brick paviors

pots on top of store

1.5m (5 ft) wall

1.5m (5 ft) wall with new trellis

overhead beams

ground cover

stepping stones

dining room door

arrive. Instead of the usual motley shed we decided to build in a double cupboard of ample capacity. This fitted neatly with the raised beds and the top acted as both a worktop and a stand for potted plants. Remember that any storage outside, although dry, is likely to be damp in the long term. Lightly oil all tools and keep your cushions indoors; they quickly grow mould if left out, even in a cupboard.

Furnishing with plants

The planting of the garden finished the picture. Climbers are of paramount importance in a town garden, helping to cover and disguise the walls. Wires for support are neater and need less maintenance than a trellis and should be secured by masonry nails driven into the joints of the brickwork.

Make your selection of shrubs and herbaceous plants with the position of sun and shade in mind. Variations of leaf tones and texture are more effective in a small town garden than brash colour, evergreens being particularly important for winter interest. The whole plant composition should thus act as a backdrop to the completed garden, giving a balanced and welcoming display

CONSTRUCTING A SMALL TOWN GARDEN

We have now outlined the methods of planning and the limitations imposed by a small town garden. Here we take a more detailed look at the construction of the various features together with planting.

The various methods of laying paving have already been covered on pages 21 and 56 but it is worth repeating that all paved areas should be given a 'fall' or slight slope away from the house and towards any available gullies. This is particularly important where the whole outdoor area is given over to hard surfacing as puddles and slippery areas are a nuisance as well as being potentially dangerous.

Raising the levels

In order to reduce maintenance and soften the dominating surrounding walls we raised the main areas of planting at the back of the garden. The bricks used for the paving were matched in the raised beds and 230mm (9 in) brick walls. Although this was not essential from a practical point of view, it gives the composition visual stability, linking with the thickness of existing walls and being neatly finished with a brick-on-edge coping. We filled the bottom of the raised beds with broken concrete from the original yard surface and this provided good drainage for the subsequent planting. It is a good idea to leave an occasional open joint in the brickwork that supports raised beds, thus allowing drainage and preventing the soil from becoming sour.

Constructing the water feature

The main focal point is the water feature situated in the corner of the garden at the end of the raised bed. We housed this within a standard polythene water tank, carefully positioned so that its top is 4cm (1½ in) above the eventual soil level. We built two 230 × 230mm (9 × 9 in) brick piers inside the tank, using a 'hard' engineering brick that would not be affected by long immersion in water. The piers stopped short of the top of the tank so that the slate that formed the feature itself stands clear of the rim and the surrounding soil. As already mentioned, the slate was a fortunate find from a demolition site, but similar materials can usually be picked up reasonably from a local monumental mason.

Offcuts of granite, slate or marble can be put to good use in the garden and the mason will usually be able to cut or drill any piece to your specification. Our slate was drilled centrally to accept a length of 12mm (½ in) copper pipe. This was pushed through the hole so that it was flush with the top, but projected about 5cm (2 in) on the underside, ready to accept the length of hose from the submersible pump. The latter was housed in the bottom of the tank and connected back to the house with the correct combination of exterior cable and sockets.

When laying a paved area it is often possible to incorporate an armoured cable underneath the slabs, thus avoiding a long run of wire above ground. Should you have any doubts concerning electrical work it is wise to seek the advice of a professional, particularly in the garden, where the hazards of moisture and accidental damage are obvious.

We left the final positioning of the slate, boulders and cobbles until the adjoining bed was filled with soil and the other features within the garden were finished, thus allowing any debris to be easily removed from the tank.

Building a worktop store

The next feature to tackle was the store cupboard that doubled as a worktop and stand for pot plants. We built the main framework with 115mm (4½ in) brick walls, each wall dividing the store into sections and acting as support for the lintels. The latter were of the 'pre-stressed' kind that are available from most large builders' merchants in various widths and lengths. The great advantage of this particular type lies in the thickness – approximately 5cm (2 in), as opposed to a cast lintel that takes anything up to 15cm (6 in) to achieve the same strength. We used three 23cm (9 in) wide lintels, (firmly bedded side by side in mortar) on top of the walls. We then laid glazed paving bricks 25mm (1 in) thick to form the top of the cupboard, the first course overhanging the front by 25mm (1 in).

The doors were constructed with tongue-and-groove boards, and then painted with a primer, undercoat and white topcoat. The hinges, catches and screws are brass, to resist rust.

The water feature, set amongst planting in the raised bed, makes a delightful focal point and, in the summer, has a cooling effect on the whole garden

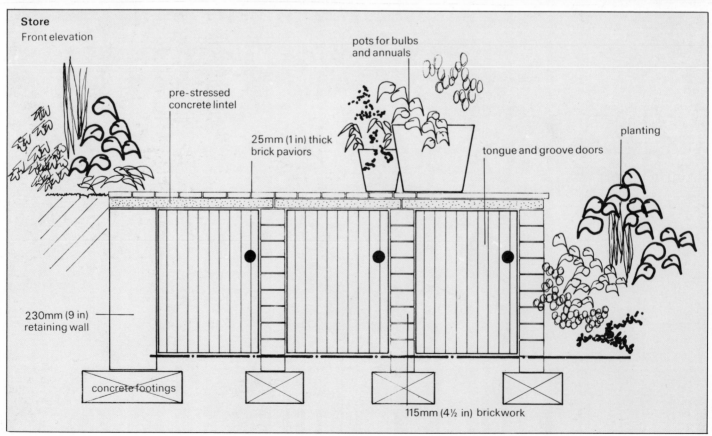

Store
Front elevation

pots for bulbs
and annuals

pre-stressed
concrete lintel

25mm (1 in) thick
brick paviors

planting

tongue and groove doors

230mm (9 in)
retaining wall

concrete footings

115mm (4½ in) brickwork

Decorating the passageway

The white beams that run over the passage to the dining room were hung next. These are constructed from 230 × 50mm (9 × 2 in) timbers and supported on the house side by joist hangers while scaffold poles form the uprights into the top of the wall.

The exact details are similar to those given for our Barbecue Garden on page 70. In order to help climbing plants onto the beams, we screwed metal eyes into the undersides and passed a wire through them. Once a plant has reached the required height it is simple enough to tuck the stems under the wire and eventually form an attractive canopy of vegetation. The wires also help maintenance as the eyes can be removed and the whole plant lowered when the beams need painting.

Filling the water tank

Before tackling the planting we finished the water feature by loosely filling the tank with large stones and cobbles. The hose from the pump we connected to the pipe inserted in the slab with a jubilee clip, and then the slate was carefully positioned on top of the brick piers. More loose cobbles and several boulders disguised the lip of the tank, the latter being filled with water to within 8cm (3 in) of the top. When the pump was switched on, water bubbled up through the slate and slid smoothly over the surface to descend into the tank in a continuing cycle.

The choice of planting

The last major operation involved planting and the preparation of the beds themselves. New soil was absolutely essential as what little there was from the original yard was of poor quality and extremely 'tired'. It is at this point that town gardeners score over their country cousins as they can virtually select the

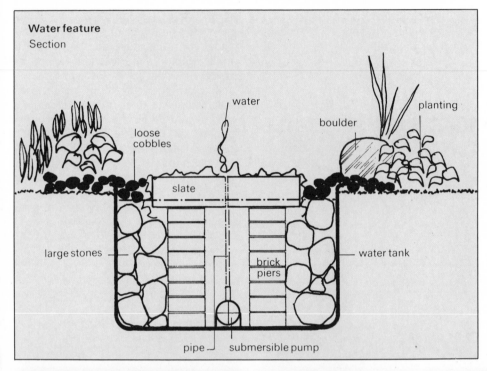

Water feature
Section

water

planting

boulder

loose cobbles

slate

large stones

brick piers

water tank

pipe

submersible pump

Far left, above: Fatsia japonica *is decorative in a shady situation*
Far left, below: the store cupboard acts as a work bench and a pot plant stand
Left: internal structure of the water feature is not completed until other construction work is finished
Below: Hydrangea macrophylla *Blue Wave*

type of soil they need. If you are a lover of rhododendrons, camellias or other acid-loving plants it is easy enough to prepare a soil of the correct pH value.

In town gardens shade is often a limiting factor but it should be remembered that the range of plants that enjoy these conditions is by no means small. In our garden, as you can see from the suggested planting plan, we have used many shade-lovers, some of which are described here. *Fatsia japonica* (fig-leaf palm of Japanese aralia) with its fine sculptural evergreen foliage is a good choice, together with *Hosta sieboldiana* (plantain lily) that contrasts with the upright form of *Iris foetidissima* Lutea.

Hydrangeas are invaluable and we have chosen one of the prettiest 'lacecap' varieties, *Hydrangea macrophylla* Blue Wave. *Viburnum davidii*, that grows into a compact rounded shrub, is another evergreen with attractive purple berries.

For vertical emphasis we have included *Rhus typhina* Laciniata, a small sumach tree of sculptural habit that can be carefully shaped to enhance its dramatic branch formations.

Climbers too are of paramount importance. *Jasminum nudiflorum* (winter jasmine), or the climbing *Hydrangea petiolaris* are particularly useful on a shady wall as is Virginia creeper, a good variety of which is *Parthenocissus tricuspidata* Veitchii. An unusual climber is featured on one of the beams, *Aristolochia durior* or *macrophylla* (Dutchman's pipe), taking its common name from the oddly-formed flowers. This, too, is happy in sun or semi-shade. Actinidia (Chinese gooseberry) is ideal for a sunny position while the many varieties of lonicera (honeysuckle) are invaluable for their fragrant blooms.

As planting is inevitably small when first introduced to its new home, it is a good idea to fill the initial gaps with bulky annuals and of course, bulbs. Nicotiana (tobacco plant) and matthiola (stocks) give the bonus of scent while helianthus (sunflowers) have more dramatic qualities to add in these early stages.

Imaginative planting clothes the composition, softening the hard line of walls and providing a backdrop to your outside room throughout the year.

Our planting plan shows one way to 'furnish' your garden with a variety of plants from bulbs to climbers. The ground plan, with details of other features, is given on page 60

Small Town Garden
Planting plan

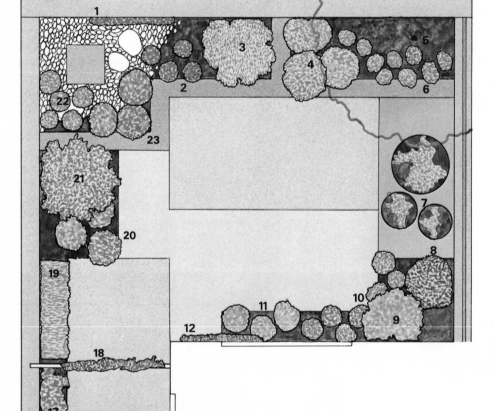

Key to planting plan

Numerals after names denote quantities of plants

1 *Parthenocissus tricuspidata* Veitchii (Virginia creeper) ×1
2 *Iris foetidissima* Lutea ×4
3 *Hydrangea macrophylla* Blue Wave ×1
4 *Viburnum davidii* ×3
5 *Rhus typhina* Laciniata (sumach) ×1
6 *Vinca minor* (lesser periwinkle) ×9
7 Bulbs and annuals in plots
8 *Rosmarinus officinalis* Miss Jessop's Variety (rosemary) ×1
9 *Salvia officinalis* Purpurascens (common sage) ×1
10 *Festuca ovina* Glauca (blue fescue grass) ×7
11 *Hebe pinguifolia* Pagei (veronica) ×3
12 *Actinidia chinensis* (Chinese gooseberry) ×1
13 *Hypericum calycinum* (rose of Sharon) ×24
14 *Hedera canariensis* Gloire de Marengo (Canary Island ivy) ×1
15 *Lonicera japonica halliana* (honeysuckle) ×1
16 *Lonicera japonica* Aureoreticulata (honeysuckle) ×1
17 *Pachysandra terminalis* ×24
18 *Aristolochia (durior) macrophylla* (Dutchman's pipe) ×1
19 *Jasminum nudiflorum* (winter jasmine) ×1
20 *Hedera helix* Glacier (common ivy), as ground cover ×3
21 *Fatsia japonica* (Japanese aralia or fig-leaf palm) ×1
22 *Bergenia cordifolia* (pig squeak) ×5
23 *Hosta sieboldiana* (plantain lily) ×3

PLANNING A GARDEN AROUND A BARBECUE

Weather permitting, there's nothing so relaxing as eating out of doors whether it be a simple 'al fresco' meal or an elaborate barbecue party. Here we tell you how to plan a barbecue garden, and then we give instructions on how to build the brick barbecue.

A tempting design for outdoor living Overleaf: ground plans showing the terrace before and after redesigning. New features include the barbecue itself, a storage space and an L-shaped seat; an extended concrete and brick-paved area that will accomodate guests and garden furniture; and two extra walls, to provide shelter

Original terrace
Ground plan

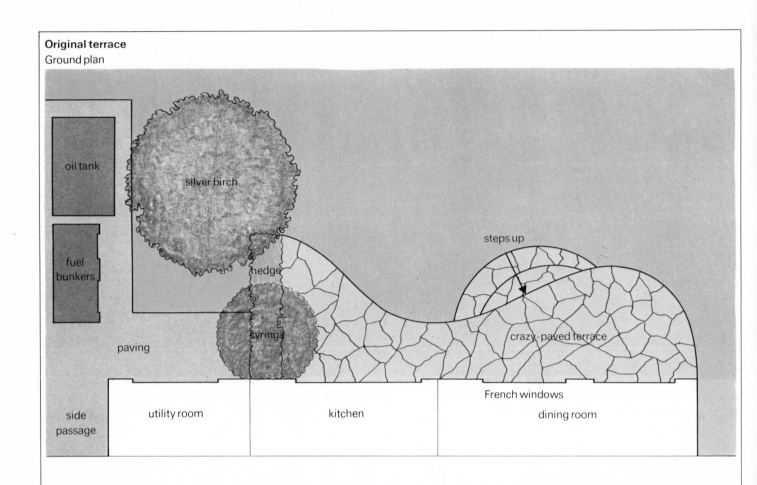

oil tank

fuel bunkers

silver birch

hedge

syringa

paving

steps up

crazy-paved terrace

French windows

side passage

utility room

kitchen

dining room

Redesigned terrace
Ground plan

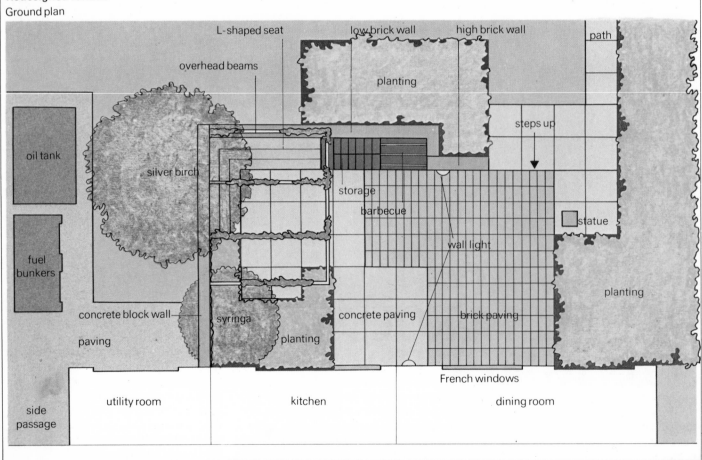

L-shaped seat

low brick wall

high brick wall

path

overhead beams

planting

oil tank

silver birch

steps up

storage

barbecue

statue

wall light

fuel bunkers

planting

concrete block wall

syringa

concrete paving

brick paving

paving

planting

French windows

side passage

utility room

kitchen

dining room

Living in the garden is not a new concept; both the Romans and the Persians built their houses around a central courtyard to benefit from shade and seclusion.

In Britain, however, it is really only during the last few decades that we have developed the 'outside room', allowing a whole range of activities, from household chores to full-scale meals, to take place in the garden.

As an occupation, barbecuing is relatively recent. The idea has been largely borrowed from the Americans who are expert at exploiting the backyard for every conceivable purpose. Barbecues do not appeal to everybody; for example, many people have been put off for life by a poorly-built model that coats both food and guests with charcoal powder.

Planning your barbecue

If you want to build your own barbecue, it is best to consider not only the barbecue grill itself, but the whole area that surrounds it. This space may be used for many different purposes, from children on bikes to family sun-bathing.

It is sometimes thought that a barbecue needs to face a prevailing wind. It is true that a good draught does help, but most small gardens are likely to be overshadowed by buildings and trees, and the subsequent turbulence means that winds may come from any direction. As a general rule, it is best to choose a site that is reasonably close to the house, but not directly under a window.

Barbecuing invariably involves groups of people, so a hard surface underfoot is essential, and the size of your paved area should not be less than 3.5×3.5m (12×12 ft). This will allow room for a table and chairs for at least four people to sit around in comfort. Ideally, it should be 4.5×6m (15×20 ft), the size of a large room inside a house.

Changing existing features

Before starting any work in the garden, have a careful look at the existing features and see how these could improve or detract from the finished design. In the garden we show, this was especially important, as the site had a marked fall away from the house, a scrubby hedge running up to the kitchen window and a view of an unsightly oil tank.

The first task was to create a level area outside the French doors that led from the dining room. As we wanted a large terrace we decided to use two paving materials: pre-cast slabs and brick. The latter material will provide contrast, in addition to visual link with the brickwork of the house.

Jasminum officinale, *common white jasmine, for softening overhead beams*

It is worth noting that the composition is built up from a series of interlocking rectangles; this design tends to extend the link visually between the house and the garden. When laying out the paving design, you should start from an obvious corner of the building and continue this pattern so that features are tied together. In our design you can see how the barbecue is strongly aligned with the French windows by the bold panel of brick. A seat in turn is held in place by the wall, while the beams bring a third dimension into play, forming the 'ceiling' of this outside room.

The area now began to take shape, but it still seemed exposed, particularly as the garden slopes away from the new side steps down from the terrace. To overcome this problem, we built another wall, at right-angles to the first one, but lower. This gave shelter on three sides and still allowed an attractive view across the lawn. The building of this second wall also gave ample room to incorporate the white seat and the barbecue itself, both becoming intentionally solid features within the overall design.

Brick for the barbecue

We built the barbecue from brick, and although this entails a reasonable amount of work, it is durable as well as being easily adapted to fit any situation. Nor need it be confined to its main function of cooking; it is large enough to have a paved worktop, set over a storage space for tools, charcoal and accessories.

It is best to use a glazed brick or quarry tile for the top, as these materials sponge down more easily than conventional bricks. However, beware of using *glazed* tiles; these look fine inside the home but frosty winters can soon shatter their surface. During the winter the grill and its supporting steel rods are best removed. This leaves a sunken rectangular space that you can then use as a tailor-made window box, filling it with bulbs or trailing plants that will provide a winter and spring display.

Plants for your terrace

Generally, planting should soften and surround the whole background area. In our garden we were lucky enough to have the lilac and, behind the new wall, a silver birch whose foliage came drooping down between the white, overhead beams. The walls themselves needed clothing and we have created new beds that would not interfere with access between indoor kitchen and outdoor barbecue grill.

Climbers are particularly useful, while the beds to either side of the steps contain a selection of flowering and evergreen plants that will provide colour and interest throughout the year. Fast and slower-growing plants are mixed and the initial gaps are filled with bulbs and annuals for colour. In this case, annuals can be quite simply hand-sown *in situ*, the drifts being thinned as they develop, a cheaper and quicker method than bedding out individual plants. Hand-sowing also results in more informal groupings that associate well with paved areas, avoiding the desperate regularity of most traditional bedding schemes.

BUILDING A BRICK BARBECUE
in your garden

The overall design of this barbecue garden was illustrated on page 67. Here we show the siting of the barbecue grill itself and give constructional details for building the major features.

For the 'floor' of this barbecue garden we chose brick or pre-cast paving and methods for laying these were given on pages 21 and 23.

Concrete block wall
The high wall running out from the house is a different matter, however, being built from hollow concrete blocks, a versatile material that could be used in the garden far more than it is. Concrete blocks come in a number of different sizes, the two most common being $115 \times 455 \times 230$mm ($4\frac{1}{2} \times 18 \times 9$ in), or $230 \times 455 \times 230$mm ($9 \times 18 \times 9$ in). They are constructed to withstand great pressure and are available in a rough or smooth finish, either of which can be given a finishing coat of stone paint.

Their size allows work to take shape quickly but it does mean that they are heavy, particularly in the larger size that you will need to use for a wall of anything over $1 \cdot 2$m (4 ft) high. Walls 230mm (9 in) thick, made either of block or brick, are visually and structurally most sound for garden work. Thinner walls of 115mm ($4\frac{1}{2}$ in) inevitably need buttresses and these detract from the appearance of the whole.

The wall here is $2 \cdot 3$m ($7\frac{1}{2}$ ft) high and for this you will need a good concrete 'footing' or foundation that will be twice as wide as the wall itself. The depth of the concrete will depend on the nature of the ground. If you are building on solid rock, virtually no footing is needed, but if the ground is marshy you will need an ample depth. On reasonable ground, as a general rule, a 75cm ($2\frac{1}{2}$ ft) trench, 45cm (18 in) wide is quite enough. This can be filled with 60cm (24 in) of concrete and allows the first course of blocks to be laid just below ground level.

You should use a simple stretcher bond, that is, lay all the blocks lengthways and stagger the joints, checking the levels as work progresses. Once five or six courses have been built, you will need a

simple scaffold or stage from which to work. Two people make the job a lot easier, with one laying blocks and the other mixing mortar and passing up the blocks as they are needed.

Joist hangers for overhead beams
As the wall nears completion you have to consider the insertion of 'joist hangers' that will hold the white overhead beams in place. These are triangular-shaped 'shoes', open at one end and with a strap that can be bedded between the top row of blocks and the brick on edge that acts as a coping. On some walls you will notice a double row of tiles just below the coping; this is known as 'creasing' and acts as a damp course that prevents water from penetrating into the top of the wall.

Low brick wall
The second, lower 1m ($3\frac{1}{2}$ ft) high wall is built of brick and will act as a host for the seat and barbecue.

On page 19 we showed a brick retaining wall built with English bond using alternate courses of headers and stretchers, or one course of bricks end on and the next one of bricks lengthways. For this wall you might try Flemish bond, where two stretchers and then a header are laid (see diagram) in the same course; this shows a pleasing finish without being difficult to build. It is essential to check your levels while working and make sure you point the joints (see page 14) at the end of each bricklaying session. With this wall you have to turn through 90 degrees behind the barbecue and, in order to marry the two angles together, you will need to cut a 'closer' brick to ensure the bond is correct (see diagram). The coping here will be brick, on edge again, but it is normal to omit the tile creasing from walls of this height.

Above right: section of joist hanger embedded in concrete block wall between top block and coping
Right: section of barbecue wall with brick laid in Flemish bond and with a 'closer' cut to accommodate the 90° turn
Far right: section of brick barbecue area showing store cupboard, adjustable cooking grill and high, sheltering wall

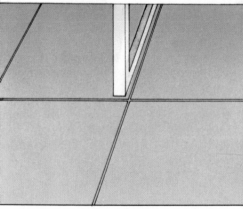

Overhead beams
Fixing on concrete block wall

- coping (brick on edge)
- tile creasing
- beam 230 x 50mm (9 x 2 in)
- joist hanger
- concrete block

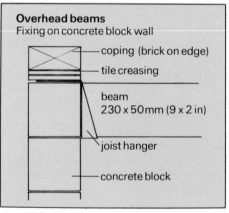

Flemish bond

closers

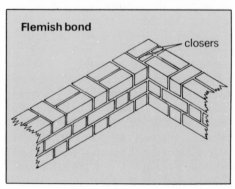

Barbecue
Front elevation

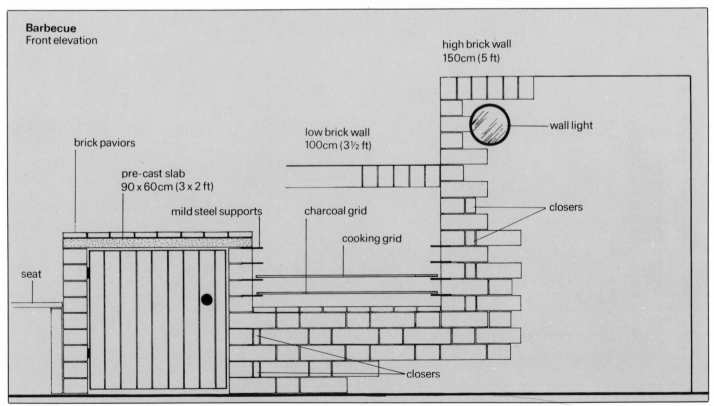

high brick wall
150cm (5 ft)

low brick wall
100cm (3½ ft)

brick paviors

pre-cast slab
90 x 60cm (3 x 2 ft)

mild steel supports

charcoal grid

cooking grid

wall light

closers

seat

closers

Brick barbecue and high wall

The barbecue and the final 1·5m (5 ft) wall are built together. The barbecue is made up of two units: the store and the actual cooker. Construct the store with a single shelf and top it with a working surface. A simple 900 × 600mm (3 × 2 ft) pre-cast concrete paving slab can act as a bed for the final finish of glazed paving bricks, or 'paviors'. Make the door from tongue and groove boards, but remember that the hinges, screws and catch should be of brass or a non-ferrous metal, to stop rust.

Below grill level, the barbecue is a solid structure and the cavity formed by the four surrounding walls should be filled with rubble and hardcore, and surfaced with glazed paving bricks. As the walls rise on either side, remember that at the sixth and subsequent courses you have to allow for the supports to hold the adjustable cooking grid. If you want a higher cooking level you must take this into consideration. Continue building the 1·5m (5 ft) wall in a Flemish bond with 'closers' as illustrated in diagram 2.

Barbecue grid

Modern foot-scrapers make remarkably effective grids and these can be held easily on several levels by 6mm (¼ in) mild steel strips bedded into the joints of the brickwork. Alternatively, a garage or local engineer will often make up a grid of any size or specification for a reasonable charge. If you are burning charcoal, a second grid or tray can be used on the lowest position, but the beauty of a brick-built barbecue is that it will accept logs that can be burned directly on the brick top; they also give the cooked food a delicious flavour.

Garden seat

Once the barbecue is finished you are ready to build the seat to the left of the store. This can have an open or closed front, the latter being a little more complicated and expensive. The top consists of six lengths of 200 × 20mm (7¾ × ⅞ in) boards which you screw into 50 × 50mm (2 × 2 in) frames (see seat diagrams). In turn, the frames are plugged and screwed into the brick and concrete walls and paving. A neatly-

Left: down support married into beam
Below and below right: L-shaped garden seat of six boards screwed into frames, secured, in turn, to walls and paving

mitred butt joint will be necessary where the boards meet in the corner formed by the high concrete wall and the low brick one. Remember to chamfer the edges of all exposed wood surfaces, that is, round them off using a plane, and then finish them with a fine grade of sandpaper. The seat can either be painted white (primer, undercoat and top coat), or stained with a wood preservative, such as Cuprinol.

Overhead beams and down supports

The final feature is the white overhead beam structure that will fit into the joist hangers already inserted into the high concrete block wall. The timbers should be lengths of 230 × 50mm (9 × 2 in) and planed all round. Do not be tempted to use smaller beams as they will only look flimsy. Climbers will soften their outline.

There is a choice of down supports: either a 50mm (2 in) square steel section, or a simple scaffold pole, dowelled at the top to accept the beams. The supports are of different lengths, the longest being bedded into a secure concrete foundation that will be surrounded by planting. Use the same method as given for erecting the pergola poles on page 23. The shorter pole is fixed into the top of the lower brick wall and can be neatly married in with the coping. This is achieved by cementing it into a 5cm (2 in) hole in the middle of the brick. Paint the supports black and maintain them, along with the beams, by giving them a rub down and a fresh coat of paint every two years.

Overhead beams
Fixing on scaffold pole

beam
230 x 50mm (9 x 2 in)

steel dowel
wooden plug

scaffold pole

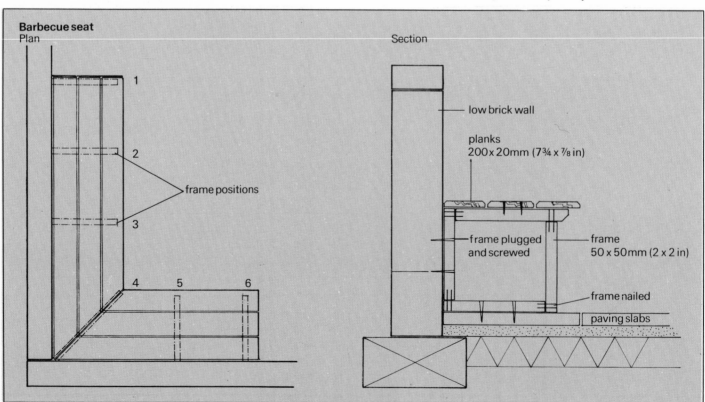

Barbecue seat
Plan

Section

1

2
3
frame positions

4   5   6

low brick wall

planks
200 x 20mm (7¾ x ⅞ in)

frame plugged
and screwed

frame
50 x 50mm (2 x 2 in)

frame nailed

paving slabs

PLANNING
A COURTYARD GARDEN

Our design for a Courtyard Garden shows how you can transform a central
area and make it into an extra 'room' clothed in vegetation, that
not only complements the house itself but facilitates indoor- outdoor living.

The success of any garden, ancient or modern, lies in its compatability with the building it adjoins. In this way the house merges with the outside room and plants and materials overlap so that it is difficult to define a precise boundary between the two elements.

A courtyard is a particularly architectural feature and it is worth remembering that the charm of such gardens was due to the ability of the designer to conceive the composition as a whole. Today, in all but a handful of situations, the opposite applies. The property may well be built as a carefully-designed unit, but the surrounding land is usually neglected.

The house and garden that we show is fortunate enough to be unashamedly urban. The low, two-storey building forms two sides of the sunny quadrangle while walls of surrounding properties close the gaps. The ensuing space is sheltered and secluded, a perfect retreat and the ideal outdoor room. Access from the house is available from the sitting room and dining room and both have large sliding glass doors, heightening the link between inside and out. In addition, the house has many windows and is in fact designed to overlook the courtyard. The brief for the garden called for an area with ample hard-surfacing, water as a central focus and enough planting to soften the harsh outlines without being a maintenance problem.

The obvious geometry of the surroundings established the theme for the design, based on a series of overlapping rectangles that extended the lines of the building. The hard surfaces are carefully chosen and help to define individual areas within the composition. Moving away from the house, we chose brick for the outdoor sitting and dining areas. The facing brick used in the building was a hard, well-fired variety and we were able to lay these, 'frog' (dent-side) down, in a stretcher bond, the bricks simply being bedded end to end, as shown in the plan.

The garden is, in fact, subtly divided in two, the pool and bed of annuals forming the link. Stepping stones cross both features and in this way you are compelled to walk over a particular route, avoiding short cuts and utilizing more of the garden as a result.

A pool as focal point

The pool is an essential part of the design, and being clearly visible from all points, acts as a pivot. Thus situated, a simple sheet of water is far more effective than a complicated series of falls and fountains. The sound of a 'bubble-jet' just breaking the water's surface is delightful and quite

Above: Eurphorbia griffithii *Fireglow adds a welcome splash of colour*
Previous page: our courtyard makes imaginative use of water and planting

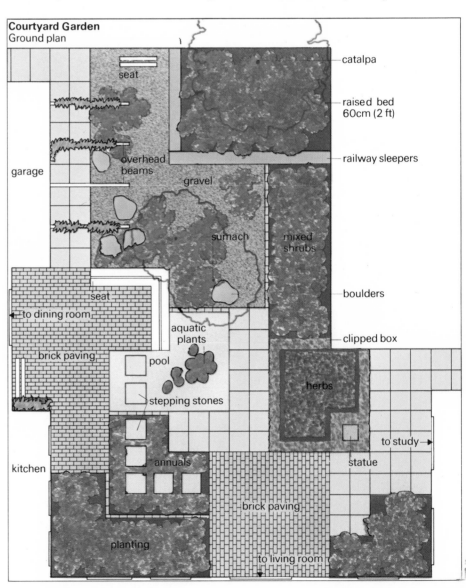

Courtyard Garden
Ground plan

adequate. In a similar way, straightforward detailing of the pool edge will produce a superb play of light and shadow, and you can enhance this by the careful positioning of aquatic plants.

As with the construction of steps and risers, slabs around a pool should overhang the water by 5cm (2 in). This is particularly important with the stepping stones that have brick supporting piers built to accommodate a similar overhang. In this way the slabs will appear to 'float' just clear of the surface.

Gravel with boulders and planting

As we considered grass to be impractical for maintenance reasons, we floored the area beyond the pool and built-in seat with gravel and highlighted it with a combination of boulders and planting, with two *Rhus typhina* (stag's horn sumach) providing vertical emphasis.

The back of the garage is perhaps the least interesting feature of the entire garden and this has become a support for a number of overhead beams forming a pergola. The beams are smothered with climbing plants and form an attractive walk that leads to the side passage and front of the house. The strong, horizontal lines of the beams are echoed closer to the ground by the raised bed built from railway sleepers. This gives initial height to young planting and has the effect of drawing attention to the *Catalpa bignonioides* (Indian bean tree) that acts as a secondary focal point.

The choice in planting

Planting is especially critical in a courtyard and not only softens the edges but adds to the feeling of form and space as well. Certain plants have definite sculptural qualities and these should be used in bold patterns to reinforce the underlying design.

Acanthus mollis (bear's breeches), the leaves of which adorn the tops of Corinthian columns, is a fine plant to grow through the gravel.

Of the euphorbias, there are three particularly fine varieties: *E. wulfenii* forms a large, rounded hummock; *E. griffithii* Fireglow has striking orange bracts, and *E. polychroma* acts as a sprawling but architectural ground cover.

Two or three yuccas with their magnificent flower spikes are invaluable, and such strong, rounded shapes are complemented by rounded forms, the shrubs cytisus and hebe being ideal examples. Herbs are included for their fragrance and culinary value and climbers are, of course, essential for training over beams and walls.

The finished composition should be planned for colour and interest throughout the year. A courtyard allows outside living over a far longer period than other garden forms as the walls provide shelter and warmth that are of benefit to plants and people alike.

Key to planting plan
Numerals after names denote plant quantities.

1 *Lonicera japonica halliana* (honeysuckle) ×1
2 *Viburnum plicatum* Lanarth (Japanese snowball) ×1
3 *Vinca minor* (lesser periwinkle) ×16
4 *Deutzia × rosea* Carmina ×3
5 *Catalpa bignonioides* (Indian bean tree) ×1
6 *Arundinaria murielae* ×2
7 *Hydrangea petiolaris* ×1
8 *Fatsia japonica* (Japanese aralia or figleaf palm) ×2
9 *Hydrangea macrophylla* Blue Wave (common hydrangea) ×3
10 *Anemone japonica* (windflower) ×4
11 *Daphne mezereum* (mezereon) ×2
12 *Spiraea × bumalda* Anthony Waterer ×3
13 *Buxus sempervirens* Suffruticosa (box) ×57
14 *Potentilla fruticosa* Tangerine (cinquefoil) ×3
15 *Yucca flaccida* ×2
16 *Cytisus × praecox* Allgold (Warminster broom) ×2
17 *Wisteria sinensis* (Chinese wisteria) ×1
18 *Euphorbia polychroma* (cushion spurge) ×7
19 *Hebe pinguifolia* Pagei (hebe) ×2
20 *Cistus × purpureus* (rock rose) ×1
21 *Lavatera olbia* Rosea (tree mallow) ×2
22 *Verbascum bombyciferum* (mullein) ×3
23 *Jasminum officinale* (common jasmine) ×1
24 *Choisya ternata* (Mexican orange blossom) ×2
25 *Salvia officinalis* Purpurascens (common sage) ×3
26 *Papaver orientale* (Oriental poppy) ×4
27 *Actinidia chinensis* (Chinese gooseberry) ×1
28 *Bergenia cordifolia* (pig squeak) ×9
29 *Euphorbia wulfenii* (spurge) ×1
30 *Rhus typhina* Laciniata (stag's horn sumach) ×2
31 *Hosta sieboldiana* (plantain lily) ×5
32 *Acanthus mollis* (bear's breeches) ×3
33 *Campsis tagliabuana* Madame Galen (trumpet creeper) ×1
34 *Hedera helix* Glacier (common ivy) ×5
35 *Aristolochia durior* (birthwort) ×1
36 *Cistus × lusitanicus* Decumbens (rock rose) ×2
37 *Lonicera japonica* Aureoreticulata (honeysuckle) ×1
38 *Euphorbia griffithii* Fireglow (spurge) ×1

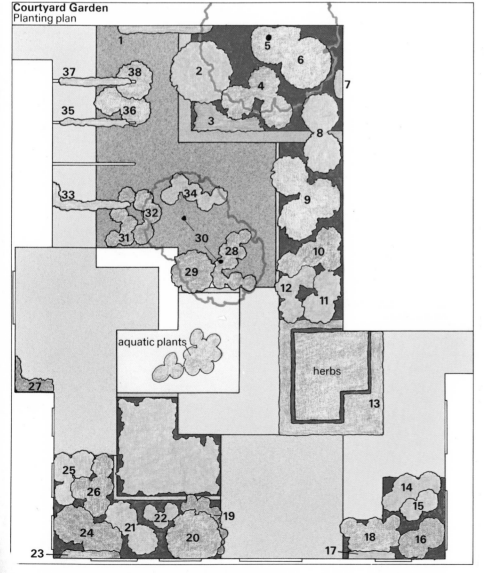

Courtyard Garden
Planting plan

aquatic plants

herbs

PLANNING A ROOF GARDEN

You don't need a ground-level site to experience the joys that gardening can bring: all that is necessary is a suitable roof and a little ingenuity.
The benefits that a roof garden can offer include a warm environment that will appeal to both plants and gardener alike; peace and privacy; and – if you are fortunate – an unhindered view.
Here we introduce our own design, and later on we describe the formation of the basic features.

To create a garden on a roof means a departure from normal gardening techniques, and often involves an entirely new set of rules. As the height above ground increases so, too, do the difficulties – seemingly in direct ratio; access, shelter, irrigation and weight: all will assume quite new proportions.

Certain problems are peculiar to roof gardens. A common one is how to hide the rash of pipes that always seems to be in the most awkward position. Another frequently concerns weight: before undertaking any work you should be absolutely certain that the existing structure is sound and capable of supporting the proposed garden. If you are in any doubt, call in an architect or surveyor to make a professional assessment of the situation – it is better to be safe than sorry!

Apart from technical considerations though, the chief factor affecting your roof garden is likely to be the wind. In a built-up area calm is normally taken for granted. However, what may seem a gentle breeze in the street can be a biting wind three floors up. Providing adequate shelter is therefore of paramount importance, both from your plants' point of view, and your own.

Plan and design

As far as design is concerned, you should tackle the initial survey exactly as you would for a ground-level garden. Views, direction of prevailing wind, aspect, position of doors and windows, and the total dimensions must all be drawn on your basic plan, together with any other relevant information. If you do this on squared paper it will be easy to establish a scale and ensure that the features are correctly related to one another.

It would be wise to position heavy features around the perimeter, where the underlying framework will transfer the load onto the surrounding walls. As soil is usually the heaviest, your planting area will be strictly regulated.

Paving, in the conventional sense, will also present a weight problem. It is usual to find either asbestos tiles or some kind of specially-laid bituminous surface where access has been previously planned, but neither would be particularly attractive over large areas.

The limitations and possibilities should now be falling into some form of pattern, possibly similar to that shown on our detailed ground plan.

Roof gardens, in general, are small and ours is no exception, measuring approximately 10·5 × 6m (35 × 20 ft). It has a high wall on one side, and a lower wall topped by chimney pots on the other. The main view is from directly in front of the doorway leading to the house below. The floor was originally laid with asbestos tiles, and unsightly pipes were visible in a number of places. A television aerial hung from the higher wall, and the prevailing wind tended to sweep over the lower wall, making sitting outdoors impossible in all but the calmest weather.

Our first task, then, was to provide some form of shelter. To this end, we constructed a strong wooden canopy, and used clear corrugated rigid PVC to form the roof. We left the front open, but fitted the side facing the wind with open, horizontally-arranged slats to form a protective screen. The latter, while breaking the force of the wind, still allows some movement of air through the garden, so helping to keep the temperature reasonable on hot days. It also hides the pipes, and creates the small utility area that houses the tiny shed and the invaluable water butt for irrigation.

Raised beds and wooden seat form focal point of design, while a rigid PVC roof and slatted wall provide shelter

A timber handrail ran along the front of the roof. As children might use the garden we decided to close it in for safety, using plate glass with bevelled edges. This way we retain the view and reduce wind velocity within the garden even more.

Structurally, in addition to the supporting walls around the perimeter, we were lucky enough to have a wall running along the line of the horizontal slats. So we were able to plant along the edges of the roof, and also incorporate a planting feature in virtually the middle of the design. This led to the creation of an interesting composition involving planting on split levels, and a seat that gives definition to the main relaxation area.

Next we turned our attention to the floor. The asbestos tiles measured 23cm (9 in) square and covered the whole roof.

After we had scrubbed them with a strong detergent their colour was a uniform grey that, although not unpleasant in moderation, was distinctly oppressive over the entire area.

As already mentioned, pre-cast paving is normally far too heavy for a roof, likewise the more traditional natural

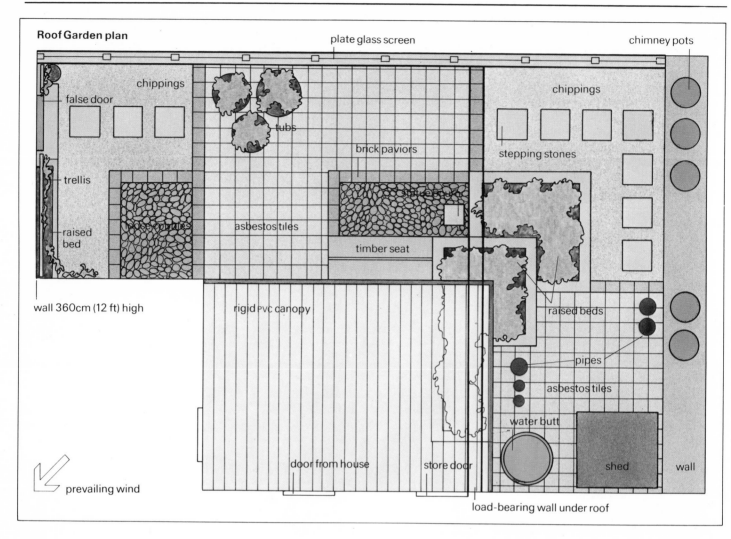

Roof Garden plan

plate glass screen

chimney pots

chippings

false door

chippings

tubs

stepping stones

brick paviors

trellis

raised bed

loose cobbles

asbestos tiles

timber seat

raised beds

wall 360cm (12 ft) high

rigid PVC canopy

pipes

asbestos tiles

water butt

prevailing wind

door from house

store door

shed

wall

load-bearing wall under roof

stone. Thinner paving bricks and quarry tiles are lighter, although where a large area is involved the weight would still be considerable.

In our design we divided the garden area into squares and worked out a simple geometric pattern. Some parts we left as the original surface, and others we edged with black paviors 25mm (1 in) thick. The resulting panels we filled with a thin covering of loose chippings – just enough to cover the tiles. As the stones were laid loose, drainage was unaffected, the occasional joint being left open in the brick surround to allow water to flow on its way to the main gutter. One word of warning: chippings come in a range of colours, but you should exercise particular care over your choice. It is advisable to steer clear of white as it can prove extremely dazzling in such an open situation; the same goes for painted surfaces. Buffs and browns are particularly restful and form a good background for plantings.

We had a bit of fun on the high wall. When the house was being converted a new front door was hung and its predecessor was due to be carted away with the

rest of the rubbish. Instead, we rescued it and screwed it into position on the wall. We laid chippings over the area in front of the door and placed stepping stones to lead up to a small and quite obvious step. With a handle fitted, the door fooled numerous visitors, who either asked what was on the other side, or actually tried the handle. We fitted the wall on each side with squared trellis, and trained climbing plants over this.

After checking with a television engineer we discovered that the aerial could be removed and replaced with an indoor model.

Planting your roof garden
A special lightweight variety of soil is available that you can actually mix in your own home and we tell you more about this on page 81. If you are thinking of using pots or tubs make sure they are of ample size, for they will dry out far quicker on a roof than at ground level, with the combination of greater heat and drying wind in that situation.

It is essential that you water pots every single day in summer, which can lead to obvious problems at holiday time. Raised

Tackle initial survey as for ground-level garden, and draw basic plan on squared paper to establish scale and ensure features relate correctly to one another

beds on the other hand, will hold a greater depth of soil and thus retain moisture longer. You could use timber as a construction material, although it will be costly and require protection from damp on the inside by polythene or asbestos. A far easier method is to use lightweight concrete blocks such as Thermalite, from which you can build beds of any shape; simply bore holes through the blocks for drainage. To protect the blocks from the weather you can render them on the outside, or give them a coat of suitable stone paint, such as Sandtex.

Choose plants that will enjoy a hot sunny position. Cistus, potentilla, senecio, cytisus and yucca will all thrive in a roof setting, provided you erect shelter, while bulbs and annuals will also grow quickly. You can group your plants in the same way as you would in a ground-level garden, choosing species to provide colour and interest throughout the year.

CONSTRUCTING A ROOF GARDEN

We have not outlined the advantages of high-level gardens, introducing our own Roof Garden design as an easy-to-follow example. We go on to detail the basic features of the design, and give instructions for making the glass screen and creating split-level planting areas. The view towards the 'false door' is shown below.

The chief factor affecting your roof garden will probably be the wind. Here we look at the construction of the two features in our own design that break the force of the wind and provide shelter for both you and your plants.

Making the canopy

The canopy protects the relaxation area from the wind and is built in three stages (see diagram on next page). First you construct a framework of beams and supports; then you add the slatted screen that acts as the principal windbreak; finally you top the whole structure with a clear, rigid corrugated PVC roof.

Use 150 × 25mm (6 × 1 in) timbers, planed all round, to construct the main framework. Make it in the form of a box, and bolt it to the two load-bearing walls with special expanding masonry bolts. The beams should finish flush with the top of the wall, allowing the corrugated PVC sheet to continue to the gutter beyond.

These PVC sheets, such as Novolux, are normally available in a standard width of 75cm (2½ ft), and can be bought with a tinted finish that is useful for cutting down glare. To ensure adequate fixing, you should space the 150mm (6 in) beams at 35cm (14 in) centres, but remember to drill through the high ribs of the corrugated sheets before screwing them into position. Standard fixing accessories – that is, screws, washers and caps – are usually sold along with the PVC sheets.

Use a 100mm (4 in) softwood post for the single down support, and fix it to the roof with either angle brackets or a single shoe.

An important point to remember when about to drill a hole in your roof is that you might cause dampness, or even leaks in the room below if you are not careful. Therefore, make as few holes as possible, and be sure always to use a sealer like mastic or bitumen. Should you have any doubts, call in professional help: it's best to play safe in such a situation.

For the horizontally-arranged wooden slats of the screen on the open side of the canopy, you can also use 150 × 25mm (6 × 1 in) timbers; screw them into the down support at one end, and to a simple 50 × 50mm (2 × 2 in) batten (screwed into the wall), at the other.

Erecting the glass screen

Erecting the glass screen at the front of the garden is a comparatively simple job. A handrail and hardwood posts were already in position on our roof-top area, so we simply had to fit brass lugs to accept the carefully-measured 6mm (¼ in) plate glass panels. A glazier will be able to bevel the edges and drill the glass for you. Use brass nuts and bolts with fibre or plastic washers to protect both sides of the glass from abrasion.

Building the raised beds

Timber will not be the best material for building the raised beds, for it is expensive and involves complicated constructional techniques. Lightweight concrete blocks, such as Thermalite, are what you need.

Right: for detailed plan see page 78
Below: section of main canopy showing framework topped with rigid PVC sheet

Buy them measuring 80 × 230 × 450mm (3 × 9 × 18 in), and lay them in a stretcher bond (lay blocks lengthways and stagger the joints). Where corners are involved a 'closer' cut to fit will be needed to adjust the bonding. An advantage of these blocks is that they can be sawn, producing neat joints.

The main feature in our garden comprises the seat and split-level beds, and is built up from blockwork two, three and four courses high respectively; the tops of the walls are neatly finished with glazed paving bricks, 25mm (1 in) thick. As lightweight blocks are porous you will have to render them with sand and

cement, and then apply a stone paint, such as Sandtex. You needn't render the inside of the bed as three coats of a bituminous paint will be satisfactory.

The highest bed is 90cm (3 ft), but it would be both unnecessary and unwise to fill with soil to this depth: 45cm (18 in) will be sufficient. Fit a false asbestos floor, which you can support with 6 × 50mm (¼ × 2 in) steel strips bedded into the blockwork two courses from the top. Drill 25mm (1 in) holes, spaced at 23cm (9 in) centres, into the floor for drainage, and similar-sized holes through the blocks just above roof level, to allow water to drain into the main gutters.

Roof Garden plan

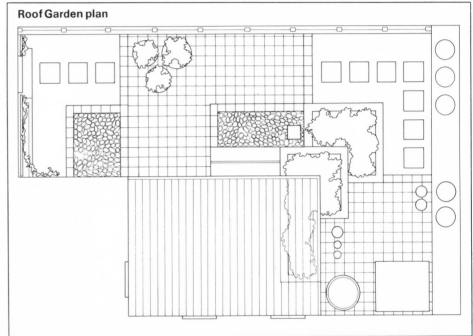

Main canopy
Section

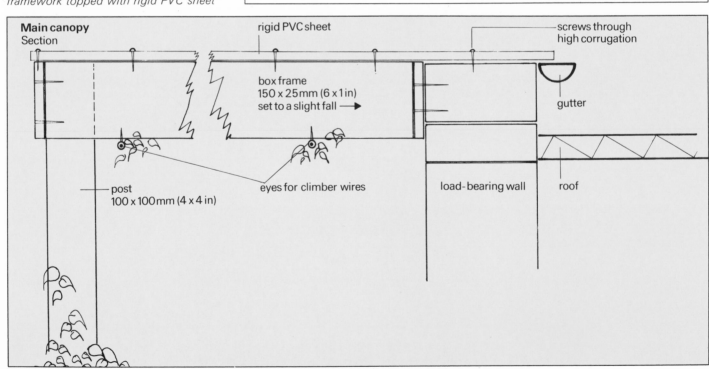

rigid PVC sheet

screws through high corrugation

box frame
150 x 25mm (6 x 1 in)
set to a slight fall →

gutter

post
100 x 100mm (4 x 4 in)

eyes for climber wires

load-bearing wall

roof

Insert plugs into the blockwork forming the bottom of the seat, and fit a 50 × 50mm (2 × 2 in) timber frame. Screw three 200 × 20mm (8 × ⅞ in) slats into this, and chamfer and carefully sand them, prior to painting.

Bedding the paving bricks

Glazed paving bricks, similar to those used on the top of the beds, are ideal for forming the retaining edges that define the areas of chippings. Bed the bricks in mortar, making sure that the joints are carefully pointed, and leaving an occasional gap to drain any trapped water. Stepping stones through the chippings will need to be approximately 25mm (1 in) thick to match the bricks, and this rules out most pre-cast slabs that are normally in excess of 38mm (1½ in). Natural stone is often available in thinner gauges, however, and slate in particular will look very handsome against the paler surrounding surface. Bed the stones in mortar in the same way as the paving bricks.

In this design we have placed stepping stones to lead up to the old front door that we screwed to the wall on the left. With a handle fitted, the door to nowhere fools numerous visitors, who either ask what is on the other side, or actually try the handle. We fitted a squared trellis to the wall on each side of the door and trained climbing plants over this.

Soil mixture for raised beds

The soil to use in raised beds in a roof garden is a specially-prepared mix, lighter than that in an ordinary garden.

An ideal mix would be made up (by loose bulk) from 2 parts medium loam and 1 part each of peat, vermiculite granules and well-rotted manure. You could also add an additional 85g (3 oz) of superphosphate of lime per 50kg (1 cwt) of soilmix, although this is not essential. The vermiculite is a very light insulation material, giving the mixture bulk and reducing the overall weight of the soil.

Before adding the soil to the beds, spread a layer of broken crocks over the bottom, making sure that the holes are protected and won't become clogged with soil. Add the soil in layers, wetting each as work progresses; this will enable the roots of the plants to take up moisture evenly as soon as they are in position.

You can plant in exactly the same way as you would in a garden at ground level, but pay particular attention to the staking and tying of plants, remembering that the wind can easily uproot young specimens. Walls and beams can be neatly wired to take climbing plants, but the wire should be closer to the wall than normal to combat the force of the wind.

Maintenance of a roof garden is very important, water being the key to healthy plant development. Few people realize how quickly beds and pots dry out, and during hot weather it is prudent to use the watering can daily, little and often being a better rule rather than sporadic floods. Try also to water in the morning or evening, avoiding the extreme heat of the middle of the day.

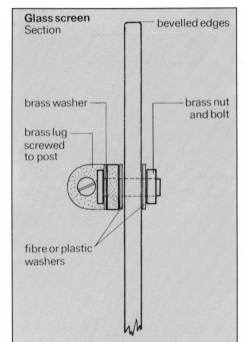

Glass screen
Section

bevelled edges

brass washer

brass nut and bolt

brass lug screwed to post

fibre or plastic washers

Left: section of plate glass screen attachment to post. Below: section of gravel area with chippings and stepping stone retained by glazed paving brick Bottom: seat and split-level raised beds

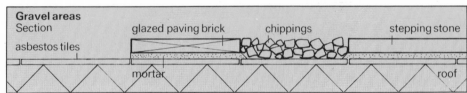

Gravel areas
Section

glazed paving brick   chippings   stepping stone

asbestos tiles

mortar   roof

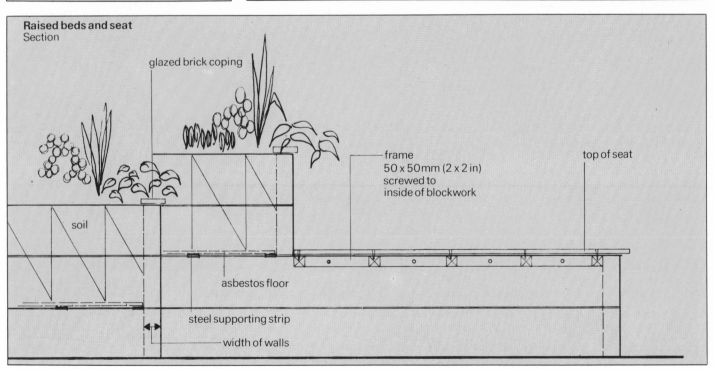

Raised beds and seat
Section

glazed brick coping

frame
50 x 50mm (2 x 2 in)
screwed to
inside of blockwork

top of seat

soil

asbestos floor

steel supporting strip

width of walls

DESIGNS FOR RECTANGULAR GARDENS

A regular-shaped plot with its formal straight lines can be just as much of a challenge as an odd-shaped plot. In the first of our designs for rectangular plots we look at ways of either turning straight boundaries into an asset or distracting the eye from them.

Although many people have odd-shaped gardens, still more possess one of standard rectangular proportions. Gardens on the whole are getting smaller – due to the demands on housing space – and the average size measures about 10m (35 ft) long by 7·5m (25 ft) wide.

With these proportions in mind, whether you start from scratch or inherit an existing garden, the approach should be the same: setting out to create an environment that is not only right for you but at the same time attractive to family and visitors alike.

To many people the ability to 'design' implies a degree of professional skill, so it is often easier to think in terms of reorganization rather than a wholly

original scheme and, again, it is often the simplest solution where an established garden is in existence.

The initial planning can fall into two stages: what you want and what you've got. Your requirements can be tackled in exactly the same way as the family shopping list, but instead of the usual groceries you may list lawn, greenhouse, shed, vegetables, terrace, barbecue, pool, sandpit, swings, roses and so on. As far as existing features are concerned it is best to make a simple scale drawing, using graph paper, and note down the north point, good or bad views, existing planting, trees, positions of doors and windows,

Left: an imaginative use of pre-cast paving links house with garden. Below: a working design to scale is invaluable

changes in level, together with any other relevant information. Your plan might not look as neat as the one shown below but it should be sufficient to give you a good idea of how to use your own available space to the best advantage.

Nor need there be only one solution to the problem, for just as the furnishing and decoration of a room in the house can vary, so can its outdoor counterpart.

For some reason people tend to have a horror of rectangular gardens, probably because most designs involving straight lines fall into the trap of rigid formality. With a small space, however, it is often advantageous to accept the shape of the boundaries, softening them by all means, but using the outline to form a frame for a geometric composition, in much the same way as a contemporary artist might do.

Planning your priorities

An average family, with several children, various pets and busy parents, will have general requirements – from somewhere to sit and have the occasional meal, a vegetable area, shed or greenhouse, flowers for cutting, shrubs and herbaceous material for interest throughout the year, to room for bike riding, games and general children's activities. But above all easy maintenance must be the aim.

Choice of planting

Whether a design is based on rectangles or curves it is sound common sense to keep the areas close to the building reasonably architectural, creating a positive link between house and garden. There are a number of ways of doing this, the most obvious revolving around a paved area that will serve as a background for the many activities that call for an easily maintained, quick-drying surface.

Numerous types of paving are available, ranging from the more expensive natural stones and brick and granite setts, to pre-cast concrete slabs of various colours and textures. As a general rule crazy paving is not the best material to use close to a house, the conflicting shapes clashing with the cleaner lines of the building. It is also worth bearing in mind that although broken paving is cheap to buy, it is far from cheap or quick to lay. Be wary also of coloured pre-cast slabs: your terrace should be a background, not a gaudy feature in itself. If you are really set on using colours, keep them simple; use two at the most and make sure they don't clash.

DESIGN THEME - RECTANGLES

In our first design we have assumed that the house is built of brick and it is logical, therefore, to use this material on the terrace. A simple squared pattern of bricks laid flat was evolved, using the corners and projections of the building as starting points. The resulting squares were then filled in with a combination of rectangular pre-cast paving, planting and a raised bed, that might double as a sandpit or pool. As the entire garden is based on rectangles the lines of the terrace were extended on our plan and another series were drawn across the page at right-angles to form a grid. The approximate proportions of the various features we needed were then shaded in: vegetables, lawn, existing shed, swing and clothes drier. A pattern was starting to evolve and by the time we had screened the bad views, created a focal point and added

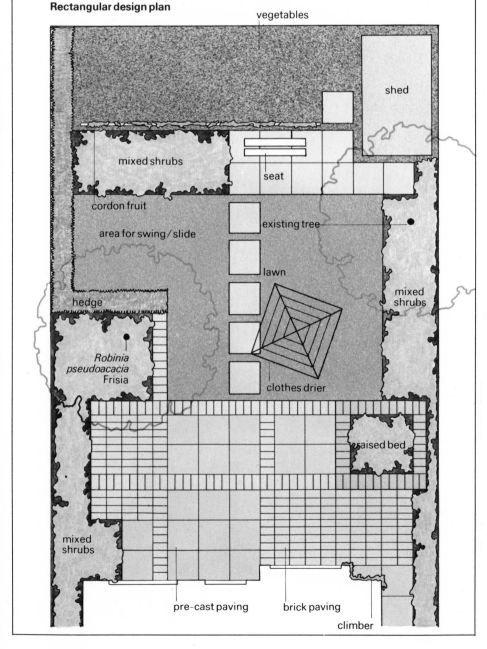

Rectangular design plan

vegetables

shed

mixed shrubs

cordon fruit

seat

area for swing/slide

existing tree

lawn

hedge

mixed shrubs

Robinia pseudoacacia Frisia

clothes drier

raised bed

mixed shrubs

pre-cast paving

brick paving

climber

trees for vertical emphasis the working design was virtually complete.

Planting within the design

Few people realize how quickly planting can soften a composition and it is therefore very important to have a strong ground plan initially, as a weak design very soon loses its line altogether. Planting also helps to reinforce the basic pattern and if you are working with rectangles, these can be linked together and enhanced by bold groupings. Whatever the size of a garden, individual specimens should be used sparingly and then only as a point of emphasis. Groups of three or four would be ideal in the size of garden shown here, while a large area could use drifts of 15 or 20 for a corresponding effect.

The treatment we have just suggested for the basic rectangular site was a plan based on straight lines which reinforced the basic pattern of the garden, with the fences acting as a positive framework. (A curved design would lead the eye away from the boundaries.)

We now put forward alternative plans, one based on diagonal lines, one based on a circle.

DESIGN THEME - DIAGONALS

However our second plan in this section turns the entire design diagonally across the garden. Diagonal lines are useful for creating a feeling of greater space as they not only direct you away from the main axis of the boundaries but also bring the longest dimensions into play, the distance between opposite corners of a rectangle being the greatest single length available.

In this garden plan the back of the house faces due north, in which case only a minimal amount of paving is needed outside the French doors, just enough in fact to give access for the side passage and room for a single bench seat on which to enjoy the shade during particularly hot weather. A simple buff-coloured pre-cast slab was used, giving a visual link with the pale brown finish of the building.

Siting of focal point

Stepping stones cross the small lawn and draw the eye to the focal point provided by a carefully-chosen urn or statue. Statuary and the like can be delightful ornaments in a garden but remember that they are dominant features in their own right and should be used sparingly as

punctuation marks in the overall composition. As a general rule they should be softened and surrounded by planting, a glimpse of a bust or figure being far more subtle than glaring nudity!

Planting within the design
In our design the urn is backed by the soft foliage and flowers of climbing roses, these forming an effective screen to the small vegetable plot beyond. The path changes direction at the urn or statue, terminating at the main sitting area that is built up from an interlocking pattern of brick and pre-cast slabs. A tree behind the sitting area would be an important element in the design, giving both shade and vertical emphasis.

Few people realize that trees can be bought in a wide range of sizes, from semi-mature specimens that are far too big and heavy for the average householder to manage, right down to small saplings that will take many years to show any real potential. Different species obviously grow at different rates but when selecting a tree for an important position, such as ours, the size known as 'extra large nursery stock' can be ideal. These trees are most usually grown by specialist nurseries and although large, can be handled by one or two people. They will probably be about 4·2m (14 ft) high and have a girth of anything up to 25–30cm (10–12 in). They establish quickly in a suitably-prepared position and have a far better success rate than the 'semi matures' that can suddenly fail after two or three years in the ground. We chose one of the vast cherry family,

Our garden with a diagonal design was planned to give a feeling of extra space, while still incorporating most of the features required in the average suburban plot.
The seating area at the end of the path is shaded by a spreading wild cherry, Prunus avium *Grandiflora (above right)*

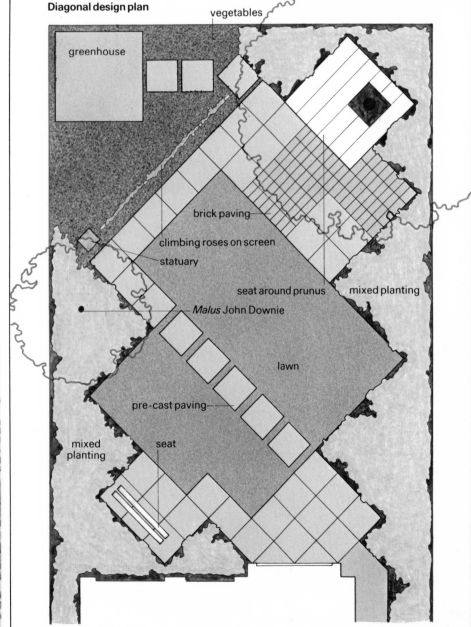

Diagonal design plan

vegetables

greenhouse

brick paving

climbing roses on screen

statuary

seat around prunus

mixed planting

Malus John Downie

lawn

pre-cast paving

mixed planting

seat

Prunus avium Grandiflora, a delightful wild cherry tree that bears double white blossoms in late spring to early summer (April to May). Because the tree was large when planted we felt that a seat around the base would not be out of place. This measured 1·8 × 1·8m (6 × 6 ft) and doubled as a table or even sun-lounger.

The vegetable area was big enough to incorporate a small greenhouse, while the strong pattern of lawn and borders was wrapped in planting designed to give variety of leaf and flower throughout the year.

DESIGN THEME - THE CIRCLE

This third alternative plan is a totally different concept; here we take the idea of using curves to create a completely circular pattern. A true circle is not the easiest design element to handle and where a major part of the garden is involved it is best to 'offset' the feature, thus giving the composition a feeling of emphasis in a particular direction. The resulting spaces between the circle and the surrounding fences are not, therefore, regular and become rather more interesting as a result.

Choice of paving

As in all our other gardens we needed a paved area at the rear of the house and here again the use of a circular design imposed certain restrictions. The shape of the paving was directly related to the geometry of the circle and became an extension of it, radii being extended until they reached and passed the line of the building. Each new circle represented a line of paving and where any circular pattern is involved small modules are the most adaptable. We had therefore a choice of brick, granite setts, stable paviors and cobbles. The last two we rejected on the grounds that they were too uneven for constant walking and the obvious use of tables and chairs. The setts were a possibility but looked a little 'hard' against the pebble dash of the building. Brick was ideal but in order to save expense and also a considerable amount of laying time we evolved a pattern of brick courses that could be filled in with brushed concrete.

For brushed concrete Lay a normal concrete mix of 1:2:3 – one part cement,

two parts sand, three parts aggregate – ensuring that the aggregate is made from an attractive selection of small rounded pebbles. Once the job has started to harden, or 'go off', brush with a stiff broom. This will expose the aggregate and produce a striking marbled effect when dry. To stop it drying too quickly in very hot weather cover the surface with damp sacking for a day or two; in frosty weather dry sacking will be sufficient.

The final planting

Climbers and planting soften the outline of the paving and house, and there is room for a small herb bed. As this garden was to be as maintenance-free as possible we decided against a conventional lawn and the main area of the circle was laid

Used with care, a circular design brings a refreshing look to a regular-shaped plot. A Japanese note is introduced with the siting of several boulders within the circle, which is surfaced with a layer of gravel on concrete and planted with two Rhus typhina Laciniata *(above right)*

with a weak mix of concrete, over which was spread 13mm ($\frac{1}{2}$ in) of washed gravel. Holes were left in the concrete to accept planting, including *Rhus typhina* Laciniata (stag's-horn sumach), while several groups of large boulders provide a sculptural and slightly Japanese feeling.

Stepping stones cross the gravel in a random pattern and lead to the shed that is neatly-screened by planting. A seat is carefully sited to one side of the sumachs, while the main border areas on the outside of the circle help to soften and hide the stiff rectangular line of the fences.

A high proportion of ground-covering plants help considerably in keeping the maintenance at a reasonable level and occasional raking ensures the gravel is free from leaves.

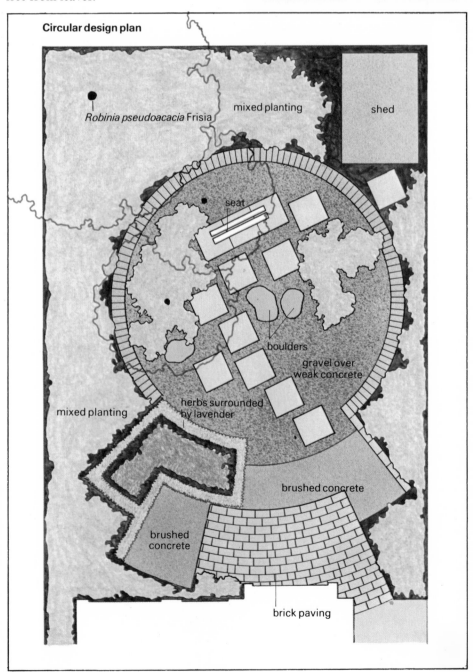

Circular design plan

Robinia pseudoacacia Frisia

mixed planting

shed

seat

boulders

gravel over weak concrete

mixed planting

herbs surrounded by lavender

brushed concrete

brushed concrete

brick paving

THE ODD PLOT
Plans for
difficult-shaped sites

Odd- or uneven-shaped sites provide plenty of problems, but none of them is insoluble if care is taken in laying out the garden. To begin with, an irregular shape often has much more character than a standard square or rectangular site. Starting with a simple ground plan you can design your garden, perhaps highlighting an unusual boundary, and gradually incorporate all the features that make up an outdoor living area.

A corner site such as this can provide a challenge, and the plan shown (far right) is one answer. The circular pattern of the layout relates to the house and ignores the outline of the site. The space between house and fence is planted out so that the shape of the garden from the terrace is incidental. Nevertheless, the basic ingredients of a standard garden are all present

For some reason a mystique has grown up and surrounds anything to do with design so that it has got itself the name of being an expensive luxury, and nowhere more so than in the garden. The down-to-earth horticulturist wants 'none of that fancy stuff'; but design should not be a fanciful, unsympathetic plan forced upon the unwilling host garden. If it is, it has missed its point, for today that valuable piece of ground surrounding your house, for which you paid so much and are probably still paying, has to do far more than grow a few flowers.

The garden is a place for all the family to use and the smaller the area the more difficult it is to fulfil this function. The average garden is often required to provide a play space, a sunbathing area and room for washing the car as well as housing the compost heap and garden shed; and all this besides beds for shrubs and colourful annuals, herb garden and vegetable patch, not forgetting paths for easy access in all weathers. Your design must permutate all these factors and make them work.

Principles of garden design

The garden should look well all the year round, not only as seen from indoors but also while wandering around different parts of the garden itself. Once this is

appreciated the shape of the plot is incidental. It is only another problem to be considered among so many and when it comes to the crunch the irregular shape often has considerably more character than the standard rectangular plot.

The main traffic of a family house usually leads directly into the garden from kitchen or living room. This is where any sort of terracing is normally laid. It makes sense that the line of any terracing, if not the texture and material of it, should relate visually to the remainder of the garden, and the resulting pattern should embrace all the desired elements of the garden. If the area is large enough it need have no relation to the odd shape of the site boundary at all as you arrange one pattern within another. The intervening area is then planted out, giving the garden a feeling of privacy and enclosure, for most families wish to create this feeling of being in their own little world, without being overlooked by the neighbours. But remember that the pattern you create

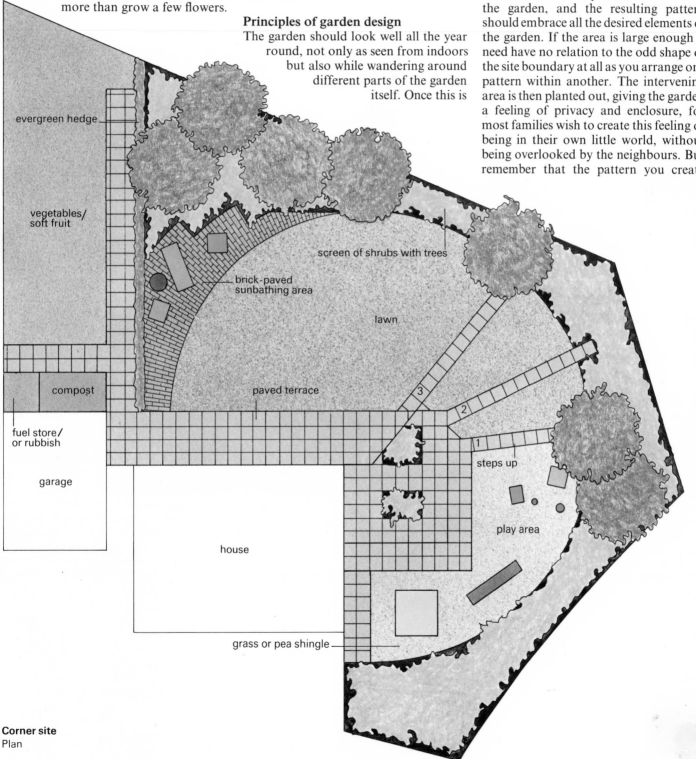

evergreen hedge

vegetables/
soft fruit

screen of shrubs with trees

brick-paved
sunbathing area

lawn

compost

paved terrace

3

2

fuel store/
or rubbish

1

steps up

garage

play area

house

grass or pea shingle

Corner site
Plan

should not be one of paths with bits left over in between, but of definite areas of different types of surfacing.

Create your ground plan pattern

Where there is not enough room to create a pattern ignoring the odd-shaped boundary line, you must accept the fact and perhaps make a feature of this limitation, relating the odd shape to the terrace in a meaningful way. Whatever the shape of the plot, the basic ground pattern should be clear and simple with no nasty little corners muffed over with the odd rock or pot. It is really a question of tailoring and the best-cut suit is the most comfortable and long-lasting because it fits the owner in every way. To a good tailor the shape of the body in front of him does not matter, the awkward one is only a little more challenging.

Your pattern, then, can run either from the house or from one aspect of the surrounding boundary: it can also be dictated by a special feature – a large existing tree, for instance, or a view to the church. More often than not you may find your feature consists of a collection of manhole covers slap in the middle of your site. Recognize your main feature, good or bad, and work with it to produce some sort of clear pattern.

To experiment with the design for your garden you will first have to measure up the site and accurately plot it, preferably to scale on graph paper. Onto this plan mark where it is convenient to have your terrace to get the sun and still see the baby from the kitchen, or whatever else is relevant to your way of life. Then site a herb patch and vegetables, if possible near the kitchen, then the dustbin area convenient both for you and the man who has to collect, the compost heap, the washing line, a greenhouse, rose bed – whatever else you want.

Taking into account all these necessities, try to devise a pattern on the principles already outlined and keep it all very simple. The chances are that as the shape of the house is regular, and usually the boundary too, your pattern will be as well. If curves are not to look weak outdoors they have to be bold and generous, which demands space. Wiggly lines that are not generous tend to look like straight lines gone wrong!

At this planning stage of your garden firmly put from your mind anything to do with plants, along with decorative pots and seats; these are first 'infill' and secondly furnishing. Only when you have a practical working plan do you infill with taller shrubs at the rear to give you privacy and shelter, scaling down to the pretty ones which are seen against them. In the average small garden, trees should be seen either as part of the overall design or as a specimen to act like a piece of statuary. Scattered about at will they fracture your basic design. Finally, introduce into your layout pots and seats as foreground interest, to give the final touch of grace.

There is, of course, no standard solution for the many different-shaped plots constituting a house and its garden, but by working to a few basic rules and getting your priorities right, you can make the best of your problem site.

Learn from interior design

You can learn quite a lot about how pattern and lines work from home decoration. You can correct your outdoor site deficiencies the same way that you would minimize an over-tall room. You would not want to emphasize the height by hanging vertically-striped wallpaper. A long, narrow site looks longer and narrower if a straight path runs down the middle whereas a pattern running from side to side will help correct this.

Where there is a pleasant view from the site, such as playing-fields at the end of the garden, concentrate on this, framing it with plantings as you would arrange the furnishings of your living room to enhance a picture or piece of furniture of which you were proud. Conversely, if your site has no view from it, turn the pattern in on itself and provide some sort of demanding feature as a full stop – a sundial, bird bath, or piece of statuary. Too many small features in a small garden fuss the arrangement, the eye is confused and the garden no longer peaceful. One of the qualities of a garden, and indeed its major function despite all the ancillary ones, should be to provide a place of tranquility for the owners – and that includes its visual appearance. Even if the garden is not used all 12 months of the year, it is still visible from indoors.

Design for a corner site

The site shown on the previous page is set in the middle of a corner plot. Outside its encircling solid timber fence, all of 1·5m (5 ft) high, there is a pedestrian path and roads that converge on the southern corner of the site. The curving pattern of the layout echoes the flow of movement around the area, although the planting inside the fence blocks out the unattractive view and, surprisingly, much of the noise as well.

The problem inside the garden was that the house faces east and the area farthest away from it gets the afternoon and evening sun, being the time when you are most likely to want to bask in the sun or just sit and have a drink. A terrace was therefore a priority in that area, away from the house but also connected to it so that the children could ride their bicycles on it and wander in and out of the house.

The next priorities were the siting of the dustbins, fuel store and rubbish, and the small vegetable area convenient to both rear door and side service passage. These and the garage are all served with a hard-paved path for easy access. It is in the cold, wet days of winter when going out to cut a cabbage or pick some sprouts that you really appreciate this, and the straight run of path would also allow for a washing line. An evergreen hedge, composed of a mixture of yew, pyracantha and the odd holly, separates the vegetable area from the rest of the garden.

A further hazard in this garden was the fact that the site 'fell away' to a downward slope on the south corner of the house. The lawn pattern could have followed suit but it would have meant that the house terrace would have been at a higher level and the children shooting along on their bicycles might have gone over the end. By stepping the terrace and lawn (as shown in the aerial view), this hazard was avoided and the steps became a feature of the layout. Where they converge they provide another little paved area on the south-east side of the house.

Below these steps the last flat area, although in fact an extension of the lawn, has been gravelled – or rather laid with rounded pea shingle. This is less sharp than gravel when fallen onto, and better than grass for a play area in bad weather. There is room for children's flowerbeds here and all the outdoor toys can be left out of sight of the main terrace. Since the area is not grassed it is easy to look after.

Between the defined outer lines of the garden and the boundary fence is a thick planting of mixed shrubs with the occasional tree sited into it. Plenty of evergreens are included here – like cotoneasters, large-leaved privets and pyracantha – to block out the noisy world outside. Colour planting, requiring seasonal attention, is confined to the sitting-out terraced area.

Design for a long, thin town garden

Typical of many town gardens behind the terraces of early Victorian houses, sometimes with a rear access, sometimes not, this site measures 30m long by 7·5m wide (100 × 25 ft). The problem is how not to make the layout seem even longer and thinner – which any sort of straight path down the middle would do – but to create a progression of small areas or 'rooms', staggered if possible, giving the ultimate view a lateral or side-to-side movement, and so apparently increase the width of the garden.

The first of these room areas behind the house is paved and used for many months of the year for eating out since it is so sheltered and surprisingly private with its old pear tree overhanging the area. It would be nice to pave such a setting in brick or old York stone. But if the expense prohibits it, you can use dark pre-cast concrete slabs instead.

The next area, down one small step, is gravelled and planted at random with perennials that seed themselves and look natural in such a setting; alchemilla (lady's mantle) and sisyrinchium (satin flower), for instance. The view is punctuated beyond this area by a piece of statuary (an old urn in fact) again to one side, and this is repeated on the other side of the garden beyond the next mown-grass room. A staggered path connects all these features and provides a dry, hard access to them.

The bottom room is allowed to be fairly wild with half-standard fruit trees planted in it and rough grass under them where spring and autumn bulbs and wild flowers can be encouraged. The borders on either side of the garden and against the old brick dividing walls are planted with a mixture of shrubs, including *Viburnum tinus* (laurustinus), syringa, philadelphus (mock orange) and choisya. When seen from the house the total effect is green and rather romantic, with the only colour being reserved for the tubs grouped on the eating terrace in the foreground. The view is a static one and planting and statuary are used to compose it. It is a garden for a middle-aged couple who enjoy pottering and the relaxed atmosphere of plants spilling out onto paving or gravel.

A strong lateral pattern progresses down this garden from one small 'room' to another. Near the house is a terrace with a gravel area beyond. A statue breaks up the pattern before the mown grass area and the last 'room' consists of rough grass with bulbs and fruit trees. The boundary fence is hidden by shrubs, and trees frame the general view ·

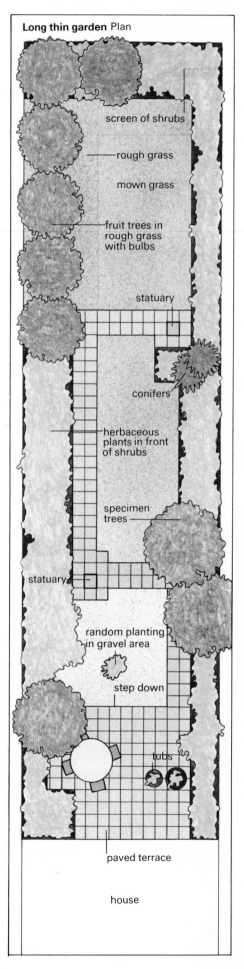

Long thin garden Plan

screen of shrubs

rough grass

mown grass

fruit trees in rough grass with bulbs

statuary

conifers

herbaceous plants in front of shrubs

specimen trees

statuary

random planting in gravel area

step down

tubs

paved terrace

house

Design for a country garden site

An irregular-shaped country garden can present just as many problems as the town gardens just described. Here we look at some possible solutions that would blend in with a less formal rural setting.

This site seemed to be the leftover bit between fields, surrounded by thorn hedges and very boggy at its farthest corner. The back of the period house was sited against the road, with the front door and main living room facing south onto the garden.

The plan shows clearly how the lines of the pattern should first start off with some regard to the shape of the house, usually with straight lines. These can then be continued on in curves to sweep about and encompass existing features and altogether be more gentle than a formal layout that in any case would not sit well within the boundary lines here.

The house is surrounded by a York stone paved terrace, so that the area outside the living room gets a long view down into the curving wild garden under a few old fruit trees. At the rear of the house the formal pattern has been broken down to form a small box-hedged herb garden conveniently near to the kitchen door. The existing hedge on this boundary has been replaced by a white picket fence along the roadside.

Where a house is set within a site the pattern of the garden should more or less follow, or at least compliment, the line of the house when surrounding it. As the pattern gets farther away it can become less regular. In our design the curves make a gentle, wild walk under old apple trees towards a summerhouse

Planting in the garden is mixed and colourful outside the front door, becoming wilder and more rampant as you progress down the length of the garden towards the pretty summerhouse.

At the side of the house facing west the grass is left rough, and bulbs are naturalized in it. The hedge has also been reduced in height so that the feeling of a neighbouring field rolling right in is encouraged and continues right up to the house. This rough grass motif is repeated in circular form to surround an old ash tree nearby. The internal pattern of this garden again pays little service to the existing boundary line, and thick intervening planting screens the discrepancy between the two.

In an old garden you tend to have old existing trees to work around. A feature has been made of the existing ash in this garden by surrounding it with a circle of rough grass containing massed spring and autumn bulbs.

The odd shape of this plot allows the summerhouse at the farthest end to be completely private from the house, approached by a winding, bordered path Below: plan, showing major features

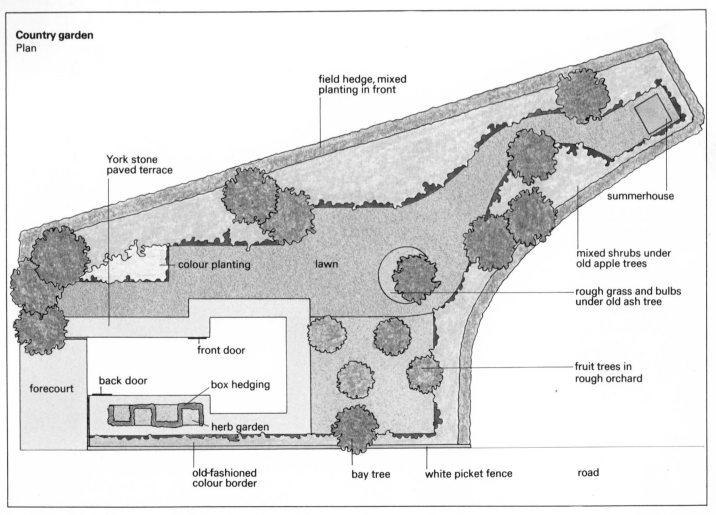

Country garden
Plan

field hedge, mixed planting in front

York stone paved terrace

summerhouse

colour planting

lawn

mixed shrubs under old apple trees

rough grass and bulbs under old ash tree

front door

back door

box hedging

fruit trees in rough orchard

forecourt

herb garden

old-fashioned colour border

bay tree

white picket fence

road

A GARDEN FOR THE ELDERLY OR DISABLED

Many people less able to cope with the normal exertions involved are still keen gardeners, and there is no need for them to be deprived of this pleasurable pastime. Here we show our ideas for an easily-worked garden and describe how to incorporate them into an existing one.

The average garden, however well planned, involves a considerable expenditure in physical energy. Mowing, digging, pruning, staking, fruit-picking, and weeding are jobs most people take for granted – time-consuming possibly, but none the less feasible.

Not everyone, however, is lucky enough to be completely fit and able to work on the construction and maintenance of a conventional garden. Some people have to spend a great deal of their time in a wheelchair, others have progressive diseases and most of us have to think of a time when we will be older and less able to cope with chores that seem easy today. Unfortunately, many people try to soldier on in a garden that becomes unattractive and completely unsuited to their particular needs; in consequence they are overwhelmed by the sheer impracticality of the situation and are never able to reap the reward of what should be a pleasant and relatively straightforward task.

Adapting the garden

The modifications needed to adapt a garden are in fact surprisingly few. Beds can be raised, steps made safer or changed to ramps for wheelchair access and paths made continuous and wide so that all parts of the garden can be easily reached. Common-sense also plays its part: paving should be completely 'true', with no poorly-laid stones that could tip or trip. Pools should be raised to minimize the possibility of accidents and to ease maintenance. Flowerbeds, if at ground level, should only be wide enough to be serviced conveniently from the adjoining path – and avoid using plants that need stakes, as these can be dangerous to an elderly gardener who may overbalance. Standard fruit trees may be too tall for easy cropping, while cordons or espaliers would be ideal in their place. Compost and rubbish should be in suitable bins of the correct height, while sheds and greenhouses can also be modified.

Hazards to avoid

Unless you can get additional help, a large garden is best avoided for obvious reasons, so we have chosen an average-sized plot measuring approximately $13·5 \times 9$m (45×30 ft). We have assumed that our garden has been inherited from a previous owner, and thus are able to show the pitfalls that a poorly-designed and badly-constructed composition might present.

Crazy paving, apart from clashing with the cleaner lines of the building, tends to have an uneven surface, and unless it is laid in mortar on a suitably-prepared base, soon becomes unsafe as the individual stones work loose. The steps are small and narrow while the meandering terrace lacks a wall, thus presenting an additional hazard. Once down the steps, the crazy paving continues, surrounding a small pool that should be raised to a height of 60cm (2 ft) to be made safe for children and adults alike.

The path is badly sited from a design aspect, chopping the garden into two unrelated sections. From the gardener's point of view it gives poor value, serving only the rose bed and failing to reach any other part of the garden. The main shrub border on the left is too wide for easy cultivation from a wheelchair – which also would be likely to bog down in the lawn after wet weather.

Giving a new look

In redesigning the garden we have tried to eliminate as many unsatisfactory features as possible. Constructional work of every type should be of the highest quality, for this will not only pay dividends in safety but also give greater pleasure in gardening terms and last a lifetime.

The terrace has been swept away and a new surface laid in a combination of brick paving and brushed concrete. Levels are particularly important in this situation

and you must always ensure that rainwater can drain away, either through pipes in the retaining walls, or to a suitable gully. Icy puddles could have unpleasant consequences.

The pool acts as a focal point from both the window and the large sliding doors. We raised it 60cm (2 ft) – which is also the ideal height for beds. A small store and worktop is sited to the right of the doors, while large tubs are ideal for bulbs, annuals and, of course, herbs.

A ramp gives access to the lower level, being safer and easier to negotiate than steps. The gradient should be no more than 1:15, as anything steeper will present difficulties for a wheelchair. The rough texture of the brushed aggregate will give the surface excellent grip. Once down the ramp, a path sweeps away round our garden, giving access to all parts of the scheme. Both paths and ramps should be at least 90cm (3 ft) wide and where the slabs are laid round the strong curve the open joints should be carefully pointed absolutely flush with the stones to make a really smooth surface.

Where both the raised beds on and below the terrace were built of 23cm (9 in) brickwork, the one jutting into the lawn was constructed differently. Here we used pre-cast concrete paving slabs, set vertically. The surrounding paving was laid first and then the area of the new bed was excavated to a depth of 30cm (12 in). The slabs, that measure 90×60cm (3×2 ft),

were then placed side by side around the perimeter of the bed, being held firmly in place with concrete and checked frequently with a spirit level to ensure they were upright. When the sides were completed the joints were covered with sheets of polythene to prevent water seeping between. The bottom of the bed was then filled with 45cm (18 in) of graded hardcore and topped with good quality topsoil. It is worth bearing in mind that any bed filled with soil will subside over the course of the first year and will need a subsequent top dressing to adjust matters. So it is best to delay permanent planting until the second year and concentrate on bulbs and annuals during this initial season.

In order to allow access around the bed we need to cross part of the lawn and here it can be a good idea to lay down screen blocks of the kind that are normally used for ornamental walls; such blocks measure $30 \times 30 \times 10$cm ($12 \times 12 \times 4$ in). To lay the path dig a trench 15cm deep and 90cm wide (6 in $\times$ 3 ft) around the two sides of the bed in question. Fork over the bottom of the excavation and lay 5cm (2 in) of coarse aggregate or gravel. The blocks can then be laid flat, side by side, so that they are flush with the existing lawn surface, finally being filled with sifted

Below: Clematis montana, *a good climber*

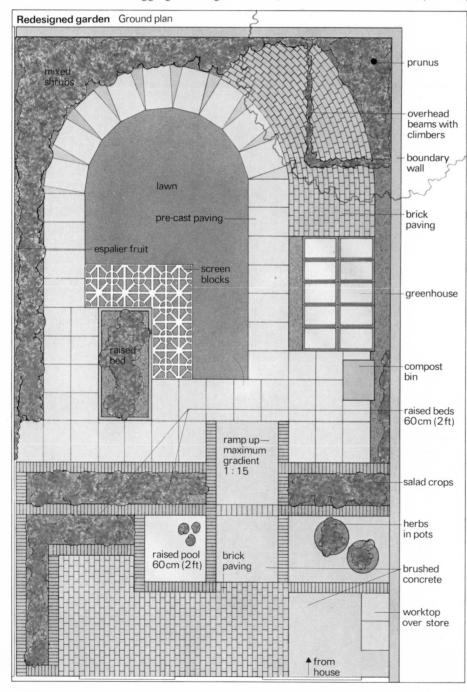

Redesigned garden Ground plan

- prunus
- overhead beams with climbers
- boundary wall
- brick paving
- greenhouse
- compost bin
- raised beds 60cm (2 ft)
- salad crops
- herbs in pots
- brushed concrete
- worktop over store

mixed shrubs

lawn

pre-cast paving

espalier fruit

screen blocks

raised bed

ramp up—maximum gradient 1:15

raised pool 60cm (2 ft)

brick paving

▲from house

topsoil. Sow grass seed and the finished product will merge into the surrounding surface and be able to support a wheelchair with ease.

Finishing touches

The existing prunus in our garden was an attractive specimen, and as it cast light shade we felt that it might form the basis for a secluded sitting area, given a suitable surface. Here we felt brick would form an ideal link with the existing walls and the pattern of courses matches the radius of the path, giving access to the greenhouse on one side. The other end is softened by planting and can be allowed to finish in a random sequence before it reaches the wall. White overhead beams frame the trunk of the tree and could be smothered with a climber such as *Clematis montana* Tetrarose.

The greenhouse could be fitted with a sliding door for easy access and there are many internal systems that can reduce maintenance and increase productivity at the same time. The small paved area between the greenhouse and the raised bed could house a compost bin, while the bed itself might be ideal for just a few salad crops.

Espalier fruit, as already mentioned, can be a real boon and the long fence on the left of the garden makes a suitable support.

Planting completes the picture and as the beds are relatively small, and the surrounding boundaries dominate, climbers will play an important part. In order to reduce maintenance it is a good plan to discard the idea of trellis which usually requires a regular coat of paint. Neat wiring is the answer here, being both permanent and unobtrusive, while self-clinging plants naturally need no support whatsoever.

As with any garden, try to select plants that will give colour and interest throughout the year, and remember that, after watering, a hose should be neatly stowed away, as one that lies at random on a path can be a real hazard.

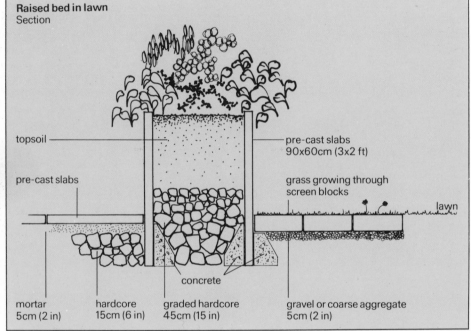

Raised bed in lawn
Section

topsoil

pre-cast slabs

pre-cast slabs
90x60cm (3x2 ft)

grass growing through
screen blocks

lawn

concrete

mortar
5cm (2 in)

hardcore
15cm (6 in)

graded hardcore
45cm (15 in)

gravel or coarse aggregate
5cm (2 in)

Left: cross-section of raised bed in the lawn, constructed from pre-cast concrete slabs. Grass grows through the ornamental screen blocks laid at right
Below: cross-section through the curved path running round the lawn. Flush joints must be very carefully pointed
Bottom: cross-section of pool raised with 23cm (9 in) brick retaining walls, together with raised flowerbed built in the same fashion. The new height of 60cm (2 ft) is ideal for maintenance as it requires little awkward bending

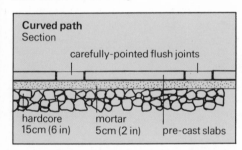

Curved path
Section

carefully-pointed flush joints

hardcore
15cm (6 in)

mortar
5cm (2 in)

pre-cast slabs

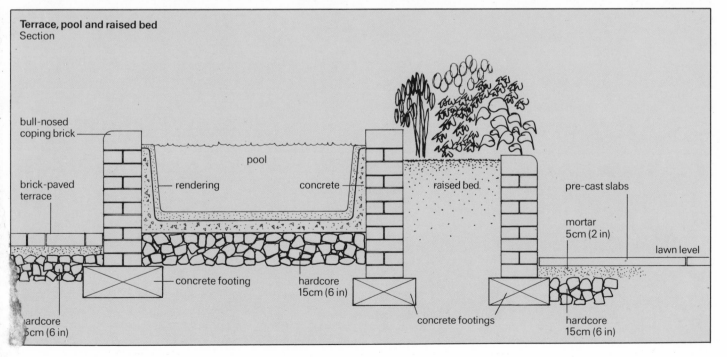

Terrace, pool and raised bed
Section

bull-nosed
coping brick

brick-paved
terrace

pool

rendering

concrete

raised bed

pre-cast slabs

mortar
5cm (2 in)

lawn level

hardcore
5cm (6 in)

concrete footing

hardcore
15cm (6 in)

concrete footings

hardcore
15cm (6 in)

A PROBLEM PLOT

Problems arise in various forms – neglected gardens, a waste ground left by developers, or a plot with curious contours – but with imagination they can all be overcome.

There is no doubt that most gardens can be planned with relative ease provided that basic design criteria are followed – largely a matter of common sense.

A very few gardens, however, are rightly called impossible – or very nearly so – conjuring up pictures of near-vertical slopes, quagmires, buried concrete paths and other equally daunting prospects. Fortunately, developers today are becoming far more conscious that the garden is an intrinsic part of the house it adjoins and that offering a building surrounded by a difficult site is not sound sales policy.

A steeply-sloping site, though not a design problem, can certainly be a financial one by the time some areas are levelled, others graded

and retaining walls are built. A garden that falls away, or slopes up, from a house in two directions is an altogether different proposition and can tax the owner's ingenuity to the utmost. Add to this a virgin site strewn with builder's rubble, devoid of topsoil, and without a whisker of vegetation, and you have a problem indeed.

Our 'problem' garden was just this – a plot of average size that fell steeply both away and across the back of the house. This was of split-level construction, with French windows leading onto a relatively level area to one side and the garage and utility room situated on the other side at the bottom of a steep bank.

The 'original site' artwork quite clearly shows the state of the site before work started. The brief called for a number of quite specific requirements: provision of a sitting and dining area, a small pond, room to grow vegetables, a greenhouse, lawns, space to park a caravan, and screening from the service road that ran along the right-hand boundary.

Although we were prepared for a good deal of initial hard work, and also to spend a sensible budget to complete the garden, subsequent labour and expense were to be kept to a minimum. This called for sound planning with an eye to both short- and long-term requirements.

The first and most important job was to carry out an accurate survey, checking existing levels and plotting these onto a scale drawing. We quickly found that the site fell into four distinct areas, upon which we could base our design. The real secret in planning a garden of this type is to recognize the existence of such divisions and to work with them to minimize expensive earth-moving and other major upheavals. We could thus create four 'garden rooms', each having its own purpose and each detracting from the long, rectangular boundaries. The back of the house was fortunate to be in full sun for most of the day and the

main sitting area could lead straight out from the sliding doors. Here we decided on a sensible combination of pre-cast paving and brick, the latter giving a visual link with the house and forming an interesting composition with the raised pond.

The existing bank was graded smoothly down to the lower level, the wall at the back of the pond giving both privacy from the service road and shelter, forming a perfect suntrap. Herbs soften the hard line of brickwork and give a pleasant aroma near the living-room.

Moving farther from the house, the low walls focus attention on the steps that drop down to the first small lawn, and from this point stepping stones cross the grass to reach the second, broader, flight. This was the point where the levels were most confused, falling sharply down and across the garden. By building a retaining wall and steps, and linking these in turn to the carefully-shaped bank, we created a series of features that were both attractive and practical.

It is worth bearing in mind that the steps in this garden, as in most others, benefit from being generous; a mean, narrow flight tends to 'fuss up' a design that is already complicated.

The lowest part of the garden was again given over to grass, the strong, flowing curve of the path giving the area a feeling of space and movement.

The vegetables and greenhouse fitted neatly into the corner, screened by either climbing roses or espalier fruit – the latter

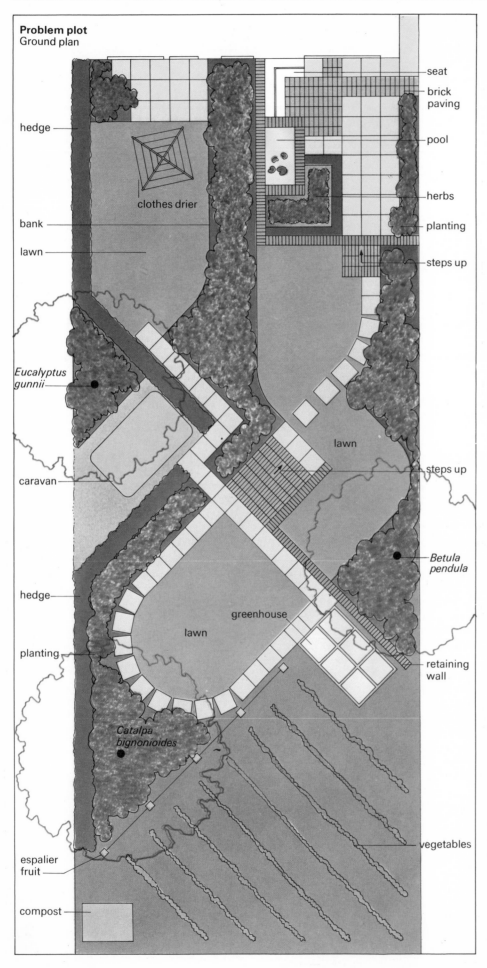

Problem plot
Ground plan

hedge

bank

lawn

clothes drier

Eucalyptus gunnii

caravan

hedge

planting

espalier fruit

compost

seat

brick paving

pool

herbs

planting

steps up

lawn

steps up

Betula pendula

greenhouse

lawn

retaining wall

Catalpa bignonioides

vegetables

undoubtedly saving space in a small garden where too many fruit trees could become oppressive. It's also worth bearing in mind that a garden full of retaining walls can be ideal for a host of climbing plants, and we took the opportunity to plant a fan-trained peach on the southern aspect of the wall to one side of the steps.

Caravans are not easy items to fit into a garden scheme, and the secret of success is to site them purposefully so that the position looks and feels intentional. There is nothing worse than a caravan, or a car for that matter, dumped at random wherever access is available.

As the service road ran the full length of the right-hand boundary we were able to make use of a flat section just to one side of the steps. A beech hedge, that echoes the main design lines of the garden, acts as an effective screen and can be clipped to just above the height of the caravan. Shade would be useful here as well, so we planted a fast-growing *Eucalyptus gunnii* that would overhang the caravan without becoming too heavy and oppressive. Such a tree is not only practical, its glaucous evergreen foliage is also a perpetual delight and invaluable for flower decoration.

With such an architectural garden there are bound to be a few hard edges, particularly during the initial seasons. This is where planting is really important, and with a sunny south-facing slope there is every opportunity for a superb display. As with all planting design, use bold groupings and drifts, the larger 'skeleton' shrubs holding the composition together. Of these, *Buddleia davidii*, *Cotinus coggygria* (*Rhus cotinus*) Royal Purple, *Choisya ternata* and *Cistus × cyprius* would be ideal. The infill planting should be more delicate and usually smaller. *Potentilla fruticosa* Tangerine, *Spiraea × bumalda* Anthony Waterer and *Hydrangea macrophylla* Blue Wave are some of the shrubs that might be used. Herbaceous material can be invaluable to highlight and brighten certain areas, and if used in conjunction with supporting shrubs needs little staking and tying.

Remember, too, that grey foliage is a great harmonizer, tying various elements of the design together. Many such plants thrive in hot, sunny positions and we could include *Senecio laxifolius*, *Phlomis fruticosa*, *Genista hispanica* and *Stachys lanata*, this last being an excellent carpeter at the front of the border.

As a final point, it's always worth including annuals to fill the gaps between the young, permanent plantings. These will add colour and maturity to the composition, as well as fragrance on a warm summer evening.

PLANTS IN DESIGN

AN INTRODUCTION TO GROUND COVER

Ground cover is a wide-ranging and diverse subject. Here we suggest two different planting schemes and with each give a comprehensive list of suitable plants.

'Gaultheria is apt to form handsome evergreen ground cover' wrote Clyde Bailey in 'The Cyclopedia of American Horticulture', published in 1900. This is the first noted use of the expression 'ground cover' that now has become a 20th century gardening cliché.

What is ground cover?

In nature the soil always becomes covered with some kind of vegetation. We choose that vegetation in a garden, or else we decide to use paving, gravel or a lawn, and our choice will determine just how much time we will need to spend working in our garden to keep it tidy and interesting. Some plants need constant attention while others virtually look after themselves, keeping the ground over which they spread free of weeds.

Ground cover plants have several attributes: the first and most important is that their foliage or branches make a covering dense enough to prevent weeds from germinating and growing through them. They can be ground-hugging plants that form a thick carpet, like saxifrage, alpine phlox, *Dianthus deltoides* (maiden pink) and thyme, or low evergreen shrubs such as prostrate juniper, santolina, erica and *Cotoneaster horizontalis*. Taller shrubs such as berberis, choisya, elaeagnus and potentilla have branches low and thick enough to stifle most weeds.

Obviously, if they are evergreen they will be more effective than if they are deciduous, but then the latter do a good job. *Spiraea × arguta*, *Elaeagnus × ebbingei*, an evergreen berberis, and *Pyracantha atalantoides* will fill a border well that acts as a break between two parts of a garden. Apart from occasional clippings and raking of dead leaves, this area needs no attention for years. In fact, this choice makes perfect ground cover.

Evergreen perennials make effective and pretty ground cover. Tiarella (foam flower), pulmonaria, *Lamium maculatum* (spotted dead nettle) and bergenia are a number of examples. Planted in groups between shrubs, or at the front of your border, they will all help to stop the weeds growing. Many perennials that lose their leaves in winter make a dense enough mass of roots to discourage weeds. Mints, marjoram, *Alchemilla mollis* (lady's mantle), *Campanula carpatica* (bellflower) and some of the hardy geraniums will do this. Others with large leaves cover the soil so successfully all the summer that the ground under them keeps weed-free. Examples are hostas, acanthus, gunnera and *Ligularia dentata*.

A very important quality, especially in the warmer months, is help in conserving moisture. Everyone who has done any gardening must have noticed how the ground under a low, spreading plant is often still moist while the surrounding bare earth may be bone dry. So, thickly-filled borders stand up to dry conditions far better than sparsely-planted ones. The plants themselves create shade and thus help to prevent loss of moisture.

impossible to disentangle them.

If the soil is full of perennial weeds and grass then give them a dose of weedkiller that contains paraquat and diquat, and kills only through the leaves that absorb the weedkiller and pass it down to the roots. The moment it touches the soil it is neutralized and so cannot spread to nearby plants. After the weeds have died, break down the soil by digging or rotavation. If another crop of weeds come through, dig again, carefully removing as many roots as you can. It is essential to do this preliminary work thoroughly so do not be impatient and plant too soon.

As for manures, newly-dug ground is sure to need an addition of organic material. If you can get it, farmyard manure or good-quality compost is ideal for digging in. Otherwise you should use

Above: santolina in the foreground, geraniums in bloom, tradescantia and euphorbia mixed with Stachys lanata
Far left: a border at Barnsley House, Gloucestershire, with (from front to back) senecio, a variegated symphoricarpos, taller, golden forms of privet, and elm
Left: Asperula odorata *(woodruff) and large-leaved bergenias shaded by a horse chestnut tree at Syon Park, outside London*

Getting ready to plant
The preparation of your borders is of the utmost importance. Just because you intend to use weed-suppressing, ground cover plants, do not leave the roots of perennial weeds such as nettles and dandelions in the ground. Before you start planting, remove them all very thoroughly or they will grow up through the roots of your new shrubs and it will be

an organic fertilizer containing peat that you fork into the top few centimetres of your soil. Both come in handy-sized bags with full instructions for quantity per square metre (or yard). By the time you have bought several bags and carried them home, you will probably want to make your own compost for future use.

Some warnings
When planning to use ground cover plants, you must bear in mind the rate at which they will increase and the manner in which they do it. You can easily find out about the ultimate height and spread to which shrubs grow. But some plants increase by underground roots, such as *Hypericum calycinum* (rose of Sharon) and the mints. These should be treated with caution or put in the right place where they cannot invade your more

treasured specimens. Hypericum can be prevented from becoming a nuisance if bordered by a stone wall and, say, the drive. In these circumstances its complete vigour is an advantage but elsewhere it could be disastrous.

Herbaceous plants that spread quickly by their roots are best planted beside each other; then it is a case of survival of the strongest, and eventually they will merge together. *Campanula glomerata, Euphorbia robbiae* (spurge) and *Anaphalis triplinervis* are three tough spreaders. Other plants increase by rooting as their new shoots touch the ground. These are usually easy to control as all you have to do is to pull up any new shoots where they are unwanted. Tiarella, *Symphytum grandiflorum* (comfrey), *Stachys lanata* (lamb's tongue) and ajuga (bugle) go into

Above: the rampant Lamium galeobdolon
Right: well-developed border of Stachys
lanata, *santolina, red-flowered* Monarda
didyma, *delphinium, acanthus, elaeagnus*

this category. Others like *Alchemilla mollis* increase at quite a formidable rate by seeding. No harm is done if you know where the seedlings are and pull them up while they are young.

As long as you know a plant's potential before you use it, all will be well. We all make mistakes and ones to avoid at all costs are putting *Saponaria officinalis* (soapwort) among shrub roses, and *Mentha gentilis* (ginger mint) in the herbaceous border. They are both so invasive that they should only be used where nothing else will grow. *Lamium galeobdolon* (yellow archangel) has the same habit and should be banned from the flower garden, except perhaps when it is used as a cascade round the edge of a tub.

The following suggestions will give you ideas for different situations where you can use ground cover.

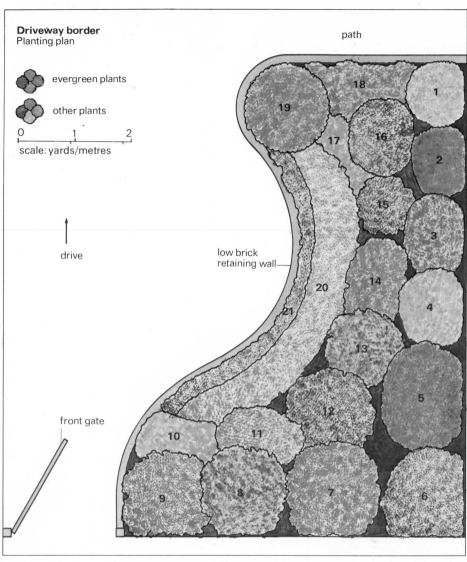

Driveway border
Planting plan

path

○ evergreen plants

○ other plants

0   1   2
scale: yards/metres

↑
drive

low brick
retaining wall

front gate

Key to planting plan

1 *Salix alba* Vitellina (golden willow)
2 *Mahonia japonica*
3 *Viburnum × bodnantense* – specimen
4 *Sorbus* Joseph Rock
5 *Virburnum tinus* (laurustinus)
6 *Chamaecyparis lawsoniana* Lutea
   (Lawson cypress) – specimen
7 *Cryptomeria japonica* Elegans
   (Japanese cedar)
8 *Potentilla* Elizabeth (cinquefoil)
9 *Juniperus sabina tamariscifolia*
10 *Tiarella cordifolia* (foam flower)
11 *Cytisus × kewensis* (broom) underplanted
   with *Ceratostigma plumbaginoides*
12 *Hebe* Autumn Glory

13 *Acer palmatum* (Japanese maple)
   – specimen – on acid soil, or *Cotinus*
   coggygria Royal Purple (smoke tree) on
   alkaline soil
14 *Hebe* Mrs Winder
15 *Pieris floribunda* on acid soil, or
   Taxus baccata Adpressa (common yew)
   on alkaline soil
16 *Cotoneaster* Hybridus Pendulus
   – specimen
17 *Helleborus corsicus* (Corsican hellebore)
18 Hostas and ferns
19 *Juniperus horizontalis* Glauca
   (creeping juniper)
20 Erica (heaths); select winter-flowering
   varieties according to soil
21 *Cotoneaster dammeri*

DRIVEWAY BORDER

The impression you get as you walk through the front gate into a garden sets the tone for what you will expect to find farther round the corner, so you want to try to make this area as well furnished and interesting as you can. Bedded-out wallflowers and petunias look fine when they are in flower but you need to do better than this in order to sustain year-long interest. Foliage ground cover, with an inter-planting of bulbs, flowers and berries, can give something to catch the eye each month of the year.

Make a list of the evergreen 'shapes' that you like, such as the low-spreading junipers and golden upright false cypresses, chamaecyparis, then go to a nursery and have a good look around, checking ultimate heights and spreads. Next, make a plan on paper to scale and fit in your various choices. Once you have defined the shape of your bed, then mark out the position of each shrub or plant with bamboos and look at your border from the front gate and again from a window to make sure that everything is sited to best advantage. It is really just like creating a picture. Do not be tempted to plant too close; for the first summer or two you can always infill with annuals or biennials.

MIXED BORDER

Today few of us have the time or inclination to look after a straightforward herbaceous border, hopefully full of colour from mid summer to late autumn (June to October). It involves too much work and the plants remain in their glory for too short a time. With experience you may arrive at a labour-saving compromise that gives a good effect virtually all the year round, that is the mixed herbaceous and shrub border. Here, with careful planning, shrubs, perennials, conifers and even annuals are incorporated to create an interesting com-

bination of shapes, colours and textures. Deep borders are much easier to make than long, narrow ones, for then you can create vistas in depth as well as length.

In order to minimize your maintenance work you must choose a framework of ground-covering shrubs and then infill between them with a few perennials and low, mat-forming plants. This infilling process is essential, and should be thought of as expendable. As your shrubs grow they will encroach on the infillers and partly take over from them.

It is interesting that the great English gardener Gertrude Jekyll (1843–1932), famous for her superb colour schemes in herbaceous borders, did not neglect these mixed types. When you are planning, remember to develop contrast using leaf shape, texture and shrub form. Round, dome-shaped bushes are soothing and lead your eye on. Upright conifers with a clear-cut edge act as exclamation marks and tend to hold your attention, taking your gaze upwards. Standard trees with light foliage are useful and need not be

put at the back. Do not despise the golden forms of ligustrum (privet) or lonicera (honeysuckle), as they both make a wonderful contribution to foliage effect.

While waiting for your shrubs to develop, you can use digitalis (foxglove), verbascum (mullein) and onopordons that make flat, weed-suppressing rosettes the first year and then flower in the second. *Polemonium coeruleum* (Jacob's ladder) and aquilegia (columbine) look good between taller shrubs. When you have found out which lilies suit your soil, invest in a few and use them in small groups. The shrubs will act as support and give the bulbs the shade they need.

If you are fond of deciduous, summer-flowering shrubs like syringa (lilac), weigela and philadelphus (mock orange), you can improve their winter and spring appearance and save weeding under them by using ground cover underplanting. Try the tough comfrey *Symphytum grandiflorum*, a rapid spreader that flowers prettily in mid and late spring (March and April) and is quite easy to control.

Mixed border Planting plan   back of border   stepping stones   scale: yards/metres 0   1   2

Key to planting plan

1 Hebe
2 Atriplex halimus (tree purslane)
3 Elaeagnus pungens Maculata
4 Euonymus fortunei (spindle tree)
5 Gleditschia triacanthos Sunburst (honey locust) – specimen
6 Ruta graveolens (rue)
7 Acanthus (bear's breeches)
8 Juniperus communis Depressa Aurea (common juniper)
9 Potentilla Elizabeth (cinquefoil)
10 Lavandula (lavender)
11 Symphoricarpos orbiculatus Variegatus (variegated coral berry)
12 Lonicera nitida Baggessen's Gold (honeysuckle)
13 Cheiranthus Bowles Variety (wallflower)
14 Anthemis cupaniana
15 Santolina chamaecyparissus (cotton lavender)

16 Stachys lanata (lamb's tongue)
17 Hebe armstrongii (hebe)
18 Viola cornuta Alba
19 Jasminum humile revolutum (jasmine) – specimen
20 Lonicera japonica Aureoreticulata (Japanese honeysuckle)
21 Origanum vulgare Aureum (marjoram)
22 Lavandula spica Munstead (dwarf lavender)
23 Euonymus fortunei (spindle tree)
24 Euphorbia robbiae (spurge)
25 Sorbus hupehensis – specimen
26 Vinca minor (lesser periwinkle)
27 Cryptomeria japonica Elegans (Japanese cedar)
28 Convallaria majalis (lily of the valley)
29 Iberis sempervirens (candytuft)
30 Ajuga metallica (bugle)
31 Philadelphus Belle Etoile (mock orange)
32 Symphytum grandiflorum (comfrey)
33 Weigela Bristol Ruby

34 Syringa microphylla Superba (rose-lilac)
35 Dorycnium hirsutum (canary clover)
36 Polygonum affine Donald Lowndes (knotweed)
37 Saxifraga umbrosa (London pride)
38 Prunus glandulosa (Chinese bush cherry) – specimen
39 Helleborus orientalis (Lenten rose)
40 Berberis thunbergii Rose Glow (barberry)
41 Geranium endressii Claridge Druce
42 Acer palmatum (Japanese maple)
43 Salvia officinalis Purpurascens (common sage)
44 Berberis thunbergii Atropurpurea Nana (barberry)
45 Campanula carpatica (bellflower)
46 Lamium maculatum Roseum (spotted dead nettle)
47 Ajuga reptans Burgundy Glow (common bugle)

Above: the aromatic Origanum vulgare Aureum (marjoram) *likes a well-drained position*

Convallaria (lily of the valley) make a thick mass of roots that deter all weeds, and they bloom before the shrubs come into leaf.

The evergreen *Euonymus fortunei* (spindle tree) varieties make splendid mounded humps that look especially good in the winter sunshine. Hellebores are perfectly happy when tucked away under shrubs; in fact it is an admirable place for them as their seedlings are then undisturbed. Bulbs cannot be classified as ground cover, but a drift of blue muscari (grape hyacinths) or scilla (squill) look just right under deciduous shrubs.

The plants suggested in the mixed border plan illustrated opposite will all grow on acid or alkaline soil.

DRY, SHADY AREA

Most gardens have a dry, shady patch under deciduous trees where planting is a problem. Grass is a possibility, but a poor one, as it would not thrive and mowing could be awkward. So what are the alternatives?

Hedera (ivy) is one obvious answer. This may sound dull and unexciting but if you choose one with a large shiny leaf such as *Hedera helix* Hibernica or *H. colchica* Dentata Variegata, you will have a year-long interest and the only maintenance will be to keep it within bounds and trimmed. Ivy can thrive in the driest of places and still look good. Small trees can be underplanted with the smaller-leaved

H. helix varieties many of which have pretty markings. They are a versatile group, as our Victorian gardening ancestors, who used them with great imagination, knew. They take quite a while to get their roots down and their top-growth on the move but once started will form an impenetrable carpet against weeds.

Another idea for the same situation would be *Cotoneaster horizontalis* underplanted with variegated periwinkle, *Vinca major* Variegata. This cotoneaster is not evergreen but in winter its mass of thin branches make a good weed barrier. The periwinkle needs a yearly clip back, which is best done just before its companion comes into leaf.

Bupleurum fruticosum is a wonderfully obliging evergreen shrub of great distinction. It manages to thrive in a really dry, shady situation, and considering its potential, it is surprising it is not better known. A group planted around a tree bole makes a heartening sight in winter. All flower-arrangers fall for its unusual green flowers and, later on, seed-heads.

It would be expensive to buy enough plants for a group so why not try to make it up from seed or cuttings? You might feel it would take too long to achieve, but this is not true if weighed against the long-standing success of your plan.

The evergreen *Mahonia aquifolium* (Oregon grape) is another star performer under trees. The rich yellow flowers open in spring and are followed by black

berries; the leaves turn scarlet in winter.

Underplanting birch trees can present a real problem. They are gross feeders, taking every bit of moisture from the surrounding topsoil. One good solution is the rather coarse-leaved *Lithospermum purpureo-caeruleum*. It has eye-catching blue flowers in early summer (May) after which the stems fan out and take root wherever they touch down. The more refined lithospermums will only tolerate an acid soil, but this particular species is best on lime.

Whatever you choose, do use groups of the same plant; do not be tempted by a mixture as this greatly lessens the effect.

DRY, SUNNY BANK

Banks are always hard to mow, so if you do not want a flowery mead (which in itself can be very rewarding) you must find suitable plants to cover the ground. This should be quite easy if you consider the conditions – dry and in full sun, in fact typical of Mediterranean hillsides. Here you find *Anthemis cupaniana*, ballota, cistus (rock rose), dorycnium, rosemary, lavender and santolina, and others that revel in the sun and a dry root-run.

These all need very little attention and will make solid, evergreen or grey clumps in their second year. If necessary, rosemary can be cut back immediately after flowering. Never cut the old wood of lavender; instead, prune it back to the new growth in late spring (April) and, of course, remove the flower-stalks before they fade completely – for the sake of tidiness; these can then be dried and used for pot-pourri. Spring-prune santolina and ballota back to the new growth; this is essential if you wish to prevent them from becoming straggly. Ballota flowers in late summer (July), and can be cut for dry decoration.

Leave the flower-heads on dorycnium as they make good seed-pods, but dead-head the anthemis; give both a spring grooming.

Cistus need no attention except for an occasional tidy. The hardiest are *Cistus × corbariensis*, with pale crimson buds that are pure white when open, *C. × lusitanicus* Decumbens, white with a maroon blotch, *C. × purpureus*, and *C.* Silver Pink. A close planting of a selection of these shrubs will make a lovely aromatic carpet by the second year.

During the first summer it would be a good thing to use simazine between the plants to prevent weeds from germinating; or you could apply a thick mulch of peat, sterilized compost, leaf mould or lawn mowings. This last will heat up, so do not put it too close to stems of shrubs.

ISLAND BEDS FOR HARDY PERENNIALS

Island beds have long been a feature of public and private gardens, but until quite recently they were used for the display of bedding plants to include roses and dahlias, as well as short-lived or tender subjects for a limited period – known as spring (or summer) bedding.

While beds with all-round access and vision continue to be used for bedding plants, they are not described as 'island beds' any more, this term being reserved for beds planted with hardy perennials.

The conventional herbaceous border of the past was invariably backed by a wall, hedge or fence, against which the tallest hardy perennials were grown, grading down to the shortest at the front, for access and visibility. However, observations over many years revealed the harmful effect of the backing, which so often reduced light and air that plants grew excessively tall, and weakly. Even with a vast amount of tedious and expensive staking, the taller plants tended to overhang the shorter, and the general effect was often disappointing and displeasing to the eye as the plants were denied natural growth and freedom in their competition for light and air.

Experimental island beds appeared at Bressingham Gardens in Diss, Norfolk in 1952. Since then, it has been proved beyond all doubt that plants respond to the light and air of an island bed with shorter but sturdier growth and need minimal staking. In over forty beds of various shapes and sizes at Bressingham, delphiniums are virtually the only plants in need of support.

While accepting island beds as the most natural and pleasing means of growing hardy perennials, there are still environmental factors to consider, including the space available, soil and situation, and, to some extent, climate. There are gardens where a severe or limited rectangular shape may appear to lend itself more readily to a boundary-backed border, with a lawn as the central feature, but an open mind and a willingness to break with convention can be the start of a new and much more satisfying dimension in gardening.

What are hardy perennials?

In the context of island beds, hardy perennials are plants (other than bulbs or shrubs) that can be relied on to survive winter, and flower year after year. Not all are truly 'herbaceous' (the strict meaning of which is 'dying back to dormancy during winter') since some retain their foliage. There is an immense selection and with careful planning, a long succession of flowering – from early spring to mid winter (February to December) – can be achieved, or alternatively a full and varied display at almost any time of year.

The majority of hardy perennials prefer an open situation and relatively few are fussy as to soil. There is a wide range of height and habit, so taller, robust plants can be used as space-fillers in large gardens, while dwarf or slow-growing ones are more suitable where space is limited. Many so-called 'rock plants', that are actually dwarf hardy perennials, are ideal for frontal positions in island beds.

Key to planting plan
1 *Anemone japonica* White Queen (Japanese anemone)
2 *Heliopsis scabra* Golden Plume
3 *Papaver orientale* Goliath (Oriental poppy)
4 *Helenium autumnale* Coppelia (sneezeweed)
5 *Sidalcea* Rose Queen
6 *Salvia × superba* East Friesland
7 *Phlox paniculata* Mount Fujiyama
8 *Hemerocallis* Pink Damask (day lily)
9 *Eryngium bourgatii*
10 *Crocosmia masonorum*
11 *Dicentra spectabilis* (bleeding heart or Dutchman's breeches)
12 *Phlox paniculata* Starfire
13 *Agapanthus* Headbourne Hybrids (African lily)
14 *Molinia caerulea* Variegata
15 *Sedum spectabile* Autumn Joy
16 *Lythrum salicaria* Robert
17 *Rudbeckia fulgida* Goldsturm
18 *Campanula carpatica* (bellflower)
19 *Solidago* Queenie (golden rod)
20 *Erigeron speciosus* Foerster's Liebling (fleabane)
21 *Oenothera tetragona* Fireworks
22 *Stokesia laevis* Blue Star
23 *Doronicum caucasicum* Spring Beauty
24 *Potentilla atrosanguinea* Wm Rollisson (cinquefoil)
25 *Geranium pratense* Johnson's Blue (meadow cranesbill)
26 *Aster novi-belgii* Jenny (Michaelmas daisy)
27 *Kniphofia galpinii* Bressingham Comet (red-hot poker)
28 *Achillea* Moonshine (yarrow)
29 *Armeria maritima* Dusseldorf Pride (sea pink)
30 *Aster thomsonii* Nana
31 *Coreopsis grandiflora* Goldfink
32 *Veronica teucrium* Crater Lake Blue
33 *Dianthus* Sam Barlow

Island Bed
Planting plan

Scale: yards / metres

28 29 30 31 32 33
27 13 14 15 16 17 18
12 1 2 3 4 5
26 11 10 9 8 7 6 19
25 24 23 22 21 20

Below: Ameria maritima, *good for edging*

Shape and site

The shape of the bed should be in keeping with the surrounding features. Use a freeform shape if the features are informal, but in most cases a rectangle or oval fits in best with a formal garden outline. The most appropriate location for an island bed is normally somewhere fairly central, in a lawn or at one end of it.

You may already have a bed that you have been using for 'bedding' arrangements, necessitating replacing the plants once and often twice a year. Although the initial outlay for perennials is higher than for bedding plants, the former group's range of form and colour, returning year after year, more than compensates for the extra cost.

Selecting your plants

Once you have decided on a site, prepare the soil by digging it over, weeding it, and – if it is of poor quality – enriching it with well-rotted manure, compost or peat, and organic fertilizer. This done, you will be ready to think about planning and selecting the contents of the bed. The vital factors to consider are varying colours and heights for contrast and continuity of flowering times. Aim to place the tallest plants roughly in the centre, and the shortest around the perimeter. Flowering time, height and habit are given in most catalogues produced by specialist firms, and in books on hardy perennials. For a maximum display of colour within a limited area you will have to sacrifice variety – and to some degree continuity – concentrating on larger groups of fewer varieties. There is no doubt that grouping gives a better general effect but if variety is what appeals to you most then you should select plants for variety.

An island bed of, say, 17 sq m (about 20 sq yd), while not large, would hold about 100 plants of the kind that produce a modest spread of growth. All the plants could be different, but three of a kind to make 33 groups would not only be effective visually but also give a fair variety to cover several months of flowering. For such a relatively small bed, space five plants over roughly 1 sq m (or 1 sq yd). This will allow for an average planting distance, within a group, of 38cm (15 in), but several centimetres more should be left between the individual groups. By this means, the vital light and air space is allowed for along with ease of access for maintenance. With larger beds you can choose more robust plants requiring larger planting distances for healthy growth.

The importance of adequate, but not wasteful, spacing will be appreciated when it is realized that on a plant per square metre basis, growth varies so that in the case of a few plants you will have to restrict yourself to one plant in the same area of space where 12 dwarf kinds can be planted as they have little outward spread. Some segregation will obviously be desirable if your selection involves plants of widely-differing growing habits. It is important, therefore, that you know what growth to expect *before* you start to order your plants.

Preparing the planting plan

It is a simple matter to make your selection if you first prepare a planting plan as in this way errors in placing are minimized. Avoid plants that grow disproportionately tall for a given space: a safe rule is to restrict heights to half the width of the bed. So if your bed is 2·4m (8 ft) wide, the tallest plants for the centre areas should not exceed 1·2m (4 ft) in height, while intermediate plantings should be from 38–90cm (15–36 in) and

Below: section of island bed, with salvia (sage) at front, geranium (cranesbill) in centre, and campanula (bellflower) on the left at back, crocosmia on the right

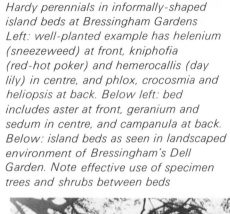

Hardy perennials in informally-shaped island beds at Bressingham Gardens Left: well-planted example has helenium (sneezeweed) at front, kniphofia (red-hot poker) and hemerocallis (day lily) in centre, and phlox, crocosmia and heliopsis at back. Below left: bed includes aster at front, geranium and sedum in centre, and campanula at back. Below: island beds as seen in landscaped environment of Bressingham's Dell Garden. Note effective use of specimen trees and shrubs between beds

dwarf plants on the outside edge from 15–40cm (6–16 in) in height.

To a large extent, the habit of hardy perennials – especially those suitable for the inner parts of a bed – falls into two categories: those that flower at more or less one level, like *Aster novi-belgii* (Michaelmas daisy) and other members of the extensive daisy family, and those that are more spiky, like lupins. To achieve the most pleasing results, and to break up uniformity or flatness, it is best to intersperse the two groups. Here and

there, something erect and spiky can be placed nearer the front than the height-to-width rule suggests, to provide focal points. However, so much depends on personal taste or choice. If at the outset you prefer to stick to the guidelines, adjustments can be made after the first season, and any errors in the planning and planting corrected.

Having made your selection, the planning is quite simple. Mark the height, colour and flowering time against each plant on your list, and add an

identification number. Transcribe these details onto labels on sticks that you can then place on the empty island bed to represent each variety. In this way, you can decide on the best planting positions before the plants arrive. It cannot be over-emphasized that you should only buy from specialist producers. They will not only have the necessary variety, true to name and type, but their plants will be of a quality that will pay off in the long run.

When to plant
The best time to plant hardy perennials is late autumn (October). Given sufficient moisture in the soil, its warmth will encourage immediate root action. However, planting may have to be deferred until the following spring, for nursery-men are sometimes unable to cope with all the orders on hand. Early winter (November) is still safe for planting out all but a few hardy perennials, but if you are planting in the spring, the earlier the better. Where the soil is dry, either in autumn or spring, surface watering should be done using a fine spray. Don't begin planting until any soil stickiness has evaporated. To avoid harmful treading in wet weather, or on sticky soils, you should stand on boards, moving them as planting proceeds.

How to maintain
After-care is not very demanding of time and energy. Weeds must be controlled, of course, and though chemicals cannot be used, the hoe will cope with seedlings, and retain the loose tilth that is so helpful to growth. Perennial weeds, if they appear, should be forked out ruthlessly. Mulching is good practice, and peat or pulverized bark is the best material to use. Apply the mulch in spring or early summer (May), 2–5cm (1–2 in) thick, and it will act both as a weed-deterrent and moisture-preserver.

Island Bed planting plan
Our own Island Bed planting plan is designed for a mainly sunny position, but its contents represent only a small fraction of the range available. It is intended to serve merely as a guide, and reliable, colourful alternatives would be possible so long as the height, habit and colour are similar. Arrangements for colour contrast or blend are likewise a matter of preference or taste. It is the basic principles that matter, and these can be reduced to the fundamental objective of allowing the plants to give of their best by providing the right conditions for growth, and making a sensible selection for whatever site you choose.

HERBACEOUS BORDERS IN THE GARDEN

There is an old-fashioned ring about 'herbaceous borders' and here we illustrate some typical ones. We then follow up with planting plans and lists of plants that would suit different seasons of the year and varying situations.

The herbaceous border has been much maligned in the labour-saving cult of recent years, admittedly with a degree of justification. But why condemn something of beauty if there are still keen gardeners prepared to undertake the work involved? A herbaceous border requires plenty of preparation and constant maintenance, but then so does a shrub border.

The herbaceous garden
The preparation for a border is not complicated and involves straightforward digging, although this isn't everyone's favourite gardening task. If the soil is sandy then you only need to dig out a single 'spit', that is, the depth of the spade being used. You should then incorporate manure in the bottom of this spit; if the soil is heavy, it may be necessary to double dig it (that is two spits deep, see Week 25) to give the extra drainage required.

Again, incorporate manure into the bottom spit. Before planting, it does no harm to scatter a general chemical fertilizer and rake it in. Spring planting is firmly recommended for herbaceous plants. There is a critical period during late spring (late March and April) when it is best to plant and this can sometimes be extended into early summer (May) if the spring season has been a wet one.

Choosing plants
There are plenty of opportunities for making notes on possible selections during the summer, when visiting gardens or flower shows. Alternatively, you could choose from books on perennials or from specialist catalogues. Personal preference must count, of course, but it is as well to consider the factors that really matter where garden worthiness is concerned. Reliability, adaptability and display potential, together with freedom from trouble, the ability to grow without a support, and not encroaching on less vigorous neighbours are the qualities to look for. Under the heading of 'display potential' preference should be given to plants that have a long flowering period, together with a reasonably good appearance when the flowers have passed.

One other category of worthiness includes plants with attractive foliage, and those that remain evergreen – for example, certain ornamental grasses and low-growing perennials. Some plants are still favourites despite the fact that they make a bright display only for a very brief period. Irises and paeonies are among these, while others – such as delphiniums and Michaelmas daisies – can be quite troublesome if you try to make them give of their best.

Most perennials prefer an open situation, but the range available is so immense that there is virtually no position in any garden – whether sunny or shady, dry or moist – where some will not grow. It goes without saying that a selection should be made in accordance with the site and soil type. A north-facing border with a high backing would best be stocked with plants that like – or will adapt to – some shade, but choose sun-lovers for a south-facing border.

These would also need to be drought-resisting plants, so any observations on behaviour during past dry spells would be worth remembering. Fore-knowledge of plant behaviour, including habit of growth, height, spread and time of flowering, is a great advantage when making a selection. Those of you who feel the urge to give perennials the chance to grow as naturally as possible will find their study fascinating. Knowledge leads to anticipation, and on to realization of the joys that perennials can bestow.

Staking and tying
One drawback to having herbaceous plants is that they need support, and staking not only takes a long time but gives an ugly appearance to the border. The least attractive form of staking is with canes and string; pea sticks are best and should be used in early summer (May),

Below: herbaceous border at Barrington Court in Somerset

Above: hardy perennials in midsummer

row plants to the middle and some middle-row plants to the front to provide a variation. You should have three, five, seven or nine plants in each clump as this enables it to have an irregular rather than a rounded shape; you can also arrange the plants to run into each other rather than leave gaps in the grouping.

In the planning you can organize an early border or an autumn border. However, unless you are especially fond of one particular group of plants, it would be inadvisable to have a border devoted to, say, delphiniums, irises or Michaelmas daisies, as the flowering period would be so brief. You might make an exception of paeonies; they do very well in a shady corner where little else will grow, and there can be few gardens that do not possess such a corner.

Widening a border

Where an old narrow border has become troublesome through competition from the backing, or because plants left in it are too tall in relation to the width, consider widening it if this is practical. If extra width can be gained by sacrificing a strip of lawn, there is no real problem. The turf removed can be used elsewhere perhaps; if not, it should be chopped up into small pieces and buried in the process of digging. If the border is fronted by a gravel path, this too can be dug and used, for not even dug-in gravel – unless it is too thick – will deter plants from growing, provided the soil is enriched and weathered. Such digging should always be done in the autumn, a rule in keeping with good husbandry in every respect.

It may occur to some readers that an old, unthrifty border – probably troublesome and unlovely as well – needs to be completely renovated and replanted with more suitable things. In such cases, the best plan would be first to mark any plants already in the border that are worth keeping. Take these out and heel them in somewhere else, so that everything remaining can be treated as weeds. Clear, and deeply-dig, the ground and shake out anything of a weedy nature: this should be burned, or made into a well-rotted compost by the addition of something that will increase fertility, such as manure or peat with organic fertilizer. Spade off any encroaching roots from the backing hedge or screening.

This kind of work is best done in mid or late autumn (September or October), especially if the soil is liable to become sticky when wet. On such soils it often pays to defer replanting until spring, but in any case start thinking about your selection of plants as soon as possible.

when growth is just beginning to rise. For a week or two, the border will look as if it is merely a collection of pea sticks. The pea sticks should be inserted close to each clump with the tops bent inwards above the clump, just below the height at which the plant will flower; the plant will continue to grow through the bent-over twigs and eventually conceals them entirely. This style of staking will withstand the onslaught of the worst weather that even a traditional British summer can produce.

An alternative is to use a form of metal support based on the same principle as the bent-over pea stick, with the plants growing through a ringed wire meshing. The rings vary in diameter but may not be large enough for bigger clumps.

Planning a herbaceous border

At this stage a precise definition ought to be given as to what exactly is a herbaceous perennial. A perennial plant is one that lasts for an indefinite period, and this applies to trees and shrubs, but they do not die down to the ground each year. Thus it can be said that a herbaceous perennial has an annual stem and a perennial rootstock. However, many plants that are very useful in the herbaceous border, such as kniphofia (red hot poker), do not die down altogether, so, by way of a looser definition, a herbaceous perennial is one that flowers perennially, but has soft stems.

The herbaceous border is probably the most artificial form of gardening that has ever been devised, but if cleverly planned it can be one of the most spectacular and colourful features in a garden. Planning the planting of the border is fairly straightforward provided one or two principles are observed: first, it would be tempting to have in a border, say 7·3m (24 ft) long by 1·8m (6 ft) deep, three rows of plants – tall at the back, medium in the middle and dwarf in the front. But this would give too uniform an effect and so, in our plan, we bring forward some back-

PLANTING HERBACEOUS BORDERS

Having, perhaps, visited other gardens and assessed the types of plants you would like in your own, you can now look at some catalogues and draw out the plan for your border. Here we detail individual plants and suggest particular border designs, and conclude this section with an alphabetical list of species and their characteristics.

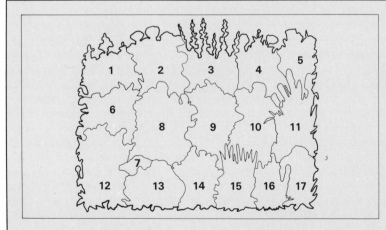

ALL SEASONS BORDER

Allow three plants of each species unless otherwise stated in brackets.

Key to border – 6 × 1·5m (20 × 5 ft)

1 *Anchusa italica*
2 *Rudbeckia subtomentosa*
3 *Delphinium*
4 *Helianthus decapetalus*
5 *Aster novi-belgii*
6 *Monarda didyma*
7 *Gypsophila repens* (1)
8 *Echinops ritro*
9 *Achillea*
10 *Chrysanthemum maximum*
11 *Kniphofia*
12 *Trollius ledebourii*
13 *Sedum maximum*
14 *Potentilla atrosanguinea*
15 *Salvia × superba*
16 *Liatris callilepis*
17 *Achillea filipendulina*

You may find it helpful to have some idea of the number of plants that will be required to fill 30 sq cm (1 sq ft) adequately. For instance, *Anchusa italica* Opel is 1·5m (5 ft) tall, with an individual spread of up to 1·2 sq m (4 sq ft). *Macleaya cordata* is 2m (6–7 ft) and has a 'thinner' style of growth, so you would plant three anchusas as against five macleayas. As a general indication, a border 12 × 1·2m (40 × 8 ft) would need 160 plants, and this can be reduced or increased in proportion as needed: for example, you would require 40 plants to begin with in a border 5 × 1·2m (20 × 4 ft). In order to provide you with a reference, we have compiled a useful chart giving you concise information, and from which the plants have been chosen for grouping in the borders as illustrated here.

As you can see from the chart details, borders can be planned for whatever time you require them and of whatever colour you want, although towards the end of the season the predominant colour, Michaelmas daisies apart, seems to be yellow. Here are three ideas for borders – for all seasons, in shade and late-flowering. If you have a particular colour or combination of colours in mind, it is easy enough to pick out from the list those you like and to make a border plan that will suit your own taste.

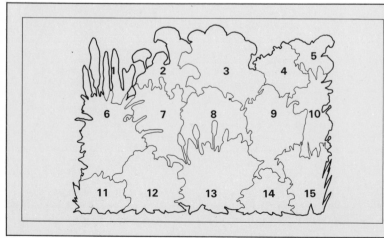

SHADED BORDER

Allow three plants of each species.

Key to border – 6 × 1·5m (20 × 5 ft)

1 *Aconitum arendsii*
2 *Thalictrum glaucum*
3 *Eupatorium purpureum*
4 *Campanula lactiflora*
5 *Thalictrum aquilegifolium*
6 *Dicentra spectabilis*
7 *Campanula persicifolia*
8 *Geranium psilostemon*
9 *Lysimachia clethroides*
10 *Anemone japonica*
11 *Liriope graminifolia*
12 *Doronicum caucasicum*
13 *Polygonum mileti*
14 *Doronicum cordatum*
15 *Iris foetidissima*

LATE-FLOWERING BORDER

Allow three plants of each species.

Key to border – 6 × 1·5m (20 × 5 ft)

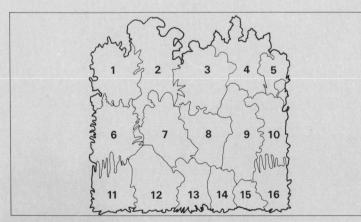

1 *Aster novi-belgii*
2 *Eupatorium purpureum*
3 *Rudbeckia fulgida*
4 *Artemisia lactiflora*
5 *Vernonia crinita*
6 *Solidago × canadensis*
7 *Eryngium × oliverianum*
8 *Campanula × burghaltii*

9 *Heliopsis scabra*
10 *Anemone japonica*
11 *Veronica spicata*
12 *Sedum spectabile*
13 *Stokesia laevis*
14 *Potentilla atrosanguinea*
15 *Anaphalis triplinervis*
16 *Physostegia virginiana*

The Gardener's Seasons

early spring (February)
mid spring (March)
late spring (April)

early summer (May)
mid summer (June)
late summer (July)

early autumn (August)
mid autumn (September)
late autumn (October)

early winter (November)
mid winter (December)
late winter (January)

NAME OF PLANT	FLOWERING SEASON/REMARKS	HEIGHT
Acanthus mollis (bear's breeches)	Late summer to early autumn. White and pink. 'Architectural' leaves. Does not like winter wet.	1–1·2m (3½–4 ft)
Achillea eupatorium (or *filipendulina*) Coronation Gold	Mid to late summer. Flat yellow heads.	90cm (3 ft)
A.e. Gold Plate	Mid to late summer. Bright yellow.	1·2m (4 ft)
A. ptarmica The Pearl	Mid to late summer. Double white.	1m (3½ ft)
A. taygetea	Mid to late summer. Primrose yellow.	45cm (18 in)
A.t. Moonshine	Mid to late summer. Bright yellow.	45–60cm (18–24 in)
Aconitum arendsii	Mid summer to early autumn.	1·2m (4 ft)
A. napellus Bressingham Spire	Late summer to early autumn. Violet-blue.	90cm (3 ft)
A. variegatum bicolor	Late summer to early autumn. White and blue.	1m (3½ ft)
Agapanthus umbellatus (or *orientalis*)	Late summer to mid autumn. Mid-blue.	60cm (2 ft)
Alchemilla mollis (lady's mantle)	Mid summer to early autumn. Lime yellow.	45–60cm (18–24 in)
Anaphalis margaritacea	Early autumn. White, grey foliage.	45cm (18 in)
A. triplinervis	Late summer to mid autumn. White, sturdy.	30cm (12 in)
A. yedoensis	Early to late autumn. White, everlasting.	60cm (2 ft)
Anchusa azurea (or *italica*) Loddon Royalist	Early to mid summer. Gentian blue.	90cm (3 ft)
A.a. Opal	Early to mid summer. Soft opal blue.	1·5m (5 ft)
A.a. Royal Blue	Early to mid summer. Rich royal blue	90cm (3 ft)
Anemone japonica (or *hupehensis*) *alba* (Japanese anemone)	Early to late autumn. White.	60cm (2 ft)
A.j.a. Profusion	Mid autumn. Soft pink.	60cm (2 ft)
Anthemis tinctoria (ox-eye chamomile) Grallagh Gold	Mid summer to early autumn. Rich golden flowers.	90cm (3 ft)
A.t. Wargrave Variety	Mid summer to early autumn. Sulphur-yellow.	75cm (2½ ft)
Artemisia lactiflora (white mugwort)	Early to late autumn. Creamy-white.	1·2m (4 ft)
A.l. Lambrook Silver	Bright foliage, sprays of grey flowers.	75cm (2½ ft)
A. nutans	Feathery silver foliage. Sunny place.	60cm (2 ft)
A.n. Silver Queen	Silver foliage. Good for cutting.	75cm (2½ ft)
Aster novi-belgii (Michaelmas daisy)	See border plans for selected named species and varieties.	
Astilbe varieties	Mid summer to early autumn. Plant in a damp spot.	
Amethyst	Lilac-purple	90cm (3 ft)
Bressingham Beauty	Rich pink.	90cm (3 ft)
Ceres	Pink and rose.	1m (3½ ft)
Fanal	Bright red.	75cm (2½ ft)
Red Sentinel	Brick-red spikes.	75cm (2½ ft)
White Queen	White.	60cm (2 ft)
Astrantia carniolica Rubra	Mid summer to mid autumn. Crimson-green flowers.	38cm (15 in)
A. maxima	Mid summer to early autumn. Rose-pink.	90cm (3 ft)
Baptisia australis	Mid summer. Blue pea flowers.	90–120cm (3–4 ft)
Brunnera macrophylla	Late spring to mid summer. Blue forget-me-not flowers.	45cm (18 in)
Campanula × burghaltii	Mid summer to mid autumn. Large mauve bells.	60cm (2 ft)
C. glomerata Superba	Mid to late summer. Purple-blue.	45cm (18 in)
C. lactiflora Loddon Anna	Mid summer to early autumn. Pink.	1·2–1·5m (4–5 ft)
C. latiloba Peter Piper	Mid to late summer. Deep blue.	90cm (3 ft)
C. persicifolia	Mid summer to early autumn. Blue. Rather weedy.	90cm (3 ft)
Centaurea dealbata John Coutts	Early summer to early autumn. Clear pink.	60cm (2 ft)
C. macrocephala	Mid summer to early autumn. Large yellow flowers.	1·2–1·5m (4–5 ft)
Chelone obliqua	Early to late autumn. Pink.	60cm (2 ft)
C.o. Alba	White form.	60cm (2 ft)
Chrysanthemum maximum (shasta daisy)	Choose well-established varieties, such as these, from catalogues.	
Dairymaid	Late summer. Cream.	90cm (3 ft)
Esther Read	Late summer to mid autumn.	60cm (2 ft)
Wirral Supreme	Late summer to mid autumn. Reliable double white.	90cm (3 ft)
Clematis recta Grandiflora	Late summer to early autumn. White.	75–90cm (2½–3 ft)
Coreopsis grandiflora Goldfink	Mid summer to mid autumn. Deep yellow.	25cm (9 in)
C. g. Badengold	Late summer to early autumn. Orange-yellow.	90cm (3 ft)
C. verticillata	Mid summer to mid autumn. Starry yellow flowers.	45cm (18 in)

NAME OF PLANT	FLOWERING SEASON/REMARKS	HEIGHT
Crambe cordifolia	Early to late summer. Panicles of white flowers.	1·5–1·8m (5–6 ft)
Crocosmia masonorum	Late summer onwards. Montbretia-like orange.	90cm (3 ft)
Cynglossum nervosum (hound's tongue)	Mid summer to early autumn. Gentian blue.	30cm (12 in)
Delphinium varieties	Mid summer onwards. Good for cuttings. Choose varieties according to desired height and colour. Belladonna group are shorter, require no staking.	
Dicentra formosa Bountiful	Mid spring onwards. Pink 'bleeding heart' flowers.	45cm (18 in)
D. eximia	Late spring onwards. Pink.	45cm–60cm (1½–2 ft)
D.e. Adrian Bloom	Late spring to early summer. Vigorous.	30cm (12 in)
D.e. Alba	Early summer to mid autumn. White form.	25cm (9 in)
D. spectabilis	Late spring. Pink, the true 'bleeding heart'. Needs deep soil.	60cm (2 ft)
Dictamnus fraxinella (or *albus*)	Mid summer to early autumn. Spikes of lilac or white spider-like flowers.	75cm (2½ ft)
Dierama pendulum (wand flower)	Late summer to mid autumn. Pink flowers on graceful stems.	75–90cm (2½–3 ft)
Doronicum caucasicum Miss Mason	Late spring to mid summer. Bright yellow.	45cm (18 in)
D. cordatum	Mid spring to early summer. Golden daisies.	15–25cm (6–10 in)
D.c. Spring Beauty	Late spring to mid summer. Double yellow flowers.	38cm (15 in)
Echinacea purpurea	Early autumn. Rose to crimson.	1m (3½ ft)
E.p. The King	Early autumn. Reddish-purple on stiff spikes.	1·2m (4 ft)
Echinops humilis (globe thistle) Taplow Blue	Mid summer to mid autumn. Dark blue globes.	1·5m (5 ft)
E. ritro	Mid summer to mid autumn. Rich blue.	1m (3½ ft)
Erigeron speciosus (fleabane) Charity	Mid summer. Light pink.	60cm (2 ft)
E.s. Darkest of All	Mid summer. Deep violet-blue.	60cm (2 ft)
E.s. Dignity	Mid summer. Mauve-blue.	60cm (2 ft)
E.s. Foerster's Liebling	Mid summer. Deep cerise-pink.	60cm (2 ft)
E.s. Rose Triumph	Semi-double, deep rose-pink.	60cm (2 ft)
Eryngium bourgatii	Mid summer to early autumn. Silvery-blue.	45cm (18 in)
E. × *oliverianum*	Mid summer to early autumn. Blue.	90cm (3 ft)
E. tripartitum	Mid summer to early autumn. Metallic blue.	
Eupatorium purpureum	Early to mid autumn. Purple.	1·5–1·8m (5–6 ft)
E. rugosum	Late summer to mid autumn. White.	90cm (3 ft)
Euphorbia griffithii	Mid summer. Orange-red.	75cm (2½ ft)
E. polychroma (or *epithimoides*)	Late spring to early summer. Yellow.	45cm (18 in)
E. sikkimensis	Mid to late summer. Purple shoots, yellow flowers.	1·2m (4 ft)
E. wulfenii	Late spring to late summer. Yellowish-green, evergreen foliage.	90cm (3 ft)
Geranium psilostemon	Late summer. Cerise.	75cm (2½ ft)
G. renardii	Early to mid summer. Light mauve.	38cm (15 in)
Geum × *borisii*	Early summer. Tangerine-scarlet.	30cm (12 in)
G. chiloense Fire Opal	Early summer to early autumn. Orange-red.	60cm (2 ft)
G.c. Prince of Orange	Early to mid summer. Double orange-yellow.	60cm (2 ft)
Gypsophila paniculata Bristol Fairy	Mid summer to mid autumn. Double white.	90cm (3 ft)
G. repens Rosy Veil	Mid summer to mid autumn. Double shell pink.	25cm (9 in)
Helenium autumnale Bruno	Early to late autumn. Mahogany-red.	1m (3½ ft)
H.a. Butterpat	Early to late autumn. Pure yellow.	90cm (3 ft)
H.a. Mahogany	Late summer to early autumn. Golden brown-red.	75cm (2½ ft)
H.a. The Bishop	Mid summer. Bright yellow, dark centre.	60cm (2 ft)
Helianthus decapetalus Loddon Gold	Late summer to mid autumn.	1·5m (5 ft)
H.d. Lemon Queen	Graceful lemon flowers.	1·5m (5 ft)
Heliopsis scabra Ballerina	Mid summer to early autumn. Warm yellow.	90cm (3 ft)
H.s. Golden Plume	Mid summer to mid autumn. Double deep yellow.	1·2m (4 ft)
H.s. Sunburst	Late summer. Double orange-yellow.	1·2m (4 ft)
Heuchera sanguinea Greenfinch	Early to late summer. Greenish sulphur-yellow.	75cm (2½ ft)
H.s. Pearl Drops	Early to late summer. Almost white.	60cm (2 ft)
H.s. Scintillation	Bright pink, tipped with coral-carmine.	60cm (2 ft)
Inula ensifolia	Mid summer to early autumn. Bright yellow, long-lasting.	25cm (9 in)
I. hookeri	Mid summer to mid autumn. Rayed, yellow flowers.	75cm (2½ ft)

NAME OF PLANT	FLOWERING SEASON/REMARKS	HEIGHT
Iris varieties	Named varieties of *Iris sibirica* and the flag iris, *I. germanica*, should be seen to judge for preference of height and colour.	
Kniphofia galpinii	Late summer to mid autumn. Delicate orange.	45cm (18 in)
K. nelsonii major	Early to mid autumn. Bright orange.	60cm (2 ft)
K. uvaria (red hot poker) Bee's Lemon	Late autumn. Citron yellow.	75–90cm (2½–3 ft)
K.u. Maid of Orleans	Mid summer to early autumn. Ivory-white.	90–100cm (3–3½ ft)
K.u. Royal Standard	Late summer. Bright red and yellow.	1m (3½ ft)
Liatris callilepis	Late summer to mid autumn. Fluffy lilac-purple.	75cm (2½ ft)
L. pycnostachys	Early to late autumn. Rosy purple.	90–150cm (3–5 ft)
Libertia formosa	Mid to late summer. White. Iris-type leaves.	75cm (2½ ft)
Ligularia clivorum Desdemona	Late summer to mid autumn. Orange flower, bronze foliage.	90cm (3 ft)
L.c. Greynog Gold	Late summer to mid autumn. Golden flowers.	90cm (3 ft)
L.c. Sungold	Mid summer to early autumn. Golden-yellow.	90cm (3 ft)
Liriope graminifolia	Mid autumn. Violet, grape hyacinth-like flowers.	15cm (6 in)
Lobelia cardinalis Queen Victoria	Mid to late summer. Good red. Not hardy. Needs a damp spot.	60cm (2 ft)
Lupinus (lupins) varieties	Early to mid summer. Choose variety according to desired colour. Place towards the back, where late-flowering plants can come up in front. Do not over-feed soil with farmyard manure.	
Lychnis chalcedonica (campion)	Late summer to early autumn. Brilliant scarlet.	1m (3½ ft)
L. flos-jovis	Mid summer to early autumn. Delightful combination of pink flowers and grey foliage.	25cm (9 in)
L. viscaria Splendens Plena	Mid to late summer. Cerise.	25cm (9 in)
Lysimachia clethroides	Early to mid autumn. White.	90cm (3 ft)
L. punctata	Mid to late summer. Bright yellow.	60cm (2 ft)
Lythrum salicaria (purple loosestrife) Robert	Late summer to mid autumn. Bright carmine.	75cm (2½ ft)
L.s. The Beacon	Late summer to mid autumn. Rosy-crimson.	1m (3½ ft)
Macleaya (or *Bocconia*) *cordata*	Early to mid autumn. Cream-white.	2·1m (7 ft)
M.c. Coral plume	Early to mid autumn. Buff.	2·1m (7 ft)
Monarda didyma Cambridge Scarlet	Mid summer to early autumn. Red.	90cm (3 ft)
M.d. Croftway Pink	Mid summer to early autumn. Soft pink.	90cm (3 ft)
Nepeta gigantea (catmint)	Mid summer to early autumn. Lavender-blue.	75cm (2½ ft)
N.×mussinii	Mid summer to early autumn. Lavender-blue.	38cm (15 in)
N.×m. Six Hills Giant	Mid summer to early autumn. Deeper blue.	60cm (2 ft)
Oenothera tetragona Fireworks	Mid summer to early autumn. Orange-yellow, red buds.	45cm (18 in)
O. glaber	Mid summer to mid autumn. Golden, bronzy foliage.	38cm (15 in)
Origanum laevigatum	Early to mid autumn. Purple.	38cm (15 in)
Paeonia (paeony) varieties	Late spring to early summer. Single or double, pinks to reds. Adapt to any soil or conditions.	
Papaver orientalis (oriental poppy) Lord Lambourne	Mid summer. Bright red.	90cm (3 ft)
P.o. Mrs Perry	Mid summer. Pink.	90cm (3 ft)
P.o. Perry's White	Mid summer. White with black blotches.	90cm (3 ft)
Phlomis samia	Mid summer to early autumn. Yellow, greyish leaves.	75cm (2½ ft)
Phlox	Late summer to early autumn. Choose according to colour preferences. Prefer good rich soil with plenty of moisture.	
Established varieties	Balmoral (rosy-lavender); Brigadier (brilliant orange-red); Hampton Court (blue); Pastorale (large pink); White Admiral (the best white).	
Physostegia virginiana Summer Snow	Late summer to mid autumn. White.	75cm (2½ ft)
P.v. Vivid	Early to late autumn. Deep rose.	45cm (18 in)
Platycodon grandiflorum	Late summer to early autumn. Blue.	45cm (18 in)
P.g. Snowflake	Late summer to early autumn. White.	45cm (18 in)
Polemonium foliosissimum (Jacob's ladder)	Late spring to early autumn. Lavender-blue.	75cm (2½ ft)
P.f. Sapphire	Early to late summer. Blue.	45cm (18 in)

119

NAME OF PLANT	FLOWERING SEASON/REMARKS	HEIGHT
Polygonum amplexicaule atrosanguineum (snake weed)	Mid summer to mid autumn. Deep red spike.	1·2m (4 ft)
P. bistorta Superbum	Early summer onwards. Does well in moist places.	90cm (3 ft)
P. millettii	Mid summer to mid autumn. Deep red. Slow-growing, likes moisture.	45cm (18 in)
Potentilla atrosanguinea (cinquefoil) Gibson's Scarlet	Mid summer to early autumn. Brilliant scarlet.	38cm (15 in)
P.a. Mons. Rouillard	Mid summer to early autumn. Deep crimson, orange blotched.	45cm (18 in)
P.a. William Rollisson	Mid summer to early autumn. Semi-double, orange.	38cm (15 in)
Prunella webbiana (self-heal) Loveliness	Early summer onwards. Pale mauve.	25cm (10 in)
Pyrethrum	Early to mid summer; if cut back at once, will repeat in the autumn. Choose from pinks to salmons and scarlets. Useful for cuttings.	
Rhazya orientalis	Mid summer to early autumn. Blue.	45cm (18 in)
Rudbeckia fulgida Deamii	Early to late autumn. Deep yellow, dark centre.	75cm (2½ ft)
R.f. Goldsturm	Late summer to late autumn.	45cm (18 in)
R. laciniata Goldquelle	Early to late autumn. Double yellow.	90cm (3 ft)
R. nitida Herbstsonne	Early to late autumn. Bright rich yellow.	1·8m (6 ft)
R. subtomentosa	Mid to late autumn. Deep yellow.	1·2–1·5m (4–5 ft)
Salvia haematodes	Mid summer to early autumn. Light lilac-blue, grey-green foliage.	90cm (3 ft)
S.×superba	Late summer to mid autumn. Violet-purple.	90cm (3 ft)
S.×s. East Friesland	Similar, except for height.	45cm (18 in)
S.×s. Lubeca	Mid summer to mid autumn. Violet-purple.	75cm (2½ ft)
S.×s. Lye End	Mid summer to early autumn. Blue.	1m (3½ ft)
S. turkestanica	Late summer. Rose and pale blue.	1·2–1·5m (4–5 ft)
Scabiosa caucasica Clive Greaves	Mid summer to mid autumn. Mid blue.	75cm (2½ ft)
S.c. Loddon White	Mid summer to mid autumn. White.	75cm (2½ ft)
S.c. Penhill Blue	Mid summer to mid autumn. Deep blue.	75cm (2½ ft)
Sedum maximum Atropurpureum	Early to late autumn. Deep purple flowers, creamy foliage.	45cm (18 in)
S. spectabile	Early to late autumn. Pale pink.	38cm (15 in)
S.s. Autumn Joy	Early to late autumn. Bright rose-salmon.	60cm (2 ft)
S. spurium Ruby Glow	Late summer to early autumn. Rose-red.	30cm (12 in)
S.s. Vera Jameson	Late summer to early autumn. Pale pink, purplish foliage.	38cm (15 in)
Sidalcea malvaeflora Elsie Heugh	Mid summer to early autumn. Soft pink.	90cm (3 ft)
S.m. Mrs Alderson	Mid summer to early autumn. Large clear pink.	75cm (2½ ft)
S.m. William Smith	Late summer to mid autumn. Warm salmon-pink.	1m (3½ ft)
Solidago canadensis (golden rod) Goldenmosa	Early to mid autumn. Large heads of golden-yellow.	75cm (2½ ft)
S.c. Golden Radiance	Early to mid autumn. Bright heads.	75cm (2½ ft)
S.c. Lemore	Early to mid autumn. Soft primrose.	75cm (2½)
Stachys lanata (lamb's tongue)	Mid summer to early autumn. Pink flowers. The entire plant is woolly-grey and spreads.	30cm (12 in)
Stokesia laevis Blue Star	Late summer to early autumn. Lavender-blue.	45cm (18 in)
Thalictrum aquilegifolium Album	Late spring to late summer. White.	1·2m (4 ft)
T.a. Purpureum	Late spring to late summer. Purple-mauve.	90cm (3 ft)
T. dipterocarpum Hewitt's Double	Late summer to mid autumn. Double mauve.	90cm (3 ft)
T. glaucum	Early to mid summer. Bright yellow, grey foliage.	1·5–1·8m (5–6 ft)
Trollius europaeus (globe flower) Superbus	Early to mid summer. Light yellow.	45–60cm (1½–2 ft)
T. ledebourii Imperial Orange	Mid summer to early autumn. Orange.	1·5–1·8m (5–6 ft)
Verbascum bombyciferum (mullein)	Mid to late summer. Yellow, silvery leaves.	90–120cm (3–4 ft)
V. hybridum Cotswold Queen	Mid summer. Terracotta.	1·2m (4 ft)
V.h. Pink Domino	Mid summer. Deep rose.	1m (3½ ft)
V. thapsiforme	Mid summer. Deep yellow.	1·2–1·5m (4–5 ft)
Vernonia crinita	Mid autumn. Purple.	1·5m (5 ft)
Veronica incana Wendy	Mid summer to early autumn. Deep blue, silver foliage.	30cm (12 in)
V. spicata Barcarolle	Mid summer to early autumn. Deep rose-pink.	45cm (18in)
V.s. Minuet	Pure pink, grey-green foliage.	38–45cm (15–18 in)
V. teucrium Royal Blue	Mid to late summer.	45cm (18 in)
V. virginica Alba	Early to mid autumn. White.	1·5m (5 ft)

PLANTS: SOIL TYPES AND SITUATIONS

GARDENING ON SAND

What an inspiration it is to wander round the Royal Horticultural Society's garden at Wisley – surely one of the great gardens of England – that has been patiently created in a notoriously poor sandy area. It is a garden that has everything – from flowering plants and shrubs, fruit and vegetables, to a rock garden and wild garden. So if you are on sand take heart from this example, which proves that with the right approach you can grow almost anything. We then give advice on the best plants for sandy soils.

Gardening on a sandy soil does have its problems, but they can be overcome by using the quite simple techniques described here. First, though, let us take a close look at sand itself.

What is sand?

Sand is composed of minute fragments of weathered rock, usually quartz. Its colour is due to chemicals present in the natural formation, iron in red sandstone, for example. Such a sand would not support plant life unless it had decaying plant remains mixed into it. Over the centuries, primitive and then more advanced organisms have lived and died on the earth's surface, forming humus in the process. Once incorporated with sand this gives us what we call sandy soil. An average soil of this type might have 60 per cent sand and 40 per cent earthy matter or humus.

Grains of sand vary in size, but are large compared with particles of loam and clay, the other main soil groups. The size of the individual grains gives sand its character, making it too loose for good root anchorage, and resulting in large air spaces through which water rapidly drains away, taking with it any soluble plant food in the soil.

Humus, on the other hand, has a large capacity for holding water, and is granular and springy. It does not stretch the imagination much to realize that its addition to sand immediately solves some of the worst problems.

The number of microscopic bacteria and other micro-organisms present in one tablespoon of good soil is said to equal the human population of the world. If you are fully to understand what is going on beneath your feet, and thus make sensible decisions that solve problems, you must appreciate something of the role of these organisms.

The microscopic population chiefly comprises bacteria (30 billion weigh approximately 30g, or 1 oz), that break down organic matter, releasing the plant foods upon which your garden depends.

Our friend the earthworm also plays an important part in the conditioning of your soil. Worms aerate the soil; their burrows provide drainage and admit air to heavy soils, but this is of less concern on sand. Their main importance is that they eat soil for the purpose of digesting the vegetable debris in it; sometimes the process ends with a wormcast on the surface. If you have ever touched a wormcast when dry you will appreciate how finely divided it is. Thus, soil and vegetable matter are thoroughly mixed.

The worms dig your soil for you. It is estimated that in a 40–50 year period the whole of the top 25cm (9 in) of soil in any garden goes through the gut of a worm and is much improved by it. So encourage the worms, and put up with a few casts on the lawn – on sandy soils they will disappear with the touch of a besom.

Although a gross simplification, it is broadly true that if you do not supply the humus and moisture that nourish the earthworm and micro-organisms, there is little chance of your garden flourishing.

How to improve sand

Since it is clear that the best way to promote happiness when gardening on sand is to change the nature of the soil, making it less sandy by adding humus, let us look at a few ways this can be done.

Fresh soil Adding fresh soil to your garden is not often considered, but it is the real short cut if you are lucky enough to find a supply. Building sites often have a surplus of topsoil if an extensive area has been stripped for a large building. But do make sure that it is topsoil and not

and colder, and generally the best on sand; and pig manure is the least popular, although it can do a good job. There is nothing wrong with a mixture of all three if you are offered it. Poultry manure is not the best way to improve sand as it is primarily droppings that can be wet, smelly and caustic to plant roots, but mixed ten parts to one with your own compost it can be useful.

If buying manure by the load ask what weight the lorry will hold before you agree quantity and price per 1000kg (1

Left: a typical corner of the RHS garden at Wisley, where all manner of plants flourish on a sandy soil
Above: formation of sand – coarse sand beneath a weathered rock face

subsoil, that it is much better soil than your own, and that it can be tipped on or very near your garden. Spread an even 15cm (6 in) over your soil and dig it in.

Animal manure Although animal manure is supposedly a thing of the past, this is probably not true save in the centre of big cities. Look in your local papers for advertisements, or ring up a stables.

You can buy it as fresh, or *long*, manure (that is, with mainly long straw), which means you have to compost it for about four months; or you can get well-rotted or *short* manure, which is the better buy.

Quality and character are much affected by the animal that has lived on the straw. Horse manure is 'hot' and rots quickly, but is the lightest and least suitable for sand; cow manure is wetter

ton), and make sure the lorry arrives full.

Spent mushroom compost Useful for helping to rot the straw if you are using horse manure. It contains very little food value, but it does provide valuable organic matter, helping with water retention on light soils.

Municipal compost A few local authorities produce this by composting paper and vegetable waste. Do not confuse it with sewage sludge, which is much cheaper but such a variable product that one hesitates to recommend it. With sludge, it is necessary to check locally that it is free from disease organisms, and from injurious metals such as cadmium, copper or lead.

Spent hops Make an excellent bulk water-retaining manure, but they do smell. Buy them straight from a brewery.

Seaweed This is only for those who live near the sea. It has a dreadful smell if you rot it down, so dig it in fresh some months before you are ready to plant.

Leaf mould Some local authorities will

deliver loads of this when the streets are being swept clear of leaves in the autumn. In 6–9 months it makes a splendid humus.
Peat Very good but expensive.
Garden compost For the cheapest and one of the best forms of organic manure there is garden compost. Keep everything rottable from the house or garden, separating those things that are quick rotting (such as lettuce leaves and grass mowings) from those that are slow rotting (hedge and shrub prunings, for example). Both make useful compost, but are ready for use many months apart.

Cultivation

The materials mentioned are of little use in improving sand unless they are thoroughly mixed in. This is best done by double digging, incorporating as much compost or manure as you have – or can afford – into the second spit, thus creating the possibility of food and moisture retention.

You are unlikely to make a good soil in one year. The measure of your success will be the colour of your sandy soil. As it darkens you will know its fertility is increasing. In digging, you may find a strange, impervious rock-hard layer. This is known as an 'iron pan', and is caused by an excess of iron salts washed down from the upper layers sealing together grains of sand. The only answer is to break up the layer, and it may well take a pick and a strong arm to do it.

Mulching

While not improving the soil directly, this highly desirable practice most certainly improves the lot of plants growing in sand. It has two forms.
1 Dry mulching, that is keeping the Dutch hoe going so that there is a layer of dry, loose soil on top of the ground. This breaks contact between soil moisture and the dry air above, and materially reduces the amount of evaporation.
2 Covering of the soil and plant roots with a layer of non-conducting material such as litter, 'long' manure, leaves, peat or partly-decayed compost. Any convenient material will do, provided it makes a dry layer that stops loss of moisture.

Conserving moisture is one of the main objectives of mulching, but it also keeps the roots cool in summer, especially surface-rooters like raspberries or rhododendrons. It provides a mild feed after rain if you have used manure as a mulch and, if applied to tender plantings like fuchsias before frost, will protect them from low temperatures. It is particularly helpful when transplanting evergreens – ideally done in late spring (April) – as it

reduces the chances of the soil drying out before the plants have been able to make a new root system.

Ground cover

This is nature's way of providing a mulch. It is not for flowerbeds or the vegetable plot, but for most other places there are plants that will cover the soil around larger plantings to the benefit of both, and incidentally reduce your work by smothering weeds.

Nature abhors bare ground and will soon fill spaces with something, so you need to be selective. You might regret planting such charmers as *Convallaria majalis* (lily of the valley), that when happy brooks no opposition, or *Campanula poscharskyana*, that can be all too much of a good thing if incautiously used on the rock garden.

There are many dozens of good plants that are both ornamental and useful in the role of ground cover. For example, on a hot, dry bank try *Hypericum calycinum* (rose of Sharon) or *Helianthemum nummularium* Rhodanthe Carneum or, if you have room, the climbing *Hydrangea petiolaris* that, if treated as a scrambler, will easily cover 1·5 sq m (2 sq yd).

Remember that ground cover only works when the plants touch each other. Therefore until they are big enough you have to keep the ground clear by ordinary

*Right: leaf mould makes a useful humus
Below: spent hops – obtained from a brewery – make a good water-retaining manure around this apple tree*

methods, but it is indeed worth it. The subject of ground cover is a wide one, and has already been dealt with earlier in the book on page 102.

Taking stock

Before you select plants for your garden you need to know whether it is acid or alkaline, as rhododenrons, for example, will not grow on alkaline sands. You can usually find out what the local soil is like by ringing your local authority or parks department, and a local horticultural society might also help.

Alternatively, you could buy a soil-testing kit, usually consisting of a fluid that changes colour when mixed with soil. You then compare this colour with a colour chart (supplied with the kit) that gives a reasonably accurate idea of the

degree of acidity or alkalinity in your soil. If acidity is excessive you can correct the balance using lime at 270g per sq m ($\frac{1}{2}$ lb per sq yd); if alkalinity is excessive any of the soil-improving forms of humus described earlier will help.

Advantages of sandy soil
By now you may well think it a good thing to move somewhere else if you have a sandy garden, but there are distinct and very definite advantages to such a soil. It is the easiest of all soils to manage. In a world where spare time is becoming increasingly more difficult to arrange, the boon of being able to dash out and cultivate at a moment's notice is incalculable. Sand is light because of the large air spaces between grains, so digging is not the back-breaking job it is on clays, and

Above: peat, though expensive, is an excellent mulch for sandy gardens
Above left: the compost heap provides good organic manure at little cost
Left: well-rotted stable manure can help to improve a sandy soil

can be carried out at any time except during, or immediately after, rain.

Given the absence of an iron pan, drainage is superb, making plant losses due to waterlogging in winter most unusual. And tender plants appreciate the absence of ice around their stems and roots in frosty weather.

The greatest advantage of sandy soil is its 'earliness'. In mid spring (March) the gardener on clay is still wondering when it will be dry enough for him to complete the winter digging, but sandy soils are already taking early sowings such as peas and lettuce. Given food and moisture, plants grow quickly and easily, and cuttings root readily in the naturally well-aerated conditions of a clean sand.

PLANTS FOR SANDY SOILS

After our look at the problems of gardening on sand, no one who has a sandy soil needs to be told that it is dry and poor in plant food.

But over many thousands of years nature has been busy adapting the physical structure of some plants to enable them to thrive in different unpromising conditions.

Making the right choice of plants if your garden's soil is sandy will therefore save you a lot of disappointment, and here we provide a selection of suitable trees, shrubs and vegetables, describing in each case the growing habit and, where relevant, giving the flowering season.

Many and ingenious are the adaptations nature has made to certain plants to reduce loss of water. In extreme cases, for example *Ulex europaeus* (common gorse) or *Spartium junceum* (Spanish broom), leaves have virtually been abandoned, but the plants remain attractive, if a little short on elegance, using green stems to carry out the function of leaves.

To make the best of gardening on a sandy soil there are a number of simple points to remember.

1 Do start with small plants, for they are much easier to cosset and nurse to the stage where they can look after themselves than larger plants. Once they are well established they will thrive virtually unaided.

2 Use pot-grown plants where possible. Prepare the planting hole with a generous supply of moist humus, then water in well, and continue to water until a root system is established.

3 Mulch well to reduce water loss.

(lady of the woods) is hard to beat, but you must choose it yourself in the nursery as the quality of the silver stem is very variable. If you prefer a golden stem then the yellow birch *B. lutea* may suit.

Pinus (pine)
In particularly windy spots pines, such as the Austrian *Pinus nigra* in one of its forms, are excellent.

Populus (poplar)
The quickest-growing of the choice of trees included here, poplars can be used both as 6–9m (20–30 ft) trees or cut back and made into a thick suckering screen, say 4·5m (15 ft) high. Excellent species are the aspen *Populus tremula*, whose leaves shimmer in the slightest breeze, and the white poplar *P. alba*, whose leaves with their white, felt-like underside are conspicuous when ruffled by the breeze. Both species have a golden autumn colour.

Robinia
All false acacias (*Robinia pseudoacacia*) will do well but you should think especially of the small but brilliant golden *R.p.* Frisia, that makes a handsome picture mixed with the purple foliage of such as *Berberis thunbergii* Atropurpurea.

SHRUBS
The following selection covers the shrubs that have adapted best to sandy soil and are therefore most likely to succeed.

Berberis (barberry)
Berberis × stenophylla comes near to being the best of the informal evergreen hedges. It forms a dense barrier up to 3m (10 ft) high out of which it throws slender arching sprays dressed in narrow, dark green leaves that in late spring (April) are clothed with small, rich golden flowers.

There are good dwarf forms like *B. × s.* Irwinii and *B. × s.* Coccinea, with one of the parents of the latter, the evergreen *B. darwinii*, making a superb formal hedge or individual specimen in its own right. Of much stiffer habit, this has shining, dark green, holly-like leaves and is profuse in its spring bloom of richest orange-yellow. It is often laden with plum-coloured berries in the autumn.

Of the deciduous berberis there are well over 100 species that could be described. Three outstandingly reliable ones are *B. aggregata*, *B. thunbergii* and *B. wilsoniae*. All are invaluable small shrubs of 90–120cm (3–4 ft) height, compact in growth, and unsurpassed for the profusion and brilliance of their scarlet, coral and red berries and spectacular autumn foliage colouring.

Far left, top: Populus alba *(white poplar) is very attractive in autumn*
Far left, bottom: Betula pendula *(weeping silver birch) has an attractive shape*
Left: Acer negundo *Variegatum*
Above: Robinia pseudoacacia *Frisia*

TREES
Although trees and shrubs are the foundation of most gardens they should be used sparingly in a small area, especially on sand. A large tree is said to evaporate 1000kg (1 ton) of water on a hot sunny day, so the moral is obvious. However, you may wish to provide shelter or hide something unsightly with one of the following trees.

Acer (maple)
Being the largest plants, trees can be used to give point to a layout or to provide a shady spot for your deckchair. A neglected small tree suitable for both purposes is the box elder *Acer negundo*. It looks like neither a box nor an elder, but is attractive and medium-sized, although you will need a stem of at least 1·8m (6 ft) if you wish to sit under it, as its boughs tend to droop. Try one of its very good gold- or silver-leaved forms – *A.n.* Auratum is bright gold and *A.n.* Variegatum a most attractive green and white.

Ailanthus
The tree of heaven *Ailanthus altissima* is extremely tolerant, even of a smoke- or fume-polluted atmosphere. Its leaves resemble an enormous ash leaf up to 90cm (3 ft) long and with as many as 20 leaflets. It makes an extremely handsome lawn specimen and can easily be kept to a desired size by careful pruning.

Betula (birch)
It is difficult to leave out the birch from any list, for it is a supremely graceful tree that succeeds in any soil. A good form of the British silver birch *Betula pendula*

Calluna and erica

Acid sands are the ideal base for a heather, heath, or ling garden, as can be seen in many commons, moors and heaths in Britain. Calluna and erica provide ground cover as well as floral beauty, and with a suitable choice of species your garden need never be without colour in any month of the year.

No heather garden would be complete without the ling native to Britain, *Calluna vulgaris*. *C.v.* Serlei is as good as any and who has not worn a bit of this white form for luck? Among the crimsons is *C.v.* C.W. Nix, and you cannot be without the double-flowered charmer *C.v.* H.E. Beale, that bejewels its long sprays with bright pink clusters.

There are golden-foliaged forms, too – *C.v.* Golden Feather, that turns a gentle orange by the time winter arrives, and the remarkable *C.v.* Robert Chapman, that is golden-foliaged in spring, orange come the summer, and red by the autumn.

The winter heath *Erica carnea* is particularly welcome, forming dense

hummocks of rosy-pink flowers from early winter to early spring (November to February). It is the originator of innumerable varieties that span early winter through to late spring (November to April). Among the best are *E.c.* King George, with carmine flowers; *E.c.* Vivellii, with deep red flowers and bronzy-red foliage in winter; *E.c.* Springwood Pink and *E.c.* Springwood White; and the very late-flowering *E.c.* Ruby Glow, that also has bronzy foliage.

Should you live on a limey sand – and there are some, especially near the sea – then only a few heaths are for you. These include *Erica carnea*, that has the most colour variants, and the excellent, slightly taller *E. × darleyensis*, *E. mediterranea* and the Corsican heath *E. terminalis*, that all bear rosy-coloured flowers.

For height among the heaths, it is worth taking a chance on the hardiness of *E. arborea* Alpina, a tree heath, from whose root briar pipes are made. 'Briar' is

Above: heather garden at the Royal Horticultural Society gardens at Wisley
Left: Erica carnea Springwood White

a corruption of *bruyère*, the French vernacular name for tree heaths. The form *E.a.* Alpina (that you should insist upon) produces a dense, upright bush that cheers you into mid spring (around March) with masses of ash-white panicles, 30cm (12 in) long, and heavy with honey fragrance on a warm day.

The common British bell heather *E. cinerea* (also known as Scotch or grey heath) is widely distributed and has produced a number of attractive varieties. Among the best are *E.c.* C.D. Eason, with flowers of a deep glowing pink, and *E.c.* Rosea, with flowers of a soft pink. Two varieties that scarcely have a flower at all, but are well worth a place in any garden for their golden summer foliage turning to red in winter, are *E.c.* Golden Drop and *E.c.* Golden Hue.

Cistus (rock or sun rose)

These rock roses are exceptionally free-flowering around mid summer (June), fast-growing, evergreen and really happy on a hot, dry bank in full sun. Many have aromatic foliage and gummy leaves that enable them to retain moisture. They associate well with heather and broom.

Low-growing *Cistus palhinhaii*, discovered on Cape Trafalgar in Portugal, is compact, unexpectedly hardy and bears 10cm (4 in) wide flowers. *C. × cyprius* is vigorous, hardy, some 1·8m (6 ft) tall and has 7–8cm (3 in) wide flowers, white in colour with five splashes of crimson around the base of each petal where it joins the central boss of yellow stamens. *C.* Silver Pink is a lovely natural hybrid.

Most rock roses rapidly become sprawling bushes and are best replaced with younger plants every seven or eight years rather than trying to keep them under control by pruning, which they dislike.

Cytisus (broom)

Brooms are remarkably well adapted to life on a hot, dry sand. A poor soil seems a positive advantage, and in full sun they will seed freely, even among rocks, and soon become as tough and unassailable as gorse. The shoots of many are green, which enables them to function as food producers when the leaves are out of action for any reason, such as storm damage or drought. They are very rapid growers, particularly the forms of the common broom *Cytisus scoparius*. Accordingly, it is a good plan to prune back the shoots regularly just after flowering so that 'legginess' is avoided.

C. albus (or *C. multiflorus*) is known as the white Spanish broom, and is a 3m (10 ft) high plant of slender grace that is best seen emerging in a fountain of white bloom from darker, more dwarf shrubs.

The common broom *C. scoparius* is an admirable plant in its own right, but unless very sheltered it needs a sound stake. We recommend *C.s.* Cornish Cream, *C.s.* Firefly, with yellow and bronze flowers, and *C.s.* Golden Sunlight, plus the sub-species *C.s.* Sulphureus, with cream and pale sulphur flowers, tinged red in the bud: all flower in early and mid summer (end of May and early June).

C. × beanii is a charming, semi-prostrate hybrid bearing golden flowers, and a great favourite is *C. × kewensis*, whose stems are only 30cm (12 in) high but that can cover a square metre or yard with myriads of creamy-yellow, pea-like flowers in late spring (April).

Genista

Botanically very close to the brooms, this is another yellow, pea-flowered family that in practical use takes over from them by flowering in late summer (July), as the brooms fade.

Genista aetnensis, the Mount Etna broom, is a tall plant of around 3–3·5m (10–12 ft) that cascades its pendant green shoots almost to the ground and studs them from end to end with tiny golden pea flowers in late summer (July).

G. hispanica, the Spanish gorse, is essential for any dry, exposed garden. It is not unlike a dwarf, close-knit gorse. Planted on a hot, dry bank (and kept watered), it rolls out an undulating carpet of green mounds that, in early and mid summer (May and June) of each year, turn bright yellow. Odd plants do die without any apparent reason, so it is as

Two plants particularly well suited to sandy conditions are Cytisus scoparius Sulphureus *(top), and the brilliantly-coloured* Genista tinctoria Royal Gold

well to have a young plant or two in reserve to fill any gaps.

The British *G. tinctoria* (dyer's green-weed) was used for the famous Kendal Green dye, and a selection from this, *G.t.* Royal Gold, is one of the best dwarf flowering shrubs available and should not be neglected.

Juniperus (juniper)

This is a most useful and long-suffering family. *Juniperus communis* (common juniper) contains *J.c.* Hibernica (Irish juniper), a column of grey-green that is admirable to give point to a formal layout; *J.c.* Effusa, a prostrate carpeting plant for a bank; and many diverse forms. The shore juniper, *J. conferta* is another

Right and far right: Mahonia aquifolium – *its berries are good for jam – is a decorative subject for underplanting*
Below right: Spartium junceum *(Spanish broom) is at home in a dry, sandy soil*
Below: Juniperus communis *(common juniper) and* Ulex europaeus *(common gorse) are hardy specimens*

excellent cover for sandy banks and originally came from Japan.

Mahonia

Mahonias are related to berberis but can be distinguished by their large pinnate leaves and spineless stems.

Mahonia aquifolium, known as the Oregon grape – after its bunches of most decorative blue berries – is one of the best plants for underplanting in dry places. It has bright yellow, honey-scented flowers

in dense, short clusters. Prune back after flowering if you want to keep it low-growing.

M. japonica is 1·8–2·4m (6–8 ft) tall, and bears clusters of lily-of-the-valley-scented flowers in chains of pendant bells in early and mid spring (February and March); there can be up to 12 chains each with up to 100 flowers. Flowering as early as it does, and growing in the most inhospitable places, it is indeed a valuable plant to have in your garden.

Spartium

Any plant such as *Spartium junceum*, that has been growing in Britain since the first Elizabeth was on the throne, must have proved its worth. The common name, Spanish broom, indicates its place of origin, where it inhabits regions of very restricted rainfall; as a result, it has almost entirely dispensed with leaves and relies on round, green, rush-like stems to carry out their function. So it is a more than useful plant for an arid sand. It is broom-like in growth up to 3m (10 ft) and apt to be 'leggy' unless hard-pruned.

One good plan is to plant in groups of an even number some 1·2m (4 ft) apart; prune every other plant close back to the crown each year. Thus the bright yellow fragrant flowers are borne in 45cm (18 in) racemes from mid summer to mid autumn (June to September) on alternate plants. This is quite sufficient to clothe the planted area, and prevents the shrubs ever becoming too large for a small garden.

Ulex europaeus (common gorse)

The plant *par excellence* for a sandy soil, and a sight to be remembered as a golden glory of gorse clothing the shelving cliffs of Guernsey against a background of blue sea. It is rarely without blossom, hence the saying 'when gorse is out of flower, kissing's out of season'. Its early flowers offer a rich bee pasture. It has a scent that to some is of coconut and to others of honey and almond; this scent hangs in the air in good weather, and to a countryman must bring back the memory of warmth, high summer and hay making.

If you have a large area to cover it may be best to sow seed in groups some 60cm (24 in) apart.

VEGETABLES

Some of the finest vegetable-growing areas are on sandy soil, due to earliness and ease of cultivation, but of course water and adequate food materials are supplied. There is no reason why you, too, should not grow vegetables successfully, provided you practise the principles already described. The following tips may also help.

Lettuce, radish and spinach These must never lack water or they become hard and run quickly to seed. A quite small area of specially-prepared soil with a high humus-content situated close to the water supply helps enormously. Don't forget that few families eat more than three or four large lettuce per week so sow short rows, say of 1·8m (6 ft), every ten days;

make the rows even shorter for radish.

Brassicas, marrows/courgettes, tomatoes When planting, after firming well, make a hole 5–8cm (2–3 in) deep a few centimetres away from the stem. Fill this when watering; it places the water where it is needed around the plant's roots.

Runner beans It is sometimes difficult to make a framework really strong on sand. Stout individual poles, say 1·2m (4 ft) apart, each with two to three plants on it may help, but drive them in quite firmly

so that the wind can pass between the columns of beans.

Onions It is difficult to get the firm seedbed beloved of onions. Sets planted in mid spring (March) do better. A row of Express Yellow onions sown in early autumn (mid August) is a good bet to bridge the onion 'gap'. They harvest in mid summer (June) of the following year. Thin to six per 30cm (12 in).

Mulching This is just as important for vegetables as for other plants on sand.

A fine crop of mixed vegetables thriving in the sandy soil at Wisley

GARDENING ON CLAY

Many people might despair when faced with the prospect of gardening on a clay soil, but in fact this is unnecessary as there is a great deal that can be done to alleviate the problem. Here we give some suggestions, explaining how to double dig and trench, and also how to improve the drainage; we then describe some of the plants that will grow happily on clay.

What we mean when we speak of clay soils are mixtures of clay and ingredients such as sand, humus, and sometimes chalk; pure clay alone cannot be used for cultivation. To some extent, the proportions of the materials in a mixture determine the character of the soil: a high percentage of clay would give a 'stiff' or 'heavy' soil, meaning that it would cling together and be difficult to cultivate, whereas a large amount of sand and humus would mean a 'light' or even 'loam' soil – the last being ideal. There are, however, other differences, and these are due to the nature of clay itself.

Potential problems

Not all clays are formed in exactly the same way, and different varieties behave in dissimilar ways when alternately wetted and dried. With some clays, the particles are so tightly bonded that their structure is not greatly altered by water, but in others the particles are more loosely attached, and as a result are forced apart when wet and close up again when dry. The effect is one of constant expansion and contraction.

When clay of this shrinkable type predominates in a soil, trouble can arise with buildings: as the soil moves, so foundations are disturbed and walls may crack – or, in extreme cases, fall down. Trees and large shrubs could well increase the rate of water removal in dry weather, so aggravating the movement of the soil, and this is why it is unwise to plant too many of them near buildings that are situated on shrinkable clay.

So much for the drawbacks of clay as a soil ingredient. But, of course, it also has many advantages, including the ability to hold moisture and plant foods – particularly those such as calcium, magnesium and potassium, the ions of which are positively charged and so are held on the negatively-charged particles of clay. So clay soils are potentially fertile, and in the words of one expert 'in most climates the most productive soils contain at least 20 per cent clay'.

Difficulties only really begin when there is so much clay in the soil, or it is of such a closely-bonded character, that it is difficult for water to pass through it or for a spade, plough or cultivator to move it.

Waterlogging can result after heavy rain if a soil contains too much clay

Then the soil may become so completely waterlogged in winter that all air is driven out, and roots, worms and beneficial micro-organisms in the soil are drowned. Even if no such disasters occur, it may be physically impossible to cultivate the soil until it has at least partially dried out in spring, and so sowings and plantings are unduly delayed. Moreover, excess water chills the soil and delays seed germination and plant growth.

Suggested solutions

All the problems so far described are physical ones, and can be reduced in severity, even if not entirely removed, by various means. Digging helps, especially if done early in the autumn, when it will expose the soil to air and frost that will help to dry it and break it up. All manner of dressings can be added to give the soil a more open texture: coarse sand and grit are excellent, and so are well-weathered boiler ashes – but not ashes from a domestic fire, as these are too fine in texture and simply become as slimy as the clay itself.

Any rotting organic matter will help, including leaves, garden refuse, partially-decayed straw, old mushroom compost, and peat or bulky animal manure – particularly the horse variety that contains a lot of litter. All of these can be worked into the soil at any time it is vacant, or – if it is permanently planted – can be spread on the surface, and left to be pulled in by worms, washed down by rain, or hoed into the top 2–3cm (1 in).

Another possibility is to use lime – though not with fresh animal manure as the two interact unfavourably. The addition of lime turns the fine, colloidal particles of clay into larger granules, and so the soil becomes more open in texture and less pasty. Fresh, hydrated lime is the best form to use, and provided the soil is not already markedly alkaline and there are no lime-hating plants (and none are planned) then it can be applied at rates of up to 1kg per sq m (2 lb per sq yd). In practice, it is usually better to give considerably less, say about 250g per sq m (8 oz per sq yd), and to repeat annually until the desired improvement has been brought about. It is seldom possible or desirable to change the character of a soil suddenly, and usually in gardening you must be prepared to be patient and make gradual improvements.

Providing drainage

Drainage should either be done thoroughly or not at all. The problem in small gardens is usually what to do with the water that has been removed by land-drains. It is generally illegal to run it into a sewer, but if a soakaway for roof water is available it may be possible to turn the garden surplus into this. An alternative is to dig a special soakaway, preferably at the lowest point in the garden and sufficiently deep to penetrate through the underlying impervious layer that is holding up the water. But that can easily prove to be a counsel of perfection impossible to achieve.

A small hole cleanly dug with a spade to a depth of one metre (or yard) or more will expose what is called a 'profile' of the soil, showing fairly clearly where the relatively fertile topsoil gives way to poorer subsoil, and where the impervious layer of clay is – and maybe even how thick it is.

In a country garden, drainage may be no problem at all if a ditch or stream is available into which the land-drains, or at any rate the main drain that takes the flow of subsidiary drains, can be run.

The best way to make land-drains is to purchase the special earthenware pipes produced for the job, and to lay these end to end and about 45–60cm (18–24 in) deep. By this means they will collect water more efficiently and are less likely to become blocked with silt if laid in stones, clinkers, or large, loose gravel. If there is a considerable area to be drained, pipes laid in a herringbone pattern will probably cover it most economically and efficiently. Drains usually need to be not more than 2·4m (8 ft) apart, and all should have a fall of at least 30cm in 12m (1 ft in every 40) so that water can flow steadily away to whatever outlet has been provided.

Double digging and trenching

Drainage can also be improved by two special methods of deep digging known as double digging and trenching. To carry out the former, excavate a trench 30cm (12 in) wide and 25–30cm (10–12 in) deep across one end of the plot, and remove the spoil to the far end of the garden. Then turn over the soil in the bottom of the open trench with a fork or spade, so that altogether soil to a total depth of 50–60cm (20–24 in) is then broken up.

Dig a second trench, adjacent to the first and to the same proportions, and again turn over the soil in the bottom. However, this time use the spoil to fill in the first trench. Continue with more trenches, each time placing the spoil in the preceding trench, until you reach the end

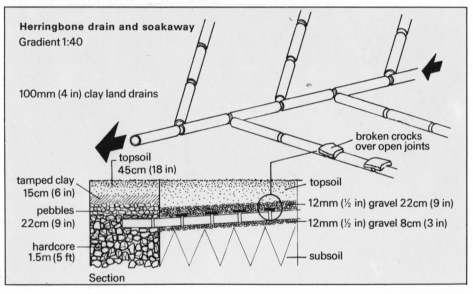

Herringbone drain and soakaway
Gradient 1:40

100mm (4 in) clay land drains

tamped clay
15cm (6 in)

pebbles
22cm (9 in)

hardcore
1.5m (5 ft)

topsoil
45cm (18 in)

broken crocks
over open joints

topsoil

12mm (½ in) gravel 22cm (9 in)

12mm (½ in) gravel 8cm (3 in)

subsoil

Section

of the plot. The last trench is then filled in with the spoil from the first.

Trenching is a little more complicated. Make the first trench at least 60cm (2 ft) wide and 25–30cm (10–12 in) deep, and remove the spoil to the far end of the plot, as before (see **2** in diagram opposite). Next dig a second trench, 30cm (12 in) wide, on the far side of the first trench, to form a step into it (**3**); this smaller quantity of soil is also left at the far end of the garden, but separate from the first pile. Then turn over the soil in the bottom of the deep, narrow trench, breaking it up to a total depth of 75–90cm (2½–3 ft) (**4**).

Now turn over the step of soil in the wide trench and place it on top of the broken-up soil in the bottom of the narrow trench (**5**), so exposing an additional 30cm (12 in) wide strip of subsoil, which in turn is broken up where it lies with a spade or fork (**6**).

The next stage is to mark out, with a line, a further strip of surface ground, but this time only 30cm (12 in) wide. Then throw the topsoil from this over the

second-spit soil in the first trench (**7**), throw the second-spit soil over the broken subsoil in the second trench (**8**), and break up the newly-exposed strip of subsoil (**9**), leaving it where it is. Proceed in exactly the same manner, with 30cm wide strips, until you reach the far end of the plot (**10–12**); then fill the last trench with the soil from the first trench – second-spit soil underneath (**13**), topsoil on top (**14**).

Double digging and trenching produce much deeper cultivation than is possible by simple digging – still without bringing the relatively infertile subsoil to the surface or burying good topsoil where it is of little or no value to feeding roots. Deep cultivation is of some direct value because it lets in air and allows surplus water to escape, but it is much more effective if bulky organic matter can be worked in at the same time to the full depth of the disturbed soil. It also allows lime to be distributed more deeply than when plain digging is practised, and this helps to improve the texture and drainage of the lower soil where most problems occur.

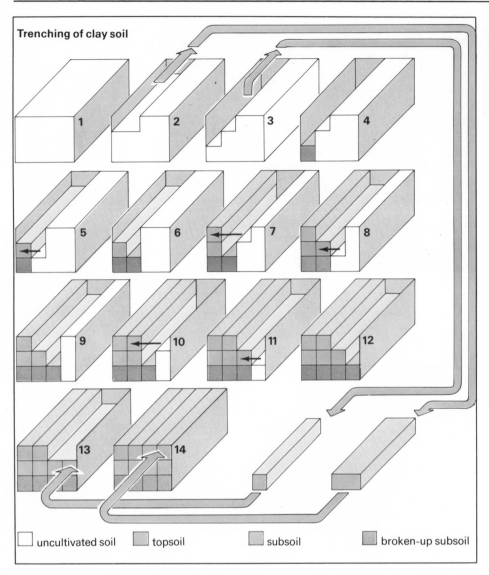

Trenching of clay soil

uncultivated soil ☐ topsoil ☐ subsoil ☐ broken-up subsoil ☐

Above: trenching improves texture and drainage of lower soil. Above right: lawn aeration and drainage are improved by spiking regularly with a hollow-tined fork

What not to do

There are some things you should never do with clay soils. As far as possible, avoid walking on them when they are very wet as this may consolidate them so much that, when they eventually dry out, they will be set hard like a brick. It is particularly important not to walk on newly-prepared seed or planting beds that have become wet; it may be necessary to put boards on the surface, even when digging, to distribute weight and avoid compacting the clay.

It is necessary to be extra cautious in the use of rollers on lawns grown on clay soils. If the lawns are not used for ball games requiring a very true surface, it is best not to roll at all, but if rolling is essential it should be as light as practicable and confined to periods when the surface is no more than just moist.

Lawns on clay are likely to need spiking, pricking, slitting, or similar means of aeration, more frequently than lawns on naturally porous soils. If hollow tining can be done, as soon as the work is completed sharp grit or sand can be brushed into the little holes that are made; finely-milled peat can be applied in the same way. Repeated treatments of this kind will produce a marked improvement in the texture of the top 5–8cm (2–3 in) of soil where most grass roots are found.

Avoid the use of nitrate of soda as a quickly-available source of nitrogen on clay as it aggravates the close texture of the soil. Try sulphate of ammonia instead, as it is almost as fast-acting, but doesn't have the same unwanted effect.

Garden features below soil level should not be attempted on clay because of the poor drainage, so steer clear of sunken gardens and paths, as these can easily become pools or streams of water. Raised features, however, are a different matter and can be very satisfactory. Among the possibilities are raised beds, banks, rock gardens built up above normal soil level, and – in the vegetable and cut flower plots – wide ridges where plants can be grown along the top. Even pyrethrum, which is very sensitive to excess water in winter, can be grown successfully on ridges.

It can be difficult to plant in clay soil, at any rate during the seasons usually recommended – that is, autumn (August to October), late winter (January) and early spring (February). In these months, clay can be so sticky that it is impossible to break it up into fragments sufficiently fine to be worked between and around roots. Of course, you could leave planting until late spring or summer (April to July) and then do it from containers, but that can be inconvenient and expensive, and will almost certainly limit your choice.

The alternative is to prepare a planting mixture, either of the best of your own soil, or of imported soil that is less binding, plus peat and sand in sufficient quantity to make it crumbly. Add a little bonemeal to the mixture, or better still some John Innes base fertilizer, to make it richer and to stimulate growth.

Once prepared, cover this heap of planting mixture with polythene or store it under cover so that it remains moist but never becomes sodden. Then a bucketful can be worked around the roots of every tree or large shrub, and a similar quantity around rose bushes and herbaceous perennials, as they are planted. It can mean the difference between success and failure.

PLANTS FOR CLAY SOILS

Earlier we looked at the make-up of clay soil and gave some suggestions for its improvement. Here we list some of the many trees, shrubs and herbaceous perennials that can be grown easily and successfully on clay.

Soils that contain a moderate amount of clay are usually highly fertile, especially if they've been well cultivated, and so there are no particular problems in selecting plants to suit them. In fact, it is easier to make recommendations about what to avoid than what to choose since the list of undesirables is quite short, and confined mainly to plants that need perfect drainage and a loose, open soil. Many alpines come into this category, but their requirements are usually so specialized anyway that they have to be grown in special beds.

There are numerous grey- and silver-leaved plants that resent excess soil moisture, especially in winter, and so they may be less satisfactory on a clay soil than on one of a more porous character unless special care is taken to ensure that there is no waterlogging.

It must be remembered that whether a clay soil is alkaline, neutral or acid will to some degree determine what can be grown in it, but then the same applies to many soils that could not by any stretch of the imagination be called clay.

Clay soils are often cold, and this can make it unwise to use them for early crops or for plants that are on the borderline of hardiness. But again, this is not a problem exclusive to soils containing a lot of clay.

The greater the clay content, the greater the difficulty that will be experienced; near-pure clay would be unsuitable for any planting and is best either paved over or converted into a pool or lake. It is in the intermediate range between the stiff but fertile loams and the impossible clays that real problems of selection occur. You can observe how the natural flora of such a place differs from that growing in other areas.

Here, then, we offer a selection of plants for clay soil starting with trees.

TREES

Quercus (oak) may continue to thrive long after the soil has become too stiff and soggy for betula (birch) or the mountain ash sorbus. Some species of acer (maple or sycamore) will survive much better than others, the worst being the varieties of *Acer japonicum* and *A. palmatum*

The dwarf campanula, C. lactiflora Pouffe, makes good ground cover on clay

(Japanese maple), and the best the strong-growing kinds such as *A. platanoides* (Norway maple) and *A. pseudoplatanus* (sycamore), and all their varieties.

Platanus (plane) is another genus that can take a lot of clay, especially *Platanus × hispanica* (London plane), a good choice for heavy soils and a first-class tree for towns, being tolerant of industrial pollution. All the salix (willow) species and hybrids do well, likewise the white-flowered *Aesculus hippocastanum* (common horse chestnut) and *A. × carnea* (pink horse chestnut). However, some other species, such as *A. indica* (Indian horse chestnut) and the much smaller, shrubby *A. parviflora*, will grow on clay but do not like late spring (April) frosts, the damaging effects of which can be aggravated by cold, wet clay soil.

Other trees that grow well, even on quite stiff clay soils, include crataegus (hawthorn or may) in almost all its species, hybrids and garden varieties; the various species of fraxinus (ash); tilia (lime or linden); populus (poplar); and all kinds of laburnum. Some malus (flowering crab) succeed, though if drainage is bad they may suffer from scab and canker. *Magnolia × soulangeana* is often seen thriving on clay soils, and all varieties of *Prunus cerasifera* (cherry plum) are usually successful. Most popular are the purple-leaved plums, *P. cerasifera* Pissardii, *P.c.* Nigra, and varieties such as *P.c.* Trailblazer and *P.c.* Vesuvius.

Among conifers, all varieties of *Chamaecyparis lawsoniana* (Lawson cypress) and thuya (arbor-vitae) are reliable. Abies (silver fir) enjoys the moisture that clay ensures, and taxus (yew) also grows well in rich, damp clay soils.

SHRUBS

Many shrubs flourish on clay, even on very stiff soils. Almost all spiraea are reliable and so are the species, hybrids and garden varieties of philadelphus (mock orange). Weigela gives no trouble, nor does deutzia – provided the situation is not very frosty in late spring (April), as this can defoliate the plants and cause considerable die-back in some kinds.

All forsythia do well, and so do the garden forms of chaenomeles (ornamental quince) that, like forsythia, start flowering in early spring (February). Both *Corylus avellana* (hazel) and *C. maxima* (filbert) actually prefer rather moist clay soils. They can be grown either for their nuts or as ornamental bushes in their coloured-leaved and contorted varieties such as *C. maxima* Purpurea (purple-leaf filbert), *C. avellana* Aurea and *C.a.* Contorta (Harry Lauder's walking stick) – this last is also known as the corkscrew hazel because of its twisted branches.

Cotoneaster of all kinds usually succeed, as do pyracantha, another genus grown for highly-coloured berries as well as decorative flowers and good foliage. Ilex (holly) will thrive in very stiff soils, and there are a great many garden varieties and hybrids from which to choose, including some with handsomely-variegated leaves, and others with yellow or orange berries.

Another large genus is viburnum. Most species thrive on heavy soil, and there is a great deal of choice in foliage, flower, berry and habit. *Viburnum opulus* (guelder rose) actually seems to prefer soils that are rather wet and close textured, and so does the variety *V. opulus* Sterile, often called 'snowball tree', because of its large, globular clusters of white flowers. It is one of the handsomest and most easily-grown deciduous shrubs. However, *V. macrocephalum*, a smaller tree than *V. opulus* Sterile, is a little tender and in many northern areas needs the shelter of a sunny wall to make it grow and flower well. Not so *V. plicatum*, a species from China and Japan, with small, snowball-like blooms, for this is a tough and adaptable plant, as is its wild form *V.p. tomentosum*, that has flat, circular clusters of white flowers along more or less horizontal branches.

Ribes sanguineum (flowering currant) loves heavy soil and so do its garden varieties *R. sanguineum* Pulborough Scarlet and *R.s.* King Edward VII, both with deep red flowers, the pale pink *R.s.* Carneum, and *R.s.* Brocklebankii, with pink flowers and yellow leaves.

Cornus alba (red-barked dogwood) likes soil that is wet, and does not object if

it is also clayey. There are numerous varieties, including *C. alba* Sibirica (also known as *C.a.* Atrosanguinea), with bright crimson stems; *C.a.* Elegantissima, with light green and white leaves; and *C.a.* Spaethii, with light yellow leaves.

Aucuba japonica is a good evergreen to grow on heavy soils either in its green-leaved or yellow-spotted forms. The leaves are large like those of *Prunus laurocerasus* (common or cherry laurel), another evergreen that likes clay.

It is commonly said that roses love clay and this is broadly true, though it does not apply equally to all kinds. *Rosa (spinosissima) pimpinellifolia* (Burnett rose or Scots briar), for instance, is a species that in Britain is at its best on sand dunes close to the sea, though its garden varieties and hybrids will grow in heavier soil. However, *R. pimpinellifolia* has for many years been a fringe interest and all the really popular roses, such as the large-flowered hybrid teas, the cluster-flowered floribundas, and all the climbers includ-

*With careful selection
you can still have a wide
range of trees and
shrubs, even on the
heaviest of clay soils.
Far left, top:* Fraxinus
exelsior *Pendula, the
weeping ash
Far left, centre:* Aesculus
parviflora
*Above left: spring-
flowering* Magnolia ×
soulangeana
Above: Ribes
sanguineum
*Pulborough Scarlet
(flowering currant)
thrives on heavy soil
Far left: all ilex (holly)
are happy on a clay soil,
so choose a variegated
one for colour value
Left:* Acer platanoides
*(Norway spruce) is a
strong-growing species*

ing the ramblers, thrive on clay soil provided it is well fed and reasonably well drained. No rose likes standing in water for long, and it is the potential richness of clay soils, not their wetness, that makes them congenial to roses.

HERBACEOUS PERENNIALS

Of herbaceous perennials for growing on a clay soil, it is those with strong, hungry root systems that are most likely to succeed, and also those that do not object to a good deal of moisture around their roots in winter and that are truly hardy.

All kinds of acanthus (bear's breeches) do well, anchoring themselves deeply in the clay and becoming quite difficult to remove once they have become established. Many species of polygonum (knotweed) do just the same, including the beautiful but notorious *Polygonum* (*sieboldii*) *cuspidatum* (also known as *Reynoutria japonica*), but this can become a nuisance, spreading far and wide, and often springing up where not wanted from underground stolons. However, the good forms of *P. amplexicaule* and *P. bistorta* (snake-weed) never give any trouble, and *P. campanulatum* (Himalayan knotweed) can be torn back quite easily if it begins to spread too far.

Several of the strong-growing campanula (bellflower) do well, none better than *Campanula lactiflora* (milky bellflower), that is normally a fairly tall plant though with one dwarf variety, named *C. lactiflora* Pouffe. *C. glomerata* is another excellent kind that spreads quite rapidly and looks delightful near the pink *Polygonum bistorta* Superbum.

Astilbe (false goat's beard) enjoys the moisture that clay brings but may not survive long if the clay dries out and

Many herbaceous perennials give excellent value on clay soils
Above left: Helleborus orientalis *(Lenten rose)*
Above: Polygonum bistorta Superbum *(snakeweed)*
Left: Phlox paniculata *Brigadier*
Top right: Aster novae-angliae *Harrington Pink*
Above right: a double variety of Hemerocallis fulva kwanso *(day lily)*
Above, far right: Doronicum plantagineum *(leopard's bane)*
Right: strong-growing Aruncus sylvester *(goat's beard) likes a damp spot*

cracks badly in summer. Its strong-growing relative *Aruncus sylvester* (goat's beard) is better able to look after itself but also prefers the damper spots.

Doronicum (leopard's bane) usually grows freely in clay soils, though it is the stronger-growing kinds, such as the varieties of *Doronicum plantagineum*, that will best be able to cope with really stiff clays. There are other good members of the daisy family, including *Aster novi-belgii* (Michaelmas daisy) and *A. novae-angliae*, most of the perennial helianthus (sunflowers) – but not *Helianthus atro-rubens* Monarch, that is rather tender – and all species and varieties of heliopsis. Some varieties of *Chrysanthemum maximum* (shasta daisy) succeed, the single-flowered varieties being, on the whole, hardier and more reliable than the double or semi-double varieties.

Solidago (golden rod) is capable of coping with the stiffest clay soils, and so is rudbeckia (cone flower), although *Rudbeckia* (*Echinacea*) *purpurea* prefers the lighter, better-drained loams. Most ligularia, still called by the old name of senecio in many gardens, prove successful, as does the less-well-known inula.

Some, but not all, achillea (yarrow) are good. It would be almost impossible to kill the garden varieties of *Achillea millefolium*, and that is also true of *A.* (*eupatorium*) *filipendulina* and *A. ptarmica* (sneezewort), but some of the grey-leaved kinds are less reliable.

Hosta (plantain lily) enjoys the moisture and richness of clay, but may need protection from slugs, as these have a fondness for hosta leaves. All the garden varieties of *Phlox paniculata* and *P. maculata* are good, and so are all lysimachia (loosestrife) and lythrum.

Hemerocallis (day lily) usually succeed, but if the soil is very stiff it will be wise to experiment first with some of the tough old varieties, such as *Hemerocallis fulva kwanso flore pleno*, before passing on to the choicer and more highly-coloured modern varieties, some of which seem to be a little less enduring. Much the same is true of iris. Old varieties of *Iris germanica* (purple or London flag) and *I. pallida* may survive where new varieties fail. The most likely of all to succeed is *Iris sibirica* in all its colour forms.

Most varieties of *Helleborus niger* (Christmas rose) and *H. orientalis* (Lenten rose) flourish on clay. The green-flowered species, *H. lividus*, *H. foetidus* and *H. corsicus* (Corsican hellebore) also manage very well. Paeonia (peony) actually prefers heavy soils provided it is not planted too deeply: the crowns should be barely covered with soil, *not* put down 5cm (2 in), as is usual on light soils.

Other possibilities are *Anemone hupehensis* (Japanese anemone), all varieties of which flower in late summer and early autumn (July and August); *Artemisia lactiflora* (white mugwort), a neglected plant with plumes of creamy white flowers; monarda in its several garden varieties; and *Galega officinalis*, an old-fashioned plant with clusters of small, vetch-like, blue and white, mauve and white, or all-white flowers that bloom throughout the summer.

Among hardy bulbs, all kinds of narcissus are very reliable, and so are both *Endymion non-scripta* (bluebell) and *E. hispanicus* (Spanish bluebell). Others that should do well are galanthus (snowdrop) – especially *Galanthus nivalis* (common snowdrop) and its varieties – and numerous species of allium.

GARDENING ON CHALK

Here we introduce our own design for a garden on chalk and describe a selection of suitable trees and shrubs; then on page 147 we turn to roses and herbaceous perennials. Given proper care and attention, a wide variety of plants will flourish in such conditions.

When grown on a chalk or lime soil, plants that originated in peat bogs or the deep leaf mould of the forest floor are inhibited by the degree of alkalinity present from taking up iron, magnesium and manganese. The result is that leaves turn yellow and the plants die back, suffering from what is known as lime-induced chlorosis. Among plants affected in this way are camellias, most heathers and other members of the ERICACEAE family, Japanese irises, rhododendrons (including azaleas), and some lilies and magnolias – they all prefer an acid soil.

However, if your garden happens to be on chalk or lime it is not the tragedy you might think. Most acid-loving plants were introduced to gardens comparatively recently as a result of botanical expeditions during the last 150 years – so if the Elizabethans in England could get along without rhododendrons, why shouldn't today's chalk gardeners? It is not all sour grapes to say that rhododendrons have their disadvantages: flowering time is short, most have no autumn colour, and the leaves – though evergreen – lack the healthy sparkle and well-polished look of holly, laurel or box.

You can grow a far greater variety of plants on chalk or limestone than on damp acid soil since the former is generally porous, dries quickly after rain, and does not get waterlogged in winter. Many reputedly tender plants only need good drainage, added to which chalk is warmer than clay soil. Lime-loving plants include a great number of lovely, medium-sized trees and shrubs, some excellent evergreens, numerous plants from the Mediterranean region, Australasia and the Cape (some of which have silver foliage), and all those that grow naturally on rocky cliffs by the sea or in the mountains. Bulbous plants, with very few exceptions, grow equally well. So while the ideal soil may be neutral, the chalk gardener is perhaps luckier than his opposite number on damp, acid soil. Remember that millions of pounds are spent yearly on liming soil, and that lime is good for most plants.

What is chalk?

Chalk is calcium carbonate ($CaCO_3$) and consists of the skeletons of minute marine animals that were laid down over millions of years at the bottom of the sea. Geological upheavals have raised these sea beds and erosion has exposed them. They run from Normandy in France to the south coast of England at Folkestone and Dover, along the South Downs, through parts of upland Dorset and the Isle of Wight, Wiltshire, Berkshire, east through the Chilterns and East Anglia, to the coast of Norfolk and up the spine of Lincolnshire to the Yorkshire Wolds. Limestone of various kinds appears all over the world, and you can safely say that anything that will grow on chalk will grow on limestone.

If you are in any doubt as to the soil structure of your garden, look at the local plants. Rhododendrons indicate acid or neutral soil, whereas campanula, clematis, dianthus (pinks) and scabiosa may mean limey *or* chalk soil.

Preparing the soil

Lime soil presents no difficulty where it has been worked as a garden or farm land. It may need feeding with well-rotted manure, compost or peat, but you can plant in it easily. Chalk is a problem when there is very little soil above it – such as you can see when driving through roadworks in chalk downs. The topsoil in a garden may vary in depth, especially if parts have been levelled or landscaped. The upper layer of chalk might already be broken, but lower down it could be solid. It is therefore vital, when planting a potentially large tree or shrub, to break up as deep and as wide a layer of chalk as you can. Use a pickaxe if necessary. Merely to scoop out a small hole to take the roots of a young plant is not enough. When the roots have filled the hole they will become pot-bound as if you had planted in a container, and the plant will suffer. There is no need to remove broken chalk: you can shovel it back and the roots will find their way between the pieces.

In a chalk garden you should feed the soil, using almost any form of humus: peat, leaf mould, animal or hop manure, or compost. A compost heap is most valuable to the chalk gardener, and good compost-making is worth studying. It is wiser to grow only calcicole plants than to try any that will be miserable. However, you can help those that are on the brink of

lime-tolerance by including 30g of Epsom salts per 5 lit (1 rounded tablespoon to the gallon) when watering. Rain water is better than that from a tap since lime is soluble and most reservoirs contain it. Once a year you can treat plants that are difficult to grow on chalk with some proprietary brand of sequestrene, but the cost is high.

Design for a chalk garden

As chalk gardens are frequently found on hillsides or near the sea our plan is designed so that it can be adapted to a sloping site. It faces south, the terrace linking house and garden being the driest, sunniest spot. This is filled with silver foliage, and the pink, blue or mauve flowers of succulents and other drought-resisting plants. A shallow, semi-circular step leads down to a level, almost circular area, gravelled for convenience, with a wooden seat built asymmetrically round a shady cherry tree.

A sloping site may have a view, but views tend to go with windy gardens – so shelter is provided by two mixed borders containing some of the shrubs and plants that grow best on chalk. The lawn starts as a wide grass path, curving in serpentine

As chalk is frequently found on hillsides or near the sea our garden is designed so that it can be adapted to a sloping site. The right-hand border screens a miniature 'gold' garden, while beyond the left-hand border is a vegetable plot. Prominent in the foreground is a flowering cherry tree Prunus *Accolade*, with a circular wooden seat built asymmetrically around it

Ground and planting plan   Size: 21·6x9m (72x30 ft)

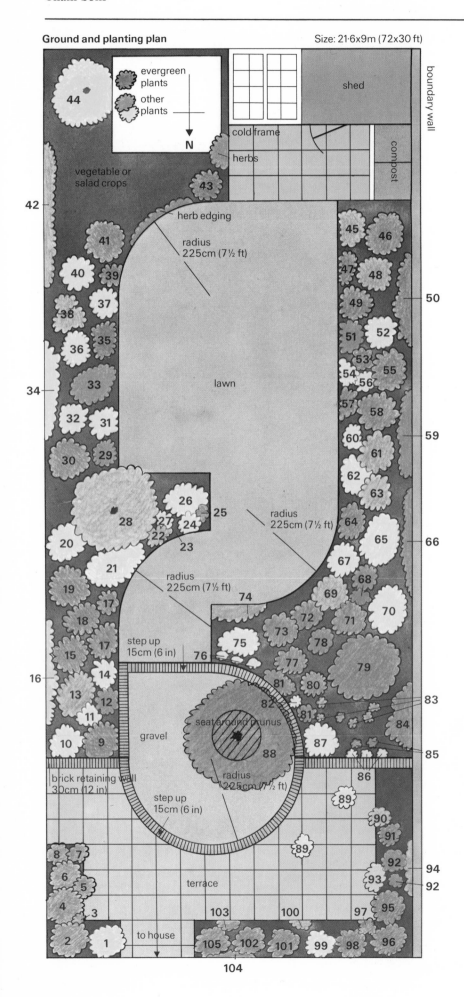

fashion between the borders, that extend from the boundaries to the central line, their relationships creating an ever-changing picture from viewpoints on the terrace. You can check on the last by holding the plan level with your chin and turning it from side to side.

The right-hand or western border screens a bed planted as a gold garden, a surprise that brightens the darkest day,

Key to planting plan

1 *Ceratostigma willmottianum*
2 *Cistus × purpureus* (rock rose)
3 *Dianthus* (pinks)
4 *Lavandula* (dwarf lavender)
5 *Hebe pinguifolia* Pagei
6 *Yucca filamentosa*
7 *Armeria maritima* (sea pink)
8 *Hebe pinguifolia* Pagei
9 *Escallonia* Apple Blossom
10 *Syringa × josiflexa* Bellicent (lilac)
11 *Lilium regale* (lily)
12 *Fuchsia* Monsieur Thibaut
13 *Hydrangea villosa*
14 *Sedum* Autumn Joy
15 *Abelia × grandiflora*
16 *Rosa* Zéphirine Drouhin (climbing rose)
17 *Bergenia purpurascens* Bellawley (pig squeak)
18 *Phormium tenax* (New Zealand flax)
19 *Hebe* Midsummer Beauty
20 *Buddleia fallowiana* Lochinch
21 *Viburnum tomentosum* Lanarth
22 *Berberis thunbergii* Atropurpurea Nana (barberry)
23 *Viola* (violets), underplanted
24 *Rosa* Felicia
25 *Narcissus* (daffodils)
26 *Forsythia suspensa*
27 *Campanula lactiflora* (milky bellflower)
28 *Pyrus salicifolia* Pendula (willow-leaved pear)
29 *Agapanthus* Headbourne Hybrids (African lily)
30 *Choisya ternata* (Mexican orange blossom)
31 *Fuchsia magellanica* Versicolor
32 *Hibiscus syriacus* Blue Bird
33 *Paeonia lactiflora* (paeony) hybrids
34 *Chaenomeles speciosa* Apple Blossom (ornamental quince)
35 *Penstemon hartwegii* Garnet
36 *Lavatera arborea* (tree mallow)
37 *Spiraea × bumalda* Anthony Waterer
38 *Eremurus himalaicus* (foxtail lily)
39 *Ruta graveolens* (rue)
40 *Kolkwitzia amablis* (beauty bush)
41 *Laurus nobilis* (sweet bay)
42 *Vitis vinifera* Brandt (ornamental grape vine)
43 *Rosmarinus officinalis* (rosemary)
44 *Sorbus hupehensis*
45 *Anemone (japonica) hupehensis* (Japanese anemone)
46 *Chamaecyparis lawsoniana* Stewartii (golden Lawson cypress)
47 *Helianthemum (chamaecistus) nummularium* The Bride (rock rose)
48 *Rosa* Maigold
49 *Helichrysum fontanesii* (everlastings)
50 *Hedera colchica* Dentata Variegata (Persian ivy)
51 *Salvia officinalis* Aurea (common sage)
52 *Weigela florida* Variegata
53 *Spartium junceum* (Spanish broom)

containing shrubs and plants with gold-variegated leaves, or white or yellow flowers. The left-hand or eastern shrub border hides the vegetable plot, that can be as large or as small as you like. The main lawn is 5·4 × 7m (18 × 23 ft), which is big enough for simple games, but can be reduced if you want to grow more vegetables. At the far end is a tool shed or small greenhouse and a compost heap.

54 *Euphorbia (epithymoides) polychroma* (cushion spurge)
55 *Euonymus japonicus* (variegated spindle tree)
56 *Lilium pyrenaicum* (yellow turks-cap lily)
57 *Helianthemum (chamaecistus) nummularium* Wisley Primrose (rock rose)
58 *Senecio greyi*
59 *Lonicera japonica* Aureoreticulata (Japanese honeysuckle)
60 *Anthemis cupaniana*
61 *Hypericum patulum* Hidcote (St John's wort)
62 *Alchemilla mollis* (lady's mantle)
63 *Rosa* Iceberg
64 *Genista lydia*
65 *Philadelphus coronarius* Aureus (mock orange)
66 *Rosa* Golden Showers (climbing rose)
67 *Potentilla arbuscula* (cinquefoil)
68 *Verbascum bombyciferum* (mullein)
69 Hemerocallis (day lily), yellow variety
70 *Cotinus coggygria* Royal Purple (smoke tree or Venetian sumach)
71 *Lonicera nitida* (Chinese honeysuckle)
72 *Santolina neapolitana* (cotton lavender)
73 *Acanthus mollis* (bear's breeches)
74 *Iris germanica*
75 *Magnolia* × *loebneri*
76 *Scabiosa caucasica* Clive Greaves (scabious)
77 *Escallonia* Donard Seedling
78 *Lilium regale* (lily)
79 *Viburnum rhytidophyllum*
80 *Juniperus virginiana* Skyrocket (pencil cedar)
81 Hosta (plantain lilies)
82 Narcissus (daffodils)
83 *Helleborus orientalis* (Lenten rose)
84 *Ceanothus rigidus*
85 *Cyclamen neapolitanum* and *C. coum*
86 *Galanthus nivalis* (common snowdrop)
87 *Paeonia suffruticosa* (moutan paeony)
88 *Prunus* Accolade (flowering cherry)
89 *Thymus serpyllum* (wild thyme)
90 *Sedum* Ruby Glow
91 *Ballota pseudodictamnus*
92 *Dianthus barbatus* (sweet William)
93 *Dimorphotheca ecklonis* (star of the veldt or African daisy)
94 *Rosa* Pink Perpétue (climbing rose)
95 *Centaurea gymnocarpa* (knapweed)
96 *Teucrium fruticans* (tree germander)
97 *Campanula poscharskyana* (rock campanula)
98 *Cistus* Silver Pink (rock rose)
99 *Caryopteris* × *clandonensis*
100 *Chrysanthemum haradjanii* (*Tanacetum densum-amani*)
101 Lavandula (lavender)
102 *Convolvulus cneorum*
103 *Dianthus alpinus*
104 *Clematis* Jackmanii
105 *Salvia officinalis* Purpurascens (purple-leaved sage)

PLANTS FOR CHALK SOILS

Here we describe a varied selection of trees, shrubs, and decorative herbs, roses and perennials to grow.

TREES
A plan can show only the horizontal plane of a garden. The verticals are provided by the walls with their climbers, and by the trees. The classic trees of the chalk downs are *Taxus baccata* (yew) and the *Fagus sylvatica* (common beech). While, fully grown, both would be too large for a small garden, it would be hard to choose which makes the better hedge. There are small-growing varieties of both, and of another good hedging tree, *Carpinus betulus* (common hornbeam).

Tilia (lime) can be pleached as a screen, and a large chalk garden might have other deciduous trees including fraxinus (ash), and most acers (maples) except the decorative Japanese ones. *Acer campestre* (field maple), *A. davidii* (snake-barked maple) and *A. platanoides* (Norway maple) are all good on chalk. *Quercus ilex* (evergreen oak) grows well, becoming a big tree in time, but makes a good, rigid hedge against sea winds. Among conifers the cypresses will flourish, as will *Cedrus atlantica* Glauca (blue Atlas cedar) and various pines and firs. Perhaps the best conifer for chalk is the juniper, that rarely grows too big. The large juniperus genus ranges from prostrate shrubs, through bushy shapes, to columnar trees – all of them in many shades of green.

When mature, Cedrus atlantica *Glauca (on right of* C. deodara*) reaches 30m (100 ft) or more in height and expanse*

Medium-sized flowering trees for chalk luckily include malus (crab apple), prunus (flowering cherry) and pyrus (ornamental pear). Smallish trees or large shrubs that have flowers and berries are cotoneaster, crataegus (hawthorn) and pyracantha (firethorn). You can also depend on the sorbus genus, with its flowers and berries, and leaf shapes that vary between the large, felted simple leaves of the aria (or whitebeam) group, and the small, pinnate leaves of the aucuparias (or mountain ashes) typified by *Sorbus aucuparia*. Laburnum is perfectly at home on chalk as are some rarer small trees like *Cercis siliquastrum* (Judas tree), with pink flowers springing from bare bark in spring, and an uncommon North American dogwood *Cornus nuttallii*, a slow grower that speeds up as it gets older, and has starry white bracts that last longer than the flowers.

In a small garden like the one illustrated here there is only room for a few trees. *Prunus* Accolade (flowering cherry) gives shade, and has masses of rose-pink cherry blossom in spring, with good colour in autumn. *Pyrus salicifolia* Pendula (willow-leaved pear) is a graceful, silvery tree, while *Sorbus hupehensis* is a pretty Chinese member of the aucuparia group with white flowers, autumn colour, and whitish berries tinged with pink that the birds ignore.

As representatives of the conifers we have a golden cypress, *Chamaecyparis lawsoniana* Stewartii (golden Lawson), and – as an exclamation point – the pencil-slim *Juniperus virginiana* Skyroc-ket (pencil cedar). Somewhere between a tree and a shrub comes the *Magnolia × loebneri*, one of the most reliable species of its genus on chalk.

SHRUBS

There is a group of large, early-flowering twiggy shrubs that grows well on chalk, but from which it is difficult to make a choice since it includes deutzia, forsythia, kilkwitzia, philadelphus (mock orange), syringa (lilac) and weigela. The best calcicole shrubs for year-round value are viburnums, some of which are evergreen and some deciduous, their flowers coming between early spring and mid summer (February and June) depending on the variety. Flowering from early to late summer (May to July) are abelia, buddleia, *Cotinus coggygria* (smoke tree or Venetian sumach), hibiscus, hypericum (St John's wort) and *Lavatera arborea* (tree mallow). *Hydrangea villosa* is the best species for chalk as it stands dry conditions, and produces blue flowers without the aid of chemicals.

The shrubs shown on our plan are closely planted for quick effect. Attention is given to leaf colour since gold, purple, silvery or variegated foliage are better value in the long run than shrubs like syringa (lilac), that flower for a few days and are dull for most of the year. However, one syringa, *S. × josiflexa* Bellicent, a delicate pink form, was chosen for its grace. Otherwise, there is gold-leaved *Philadelphus coronarius* (mock orange), set off by silver-leaved *Buddleia fallowiana* Lochinch, purple-leaved *Cotinus*

Above: wide-spreading Cercis siliquastrum
Above right: Cotinus coggygria *in flower*
Right: Ceratostigma willmottianum
Left: distinctive large bracts surround flowers of slow-growing Cornus nuttallii

coggygria Royal Purple, and gold-variegated *Weigela florida* Variegata. *Hypericum patulum* Hidcote (St John's wort) and *Potentilla arbuscula* (cinquefoil) provide golden flowers. Evergreens are represented by ceanothus, *Choisya ternata* (Mexican orange blossom), escallonia, euonymus (spindle), gold-flowered *Genista lydia* and hebe.

The buddleia should be cut down in late spring (April) to encourage new growth. This is called stooling and keeps many shrubs that flower on the current year's wood neatly in their station. It should be done with blue-flowered, grey-leaved *Caryopteris × clandonensis*, blue *Ceratostigma willmottianum*, fuchsia, pink *Lavatera arborea*, yellow *Spartium junceum* (Spanish broom), and

Spiraea × bumalda. Some other shrubs – like deutzia and syringa – need the deadheads cutting back after flowering so that they will put their energies into new wood instead of seeds. If you do this with euphorbia (spurge), don't get the poisonous white juice on your hands – or if you do, wash very thoroughly – and don't cut lavandula (lavender) back into the old wood or it will die.

Some climbers are indicated on the fences or walls: *Vitis vinifera* Brandt (ornamental grape vine) for autumn colour; *Chaenomeles speciosa* Apple Blossom (ornamental quince) for spring; evergreen, blue-flowered *Ceanothus thyrsiflorus* for summer; mauve *Abutilon vitifolium* and *Solanum crispum* Glasnevin (Chilean potato tree) for the terrace; rose-pink and yellow climbing roses, and gold-leaved hedera (ivy) and lonicera to back the gold bed. Clematis, that grows so well on chalk, is represented by *Clematis* Jackmanii, the sturdy, purple favourite.

It is impossible here to cover all the plants and bulbs that grow on chalk or lime soil, but our plan includes representatives of most of the main types. Some have been omitted because they can be uncomfortable in a small garden. Among them are the prickly, thistly plants that grow in the driest soil, often by the seashore, such as eryngium (sea holly) and echinops (globe thistle), and tall, grey *Onopordon arabicum* (ghost thistle).

Conditions in a chalk garden seem to suit the shrubby plants from the warm, dry shores of the Mediterranean region. Many with aromatic foliage have been used as herbs (and still are), but are included here mainly for their decorative effect: for example, rosmarinus (rosemary), lavandula (lavender), blue-leaved *Ruta graveolens* (rue or herb of grace), and the culinary sage in its purple- and gold-leaved forms, *Salvia officinalis* Purpurascens and *S. o.* Aurea. *Thymus vulgaris* (common thyme), *T.* × *citriodorus* (lemon thyme) and *T. serpyllum* (wild thyme) can be used to fill gaps, the last-named – in bright-flowered varieties – being ideal for cracks in the paving, though it may ramp in a warm, dry flowerbed.

The cistus (rock rose) genus also comes from southern Europe, and does very well in dry conditions. There are two on the terrace in the plan, one being *Cistus* × *purpureus*, with bright cerise flowers 8cm (3 in) across, the other, *C.* Silver Pink, is a hybrid of great stamina. Helianthemums, too, are known as rock roses, and are similar plants in miniature, spreading to make ideal cover at the front of a border. We suggest *Helianthemum* (chamaecistus) *nummularium* The Bride, a white variety with grey leaves, and *H. n.* Wisley Primrose as being good for the gold border. Another shrubby plant that likes sunshine and sharp drainage, and is

well worth a place on the terrace, is the less well-known *Convolvulus cneorum*, a crevice plant from the southern Alps. Its grey, satiny leaves have been described as chromium-plated, and the white, pink-backed flowers come out for weeks.

Plant evergreen Ruta graveolens *(above left) as a scenting border shrub*
Mixed border (top) includes verbascum, dianthus (pinks) and stachys
Evergreen Convolvulus cneorum *(above) likes a well-drained soil in full sun*

ROSES

Roses are essential in any garden, but hybrid teas find the going on chalk too hard, so you will have to stick to the tough floribundas like Iceberg, or shrub roses such as the repeat-flowering musks, of which the most reliable is probably pink Felicia. Maigold, a hybrid with strong, glossy foliage and delicious fragrance, is shown in the gold border.

Climbing roses grow well on walls where they can find a cool root run, but many are strong enough for a fence or pergola. Two suggestions are Pink Perpétué, that echoes the colour of *Cistus × purpureus*, and the true rose-pink Zéphirine Drouhin, the rose without a thorn. Golden Showers is a fine repeat-flowering climber to back the gold border.

HERBACEOUS PERENNIALS

An enormous variety of herbaceous perennials grow well on chalk, and many have daisy-like flowers. There is the strongly-spreading, grey-green-foliaged *Anthemis cupaniana*, for example, the white flowers of which appear at the same time as cheiranthus (wallflower) – the latter being a useful filler. The *Anthemis tinctoria* E. C. Buxton (ox-eye chamomile) is a lovely, lemon-yellow 'daisy' for late summer (July), but it has been omitted from the gold border as it needs staking. *Dimorphotheca ecklonis* (star of the veldt or African daisy), 45cm (18 in) high, with white flowers and a blue disc, and *D. barberiae*, 30cm (12 in), with pink flowers, are two South African 'daisies' that are magnificent in a chalk garden and will not grow in a soggy site. Erigerons (fleabane) and *Aster novi-belgii* (Michaelmas daisy), both in the mauve/pink range, are other 'daisies' that do well.

All paeonies like chalk, although they benefit from a good dressing of leaf mould every year. There are the herbaceous named forms of *Paeonia lactiflora*, and the gorgeous tree paeonies or moutans, mostly hybrids of *P. suffruticosa* or the yellow *P. lutea*. Their flowering time is short but the elegant leaves make up for this and often have fine autumn colour. Scabiosa (scabious) is a typical flower of the chalk downs, and there are many kinds – from choice alpines to the excellent *Scabiosa caucasica* Clive Greaves, which has pale blue flowers, and the annual *S. atropurpurea* (sweet scabious or pincushion flower) in a variety of colours.

Two roses for the chalk garden are vigorous, lightly-scented floribunda Iceberg (above right) and double-flowered climber Pink Perpétué (right)

Above: spring-flowering Anemone blanda
Summer-flowering evergreen Euphorbia
wulfenii *Lambrook Gold (below right)
reaches a height of roughly 1·2m (4ft)*

Another comparatively large perennial plant is *Anemone (japonica) hupehensis* (Japanese anemone). This is one of the most useful flowers for a chalk garden as it starts to come into bloom in late summer to early autumn (late July to August) – after the mid summer flush – and goes on into mid autumn (September). It stands 60–90cm (2–3 ft) high and has pink or white flowers with great delicacy of form. *A.×hybrida* Louise Uhink is the one most often recommended, but several other anemones grow equally well, notably the brilliant blue or white woodland carpeter, *A. blanda* (mountain windflower of Greece), 15cm (6 in), and *A. fulgens*, 23cm (9 in), a scarlet flower, astonishing in spring. Spring anemones disappear in summer and care must be taken when weeding or planting around them. Pulsatillas used to be known as *Anemone pulsatilla*, but now have a genus of their own, and can form fine clumps on chalk.

Tubular-flowered penstemons are usually successful on chalk, though not considered reliably hardy in cold, damp gardens, where it is advisable to take cuttings in early autumn (September) for planting out the following year. A strong *Penstemon hartwegii* variety like Garnet or Firebird will flower from late summer to mid autumn, and has the advantage of being evergreen. Penstemons make good cover in early summer for that magnificent bulbous plant *Eremurus himalaicus* (foxtail lily), that can send its white spikes up to 1·8m (6 ft), but can also look rather silly if it is allowed to spring from an expanse of bare earth.

Many flowers loved by flower-arrangers will grow on chalk, among them *Alchemilla mollis* (lady's mantle), a good, perennial, front-of-the-border plant with acid-yellow clouds of bloom and sea-green leaves of interesting scalloped shape. All dianthus, including *Dianthus barbatus* (sweet William) and pinks, grow well on chalk. The former is not long-lived and should be treated as a biennial, but it would be a foolish chalk gardener who did not take advantage of the possibility of growing it really well.

A totally different type of plant is *Phormium tenax* (New Zealand flax). It has great, tough leaves that rise 1·2m (4 ft) from the ground like a bunch of swords, and makes a magnificent architectural focal point in a border. It needs protection from strong winds that can split and shred the leaves, and it flowers rarely – but when it does the effect is striking. Similarly the yuccas grow well on chalk, and are represented by grey-leaved *Yucca filamentosa*, that produces dramatic spikes of white bell flowers in most years and has a place on the terrace. *Y. flaccida* has leaves that curve down gracefully.

The large family of euphorbias (spurge) will grow elsewhere but is sometimes collected by chalk gardeners for its great decorative quality. *Euphorbia wulfenii* and *E. characias* are large plants with evergreen leaves of a good blue-green. The flower-buds appear from mid to late winter (late December) and slowly uncurl until the flowers, really bracts, unfold into great lime-yellow heads that remain until late summer. When these are dead, cut the stems down to the ground but do not get the white 'milk' on your hands as it can cause skin irritation. *E. (epithymoides) polychroma* (cushion spurge) makes a 45cm (18 in) mound of brilliant yellow in the spring and often has autumn colour. *E. myrsinites*, a rock plant that looks like a succulent, has sharply-carved, bluish-jade leaves that set off the acid-yellow flowers. Others include the taller *E. lathyrus* (caper spurge), 60cm (24 in), that is reputed to keep moles away, and the spreading *E. cyparissias* (cypress spurge or ploughman's mignonette).

While dealing with architectural plants we must not forget *Acanthus mollis* (bear's breeches), that gave the inspiration to the classic Corinthian capital. Its deeply-cut, glossy green leaves brighten the garden in winter and die off in late summer and early autumn, while the flower spikes are tall, prickly, and in colour a mixture of white petals (corolla) and purple outer leaves (calyx). Coming

Rampant Campanula poscharskyana *(above) flowers through summer and autumn*
Summer-flowering Sisyrinchium striatum *(below) prefers a sunny position*

from southern Europe they enjoy quick drainage and withstand drought without ill effects – but they like a winter mulch.

Coming down to smaller plants, the bergenias (pig squeak) are dependable, and hybridizers are producing many varieties of these huge evergreens with spoon-shaped, leathery leaves. *Bergenia stracheyi* Schmidtii flowers first, followed by *B. purpurascens* Bellawley, with rose-red flowers, *B.* Margery Fish, a nice pink, *B. stracheyi* Silberlicht, white and pink, *B. s.* Evening Glow, with purple flowers and purplish winter foliage, and many others. Most bergenias produce a few scarlet leaves in winter. Often bracketed with them because of their equally big leaves are the hostas (plantain lily) of which there are dozens. Their flowers are lily-like on strong stems and the leaves are ribbed longitudinally. As they die off completely in winter they are good companions for narcissus (daffodil) and other spring bulbs, including *Eranthis hyemalis* (winter aconite). Their leaves are dormant when narcissus are out, and then unfurl to hide the dying leaves.

Another showy plant for a chalk or lime garden that seems indifferent to sun or shade is hemerocallis (day lily). Again hybridizers have been at work and these can now be obtained with their 90cm (3 ft) stems rising from wide, strap-like leaves with a succession of flowers in every shade, from yellow – through apricot and orange – to deep mahogany.

Campanulas (bellflower) that flower in mid summer do well on chalk, tending to seed themselves all over the place, but they are easily controlled when small. They range from little rock plants that can be invasive, such as *Campanula poscharskyana* and *C. portenschlagiana*, to taller border plants, forms of *C. lactiflora* (milky bellflower), *C. latifolia* (great bellflower), *C. latiloba* and open-belled *C. persicifolia* (peach-leaved bell-flower). *C. glomerata* is a magnificent rich purple but may ramp through other plants. All of the campanulas mentioned so far grow in sun or shade. *C. pyramidalis* (chimney bellflower), if it is brought inside the house and treated as a pot plant, will last longer than in the garden where the flowers fade as soon as they have been fertilized by the bees.

Many irises grow well on chalk, particularly *Iris germanica* and its many hybrids. This is the fleur-de-lis, its great, flambeau-shaped blooms having been known to heraldry since they became an emblem in Renaissance Italy. In Tuscany they can be seen everywhere, their pale, sword-shaped leaves springing from the dry soil. *I. sibirica* grows well as a border plant, while iris-like leaves but spikes of starry yellow flowers are found on another chalk gardener's friend, *Sisyrinchium striatum* (satin flower). This seeds itself freely so that once you have it you need never be without it. The same useful quality is shared by the verbascums (mullein), that produce attractive rosettes of pointed leaves in their first year, and spires of yellow flowers in the second year. *Verbascum bombyciferum* has white, woolly foliage that is most attractive.

Hardy succulents grow well on chalk, the two most useful groups being the sempervivums (houseleek) with neatly-spreading rosettes, and the sedums. The latter are a huge family, from tiny, ground-covering *Sedum spathulifolium*, to medium-sized *S.* Ruby Glow and blue-leaved *S. cauticola*, and to taller varieties like *S.* Autumn Joy, and the type species *S. spectabile*. Their showy red or pink flowers that appear in mid to late autumn are useful.

There are many bulbs that find chalk conditions ideal: galanthus (snowdrop), all the narcissi and crocuses, the little blue flowers of spring like muscari (grape hyacinth), chionodoxa (glory of the snow), scillas (squill) and puschkinias. There are also many early-flowering bulbous irises of the reticulata type, the earliest being *Iris histrioides* with the *I. reticulata* species following on. Cyclamen have corms not bulbs. *Cyclamen neapolitanum* flowering in autumn, and *C. coum* in spring are jewels of the chalk garden and grow best in dry shade.'

Many lilies grow on chalk, particularly the beautiful, white *Lilium regale*, the shade-loving martagon group, the early *L. pyrenaicum* (yellow turks-cap lily), the orange *L. henryi*, flowering in late summer, and the hybrids of *L. × aurelianense*. Indeed most hybrids grow well on chalk but not those based on the Japanese kinds, like *L. auratum* (golden-rayed lily of Japan or goldband lily) and others.

Belonging to the lily family but growing from a fleshy root is perhaps the most beautiful chalk-loving flower, the agapanthus (African lily), with heads of glorious blue in late summer. Look for *Agapanthus* Headbourne Hybrids growing 45–75cm (18–30 in) high.

Chalk-loving plants come from many places, viola (violet) and helleborus (hellebore) from the woods, armeria (thrift) and mesembryanthemum (Livingstone daisy) from the seaside, and the brilliant blue *Gentiana acaulis* (trumpet gentian) from the Alps. If you know where a plant comes from it is often the greatest help when it comes to growing it, and its name sometimes gives you a clue.

Above: Sedum *Ruby Glow in foreground,* Centaurea gymnocarpa *and* Ruta graveolens *behind* Agapanthus africanus *(right) grows up to 60–75cm (2–2½ ft) tall*

ROCK GARDENING

Creating a focal point of interest in your garden can be a problem, particularly if you live on one of today's many housing estates. Often there are no fences between sites, and sometimes there are restrictions on having trees, or indeed any plant that grows above a certain height. One answer could be to create your own rock garden, and here we explain how to do it. Later on we tell you about scree gardens, and include a selection of rock and alpine plants.

Before you make any final decision on whether to proceed with a rock garden, you must first consider the conditions that will most suit rock plants and alpines. Ideally, a rock garden should be situated on a gentle slope, preferably facing south or south-west, and sheltered from strong winds. It should be close enough to any trees to benefit from the sunlight that will filter through the leaves in summer, but not so close as to suffer from the continual dripping of rain. A well-drained, sandy loam is the best soil for this type of garden.

Obviously, many sites will fail to meet at least one of these requirements, but don't worry. In fact, one of Britain's best-known rock gardens, at the Royal Horticultural Society's establishment at Wisley, is on a north-facing slope, but by clever construction parts of it have been 'turned' to face south. How this was done is explained in the section headed: Forming an 'outcrop' rock garden.

The worst places you can attempt to create a rock garden are in a dry corner, near a hedge, or in very dense shade. But the more determined you are, the more you can do to combat difficulties.

In this typical 'outcrop' garden large, weathered rocks have been set into a slope in an informal manner to create a series of 'steps' and colourfully planted

Preparing the site

Once you have settled on where to situate your rock garden you must turn your attention to the preparation of the site. First dig the area over and, if it is a heavy soil, trench it. Remove any perennial weeds, by chemical means if necessary.

Clay soils must be drained (see diagram next page), and to do this dig trenches approximately 45cm (18 in) deep and 90–180cm (3–6 ft) apart, according to the state of the clay. Half-fill the trench with rubble or large stones, cover these with upturned turf or very coarse compost, and fill up with soil.

Rock used in the garden includes cold, hard granite (top) and mellow sandstone (above) which is soft in texture

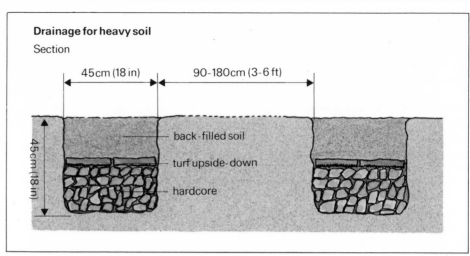

Drainage for heavy soil

Section

45cm (18 in)   90–180cm (3–6 ft)

45cm (18 in)

back-filled soil

turf upside-down

hardcore

Natural lie of rocks

1

2

soil level

Bed the rocks in a soil mound comprising 2 parts 6mm ($\frac{1}{4}$ in) down rock or gravel chippings – to provide drainage – and 1 part each of loam and moss peat. If only 10mm ($\frac{3}{8}$ in) down chippings are available, these will suffice. The mound will subside after a while, even though you firm the soil down, so keep a reserve of the mixture for topping up after about ten days – or sooner if it rains.

Finally, add a top-dressing of 6mm ($\frac{1}{4}$ in) down chippings, making it about 2–3cm (1 in) deep, and rake flat. The chippings have a three-fold purpose: to retain moisture; to protect the necks of plants from rotting; and to prevent rain splashing soil onto the flowers, some of which – although hardy – are delicate.

Other badly-drained sites will require the same approach. A rock garden built on chalk should present no problems, provided you follow the same drainage

*Above: an outcrop rock garden should imitate nature to be effective. In **1** rock lies flat in the earth's surface, but in **2** geological upheaval has set it at an angle of about 45 degrees*

procedure as for clay. But your choice of plants will be limited, and you may need to add a chemical agent to the soil to prevent the foliage turning yellow.

Choice of rock

You should give extremely careful thought to the choice of rock. It is not a cheap commodity, and you will have to balance aesthetic considerations with the availability of the stone you choose.

Two important factors to bear in mind when making your decision are the type of soil in your garden, and whether any local stone is available. Matching the rock with the soil is very important if your

rock garden is to look authentic. Nothing looks more out of place than, say, a water-worn limestone in a sandstone area or, indeed, vice versa. In some urban areas limestone tends to wash white and become rather glaring, although it will prove excellent if used in conjunction with a stream, pond or waterfall.

If you are unable to get any local stone, or if none exists, you will have to look around and see what you can find. Sandstone will be kindest to your plants, and is available in the south of England. Sussex sandstone is very popular, and Kentish Rag sandstone is quite easily obtained. Cotswold stone has a warm appeal, but although a sandstone, it contains an element of alkalinity, so a careful choice of lime-loving plants is necessary. Granite is cold, hard and heavy, and plants will not really grow well around it, but it can make quite an attractive garden.

As far as cost is concerned, the amount you will have to pay will be determined primarily by the distance the rock has to travel from the quarry and the quantities that are to be conveyed.

How much rock will you need?

When you have decided which rock to use, and discovered the cost per tonne, the next thing is to calculate how much you will need. For a rock garden measuring 4·5 × 3m (15 × 10 ft), 1½–2 tonnes of rock should be sufficient. Individual pieces of different types of stone will vary in size, and you will get a slightly larger volume of sandstone per tonne than you will limestone. Ideally, of course, you should be able to pick out the particular pieces of stone that you want, but this is not always possible.

In a small garden, an economical use of stone is essential if you are to keep the overall effect in proportion. Judicious placement can often make the end result appear rather more than the number of stones might indicate.

Rock in nature

All rock starts life as a large lump – be it in the shape of a mountain or a range of mountains. The action of various strains and stresses in the earth's behaviour causes this lump to crack and split. Splitting occurs in parallel lines, vertically and horizontally, but not diagonally. Moisture which permeates into these cracks expands and contracts under the alternating effects of cold and heat, eventually causing the rock to split further and to crumble. Some parts disintegrate to the extent of forming soil, but others protrude from the earth's surface as an outcrop, and it is this that is often imitated in the rock garden.

Forming an 'outcrop' rock garden

The important thing to remember when forming an outcrop rock garden is that it should appear natural. In nature, geological upheavals can mean that rocks lie at an angle in the soil, so when positioning the stones in your garden make them slope gently into the ground: this will

Below: densely-planted outcrop rock garden at Dinmore Manor, Herefordshire

have the added effect of guiding moisture to your plants.

If you already have a slope suitable for a rock garden then clearly your task will be much simpler than if you don't. However, if your slope faces north, you would be well advised to turn it so that it faces south. This is achieved by setting large rocks into the slope at such an angle that they face north, thus providing a protected area behind them – facing south – where you can place your alpines and rock plants.

If your garden is flat, you will have to create an artificial slope, but at least you can point it in the right direction, and make it an appropriate size.

All rock has strata lines, that indicate successive layers of deposited substance, formed over millions of years. In some rocks, these lines are barely distinguishable, while in others they are fairly well defined. When arranging the rocks in your garden, try to ensure that the strata lines are horizontal and never vertical.

Remember, too, that if your particular design requires you to place one rock on top of another, you should follow nature's example and avoid the brick wall principle of overlapping.

Forming a tufa rock garden

Another type of rock used for building a garden is tufa. If weathered it will be grey in colour, but direct from the quarry it is bright creamy-white.

It is basically a porous limestone, formed by the action of water passing through limestone rocks and collecting particles that, together with decaying plant life of a primitive nature, form the original tufa. The porosity is brought about by the decaying and eventual washing away of the primitive plant life.

The advantages of tufa over the other types of rock mentioned are numerous. From the construction point of view, it has little or no strata lines. Many plants will actually grow *on* it, as roots can penetrate its porous form. Saxifrages and draba will both do very well here.

As with an outcrop rock garden, drainage is essential. Tufa should be arranged on an informal basis: you simply 'mould' the stone to the existing contours of your garden, or use it to create a rise and fall on flat ground. When you have laid the rocks and filled in with soil, the ground can be top-dressed with the left-over 'dust' from the rock, or with limestone chippings. The cost per tonne is rather high in comparison with other stone, but its porosity makes it light in weight and, therefore, good value for what you have to pay.

SCREE GARDENING

When building an informal rock garden we compared different types when we compared the different types of stone available in Britain. Here we look at the use of stone chippings, or scree, in the rock garden, and include a selection of suitable shrubs and alpine plants.

A scree in the context of a rock garden is simply a reconstruction of the conditions in which rock plants grow in their natural habitat throughout the mountains of the world. Plants that will often prove difficult to cultivate in a normal environment positively thrive in a bed of stone chippings. The scree provides perfect drainage, a cool root run, and moisture during dry periods.

A scree can be created on any soil: alkaline or acid, heavy clay or light sand. It can form an integral part of a rock garden, or it can be a feature on its own, but always remember that in nature a scree emanates from a rock formation and usually 'fans out' from a fairly wide fissure or valley in the rocks. Examples of scree can be found in botanic gardens all over Britain, and there is a particularly good one at the Royal Botanic Garden in Edinburgh.

In a rock garden, the most suitable place to form a scree is between two rising outcrops, but it is also possible to lay special scree beds, either as an edge to a rock garden, or as a completely separate bed on a lawn.

Making a scree bed

To make a scree bed you must first mark out the area you propose to use and excavate it to a depth of approximately 90cm (3 ft) on a heavy subsoil, or 60cm (2 ft) on a light, well-drained soil. Slope the floor gently on a well-drained soil, but more sharply on a heavy soil, where you should also add a layer of rough drainage material – something like brick rubble or broken pot would do the job. Over this, place either rough peat, compost, half-decayed leaves or rotted turf, and tread firm. Finally, the scree itself is laid.

Opinions differ on the ideal make-up of a scree, but basically it is agreed that too much drainage is worse than too little. Make your scree of roughly 50 per cent chippings, 25 per cent sandy loam and 25 per cent peat or leaf mould, and you should be all right.

To add interest to the surface, as well as create a more natural finish, you could dot a few rocks here and there, building up the scree around them for greater effect. It is a good idea to add a modest top dressing of leaf mould or peat once a year.

The chippings should be no larger than the 6mm ($\frac{1}{4}$ in) variety if possible, although the standard 10mm ($\frac{3}{8}$ in) might be the only one available at your local supplier. If the colour of the chippings does not blend with the stone in your rock garden, you can cover the chippings with a thin top dressing of whatever will match, be it granite, limestone or tufa.

Raised scree beds

One form of rock garden leads to another. A raised scree bed can be constructed from broken paving stone comparatively cheaply, and can, in fact, form quite a feature in a garden that has been terraced. Alternatively, the raised scree can be free-standing, particularly in an environment containing a great deal of paving or concrete.

A raised scree won't usually exceed 45cm (18 in) in height, but a normal raised bed can be up to 90cm (3 ft). It makes an excellent form of gardening for the elderly, or those confined to wheelchairs, as it is not necessary to crouch to reach the planting area. It is also a controlled form of gardening, for the soil mixture can be specially chosen to suit whatever group of plants you plan to cultivate.

The construction of a raised scree bed differs from that of the other forms of rock garden so far described, in that, for strength and rigidity, the rocks or paving forming the wall can be interlocked on the brick wall principle.

The walls should not be exactly vertical; each stone should be set back gradually to form a slight slope. If you can also tilt the stones slightly to cause the rain to percolate through to the centre, so much the better.

You will have to insert plants for the sides of the bed at the same time as you build the wall. For extra security you might decide to cement the stones into

Top right: section of scree bed excavated to total depth of 90cm (3 ft) with a base slope at 20° to horizontal for poorly-drained soil, or 5° for well-drained soil
Centre: make hardboard, triangular template to measure the 20° angle of slope; for a 5° angle, the short side of the triangle should be 5cm (2 in) long
Right: section of raised scree bed with supporting side wall of paving slabs, tilted to allow water to run into bed

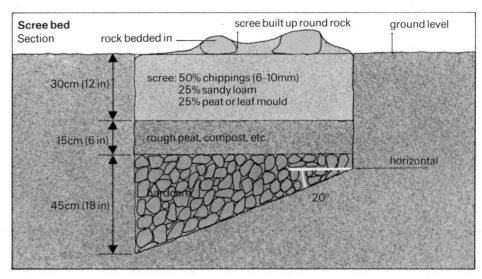

Scree bed
Section
rock bedded in
scree built up round rock
ground level
30cm (12 in)
scree: 50% chippings (6-10mm)
25% sandy loam
25% peat or leaf mould
15cm (6 in)
rough peat, compost, etc.
horizontal
45cm (18 in)
hardcore
20°

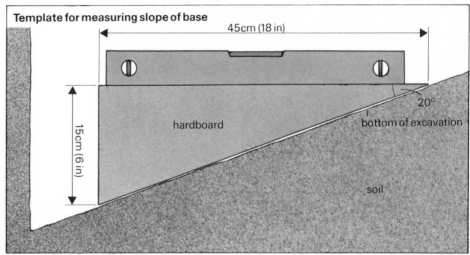

Template for measuring slope of base
45cm (18 in)
15cm (6 in)
hardboard
20°
bottom of excavation
soil

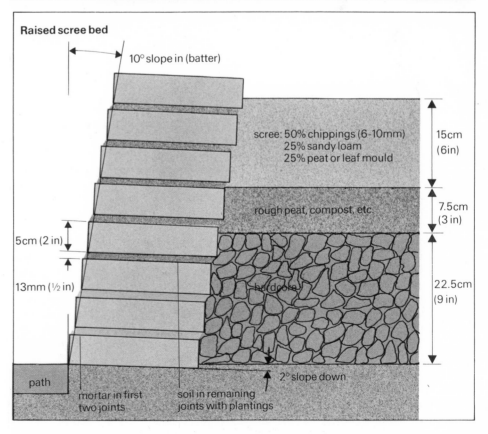

Raised scree bed
10° slope in (batter)
scree: 50% chippings (6-10mm)
25% sandy loam
25% peat or leaf mould
15cm (6in)
rough peat, compost, etc.
7.5cm (3 in)
5cm (2 in)
hardcore
22.5cm (9 in)
13mm (½ in)
path
2° slope down
mortar in first two joints
soil in remaining joints with plantings

Top: free-standing, raised scree bed looks attractive in a paved area
Above: a finished scree bed, planted out

place, but the most satisfactory results will be achieved by setting them in soil, apart from perhaps the first few layers. This will allow plants like ramonda and lewisia to grow happily on their sides in the wall, rather than upright on the flat area below the wall, where they will collect rain in the centre of their rosettes.

Instead of paving or rock, you could use discarded railway sleepers to make the wall of the bed. Lay them one on top of another, to form a square or rectangle, and drive iron stakes into the ground around the edge to keep them in position.

Planting in rock and scree
There is an almost unlimited range of rock plants and shrubs, but it is important that, when making your selection, you

also consider where you are going to put each plant. A visit to a specialist nursery-man is well worth the effort, as he will be able to advise you on what will be best for your particular soil. You will also be able to see the plants in flower. Alpines are always grown in pots and are thus easily transplanted at any time of year, although spring is naturally the best time for planting.

Never put fast-growing plants close to slow growers, otherwise the former will tend to overrun the latter. Try to arrange things so that your rock garden has some colour all through the year, rather than just in one season. The best plan is to plant the miniature shrubs first, and then select the most suitable positions for the other plants.

Evergreen conifers are particularly useful in the rock garden, providing variety in colour, height, form and texture. Often, a conifer can be used to

enhance the appearance of another plant, but follow the directions of nature when deciding on the appropriate places for planting. You would never see a tall tree on top of a mountain – it will always be at the base – and so it should be in your garden. On the same principle, a prostrate conifer or shrub would best be planted to fall over the edge of a rock.

To provide a continuous and colourful display throughout spring and summer, you can plant aubrietia, alyssum, iberis, helianthemum, some campanula and the more vigorous dianthus: position them to cascade down a dry wall or bank. If you add *Polygonum affine* and *P. vacciniifolium* to this group, the display will continue through to the autumn.

Bulbs, in general, will not do well on a scree, but a selection of those which are suitable adds interest. Plant them so that they peep through mats of ground cover such as thyme or acaena. Tulips come in all sizes and colours, with the many hybrids and varieties of *Tulipa kaufmanniana* being particularly suitable. Then there are the numerous dwarf species and cultivars of narcissus. Crocuses will make an attractive show early in the year, and *Crocus speciosus* will start again in the autumn.

As already explained, it is not advisable to grow the more vigorous rock plants on a scree because they would soon choke more delicate and choice species. So while, for instance, *Campanula allionii, C. pulla, C. arvatica, C. cochlearifolia* and other small campanulas would all do well, larger plants such as *Campanula portenschlagiana* and *C. poscharskyana* would be out of place and a menace. The latter two would be best situated on a dry wall where it will not matter if they spread rampantly. Kabschia saxifrages are a good choice for a scree, particularly the yellow-flowered *Saxifraga × apiculata* and *S. burseriana*, with its many hybrids. Careful siting is vital, for unless they occupy a shady position in summer, they can be scorched in a single day. Autumn rains will tend to rot them, so glass protection may also be necessary. Otherwise they are completely hardy.

Of the other saxifrages, *S. aizoon* and its forms create silver-encrusted mats of rosettes, while *S. cotyledon* and *S. longifolia*, particularly the form of the latter called Tumbling Waters, provide handsome sprays of flowers, some 30cm (12 in) long.

The alpine aster *Aster alpinus* will thrive, and the alpine catsfoot *Antennaria dioica rosea* makes an attractive grey carpet with short pink flowers. *Armeria caespitosa*, a form of thrift, will form little

Above: scree at Edinburgh Royal Botanic Garden. Right: Cotyledon simplifolia *thrives on well-drained, rocky surfaces*

hummocks and produce heads of pink flowers. The European aretian androsaces would be too vulnerable in this sort of situation and is best kept in an alpine house, but the rock jasmine from Kashmir, *Androsace sempervivoides*, again with pink flowers, would enjoy scree conditions. Some of the gentians will give a good display, notably *Gentiana gracilipes* and *G. septemfida*, two summer-flowering species. The well-known *G. acaulis* and *G. verna* would also be happy, and although the latter is a short-lived plant, it will seed freely. A dwarf flax *Linum salsoloides* Nanum, bears slightly opalescent pearly-white flowers during the summer, and might also be considered suitable.

Among other bulbs that will do well

Above: the hardy Saxifraga × apiculata
Below: Erinus alpinus *with starry flowers
that are borne throughout the summer
Bottom left: an alpine dianthus hybrid
Centre:* Ramonda myconii, *a native of the
Pyrenees suited to north-facing slopes
Bottom right:* Linum salsoloides

in scree are the rhizomatous irises, including *Iris innominata, I. cristata* and *I. mellita*. The latter is a miniature flag iris, only 8–10cm (3–4 in) tall, and it can have either smoky-purple or yellow flowers. The other two are 13–15cm (5–6 in) tall, are natives of America, and – like most American iris – detest lime.

Dianthus go well in rock gardens. *Dianthus alpinus*, with its deep green, strap-shaped leaves, and its large, deep-rose flowers that appear in early summer, will like the cool side of a rock. Another European dianthus worthy of your consideration is *D. neglectus*, which has a distinctive light buff reverse to its petals, and will form a dense cushion of fine green linear foliage, almost indistinguishable from grass. *D. freynii* is yet another from Europe, and has more typical greyish foliage, and small pink flowers on 3–5cm (1–2 in) stems. Dianthus will not object to lime and neither will *Linaria*

alpina (toadflax), although the latter will be happier on a scree, where it will form a compact mat of blue-grey foliage and produce little mauve snapdragon flowers with orange markings.

Although it tends to seed itself freely, the pink-flowered *Erinus alpinus* and its hybrids will not become objectionable. An interesting miniature relative of the cabbage family is *Morisia monantha* (or *M. hypogaea*), which has a long taproot and will form a flat rosette of glossy, dark green leaves in which will nestle golden-yellow flowers in the spring. *Wahlenbergia serpyllifolia* Major and *W. pumilio* are two cousins of the harebells. They form prostrate mats and produce deep purple and lavender bells respectively in mid summer (June). They are sometimes considered temperamental plants and are often short-lived, but they are still worthwhile.

You can bring a touch of colour to the scree in the autumn by planting two cyananthus. *Cyananthus microphyllus* (also known as *C. integer*) can become over-large for a scree, but *C. lobatus* and *C. l. albus* will both do very well.

Shrubs can also be grown in the spartan conditions provided by a scree. *Daphne arbuscula* is a fragrant-flowered, 15–25cm (6–10 in) tall shrublet that will flower in June. *Juniperus communis compressa* (common juniper) is a greyish-foliaged conifer that will slowly reach to over 60cm (24 in) in a slim, columnar manner. Other suitable conifers are *Chamaecyparis obtusa caespitosa* and *C. o. minima*: both produce dense, dark green foliage, and are very slow growing, taking several years to reach 30cm (12 in).

This, then, is but a small selection of what will grow in rock and scree conditions. As already indicated, a visit to your local nursery will give you a much better idea of what is available and which plants grow best in your area.

GARDENING WITH PEAT

We have explained how scree can be used to enhance your rock garden and added a list of suitable alpine plants and shrubs. In this third part we tell you how you can build your own peat garden.

A further variation on the rock garden theme is the peat garden which, although less tidy than other rock gardens, should reflect nature just as keenly in its appearance.

Lime-hating, acid soil plants, such as erica, that are too small for the wilder parts of a woodland garden, and some of the smaller rhododendrons, will all do extremely well in a peat garden, provided you create the right conditions. All of these plants will require a moist soil, and frequent overhead spraying will be essential during summer months to prevent any drying out. Adequate drainage is imperative – although don't overdo it. And there should be plenty of light around the peat garden with, ideally, a nearby tree to cast a dappled shade across the bed in summer, without completely overshadowing it.

Laying out your peat garden

The design of your peat garden should resemble that of other informal rock gardens. Aim simply to create a series of rising beds, each capable of accommodating peat-loving plants, and you won't go far wrong. You won't be able to achieve the same height as with other rock gardens, for a small block of peat will naturally lack the strength of a piece of rock.

The ideal site for a peat garden is a gentle slope, so if your garden is flat you may wish to create an artificial slope. But remember that you must first ensure adequate drainage, so be prepared to trench the ground if necessary.

When you have formed a mound of suitable height and shape, you will have to consolidate the soil thoroughly before starting to position the blocks of peat.

On the matter of aspect, it is very important that your garden faces north – a southern aspect could prove disastrous for peat-loving plants in the heat of summer, especially if there is no tree to cast a shadow over the beds.

A moderate-sized peat garden made from large peat blocks that have been rounded, set one on top of another and covered with a selection of moisture-loving plants

Above: the RHS's peat garden at Wisley
Right: bed peat blocks into soil mound
to form series of gradually-rising beds

Peat blocks

In Britain blocks are available from suppliers in Somerset and Scotland, and you can order them at most garden centres. Frequently, you will receive the blocks in a dry state; as it is important that they be wet before you bed them in the soil, you should give each block a soaking prior to use.

Firm placement will be necessary when you set the blocks in position, so ram moist peat between them for rigidity.

Although you can adapt an ordinary rock garden to the needs of peat-loving plants, this will never be entirely satisfactory; rocks can become very hot in the summer, and at such times plants will be happier in the cooler environment of a peat garden, where they can spread their roots through the peat blocks.

Plants for your peat garden

Two groups of plants immediately spring to mind: one the rhododendron, the other the erica, including heaths and heathers. Take care if you buy the latter, for while a small heather can look most attractive, particularly if purchased in flower, when it has covered an area of some 3000 sq cm (3 sq ft) and engulfed other more choice plants, it will lose much of its appeal.

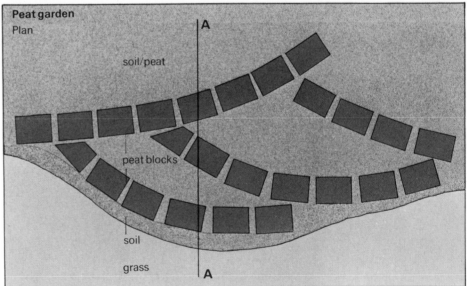

Peat garden
Plan
A
soil/peat
peat blocks
soil
grass
A

Erica can be used initially to fill in empty spaces but with one exception should not be regarded as permanent plantings. The exception is *Calluna* Foxii Nana (ling), that will form a tight symmetrical hummock 10–15cm (4–6 in) across.

The number of suitable rhododendrons is almost countless: the free-flowering pink *Rhododendron pemakoense* flowers in late spring (April) and grows to a height of 30–38cm (12–15 in). Unfortunately, because of its early flowering its blooms will sometimes be frosted. *R.*

scintillans, although officially reaching 75–90cm (2½–3 ft) height, does this slowly; it is upright in habit, evergreen, and has mauve-blue flowers that are quite hardy.

The dwarf *R. impeditum* has a tendency sometimes to ramp, but you can usually rely on the quality of its blue flowers. One of the most attractive of all rhododendrons is the deciduous *R. camtschaticum*, with pure-pink, saucer-shaped flowers appearing in early summer (May), and reaching only 20–25cm (8–10 in) in height. *R. repens* is not very free flowering, but its cultivar, Carmen, will

Peat garden
Section A A

peat rammed into joints

peat blocks

7-8cm (3 in)

soil/peat

subsoil

A

10cm (4 in)

A

Plants for peat — above left: Gentiana
sino-ornata; *top:* Hylomecon japonicum;
and above: Rhododendron pemakoense
*Left: tilt blocks slightly to help retain
water, and ram moist peat between them*

develop a mass of dark red bells on a
fairly compact evergreen bush.

Cassiopes are attractive evergreens, in
particular *Cassiope lycopodioides*, which
produces a dense mat of whipcord-like
foliage and a mass of miniature white
bells.

Hylomecon japonicum, a native of
Japan, will display numerous golden-
yellow flowers on 20–25cm (8–10 in)
stems if grown in a rich soil.

Although all shrubs in the gaultheria
genus are dwarf, different species vary in
shape and size, and some species tend to
be invasive. *Gaultheria procumbens* (part-
ridge berry) has pinkish, globe-shaped
flowers and bright red fruits, while *G.
trichophylla* has deep pink, bell-shaped
flowers and blue fruits. *G. cuneata* is
rather more vigorous, reaching a height
of 30cm (12 in), and a spread sometimes
exceeding this. It has racemes of white
flowers and in the autumn produces
globose white fruits.

Of all gentians, *Gentiana sino-ornata*
will go best in shade and peat, but you will
need to divide the plants every second
year for continuous success. The clear
blue, trumpet-shaped flowers will provide
a spectacular display in the autumn.

Most phlox will only grow in an
outcrop rock garden, and as a general rule
you can take it that the smaller the leaf,
the more sun the particular species will
tolerate. *Phlox subulata* (moss phlox) and
P. douglasii, both prefer a well-drained
sunny site, but *P. stolonifera* Blue Ridge
will enjoy a peat garden, although it has
an untidy rampant habit, partially com-
pensated for by the blue flowers on 10cm
(4 in) stems that will appear in the spring.

Of saxifrages, *Saxifraga moschata*
Cloth of Gold will add a patch of colour
to your peat garden if you can find it a
shady corner – it dislikes bright sunlight.

A plant that has had several names in
its time is *Cotyledon simplicifolia* (*Chias-
tophyllum oppositifolium*), that will be
happy in peat, and produces catkin-like
inflorescences of tiny yellow flowers in the
summer. Its succulent leaves are basal
and slightly coarse.

You can grow certain of the smaller
primula if your peat garden is damp
enough, but some Asiatic species will be
extremely difficult to cultivate in dry parts
of Britain, although they grow like weeds

in western Scotland. *Primula gracilipes*, *P. bracteosa* and *P. edgeworthii* are all very beautiful, with *P. gracilipes* perhaps the easiest to grow in Britain. The Balkan *P. frondosa* will be a simpler proposition to cultivate, and will produce lavender flowers and leaves with a covering of white hairs. *P. denticulata* (drumstick primrose), although even easier to grow than *P. frondosa*, has really too gross a form for the peat garden, and tends to seed freely.

An attractive native of Manchuria is *Jeffersonia dubia*, that produces large blue flowers very close to the ground, followed by kidney-shaped leaves.

Corydalis cashmeriana, as its name suggests, originated in Kashmir, and is reputed to be intractable, although it seems to do satisfactorily in peat conditions. It has delightful blue flowers similar to those of the British fumaria (common fumitory).

Some bulbs will do well in the peat garden. Erythronium are very colourful, with the easy-growing *Erythronium tuolumnense* a good choice, producing deep yellow flowers. The rose-pink-flowered *E. revolutum* (American trout lily) has a number of named forms, Pink Beauty being outstanding.

Cypripedium (lady's slipper orchid) are rather expensive, but worth it for the handsome display they can give. *Cypripedium calceolus* is a native of Britain, but rarely found growing in the wild. Its flower has chocolate sepals and, in common with all cypripedium, a distinctive pale yellow 'pouch'. *C. reginae* is of North American origin and has a rich rose pouch and pink-flushed sepals.

A charming miniature daffodil that will flower in early spring and grow to a height of no more than 15–20cm (6–8 in) is *Narcissus cyclamineus*. If it likes its situation it will seed and spread freely.

Among rhizomatous plants are the North American *Uvularia grandiflora*, a relative of the lily, displaying pale yellow, bell-shaped flowers on 25cm (10 in) stems in early summer (May), and *Iris gracilipes*, a small lavender-blue crested species with wiry stems and spear-like foliage.

Left: moisture-loving Primula frondosa
Below left: easy-growing Erythronium tuolumnense *will flower in spring*
Below: North American Cypripedium reginae

PLANTS FOR SUN

Most plants growing in a sunlit garden will revel in the experience, though problems can arise when there is too little moisture, such as during periods of drought. Add to this poor, hungry soil, as is found in sand, gravel and limestone districts, and gardening becomes a battle to keep things alive. The answer is to work with nature rather than against it, sticking to plants that flourish on hard living.

There are many plants adapted to hot, dry conditions that will furnish the garden throughout the year. Dry, sunny borders are often near the sitting-out area of the house – for example in the patio garden, that needs to look well dressed to provide a relaxed atmosphere. You can achieve this with proper planning and planting.

Preparing the soil

If drought is a problem, then thorough preparation before planting is essential, regardless of the type of soil. Incorporate whatever moisture-holding material you can lay your hands on. Well-rotted garden compost, old turfs, kitchen waste – even rotted-down newspapers, muck, and well-wetted peat with added bone-meal – any or all of these can be used. Most people know the value of these things, but the response from plants still seems little short of miraculous. No amount of watering, or sprinkling this and that on top, has the same result.

When the bed has finally been planted, a thick layer – 5cm (2 in) if possible – of a mulching material like peat or pulverized bark can be put down to stop excessive evaporation and smother germinating weed seeds. Thick straw spread around larger plants at the back of the border, such as trees and shrubs, makes a splendid mulch, protecting the roots with the most rewarding results.

Among the very small plants, especially some of the delicate silver ones, a good

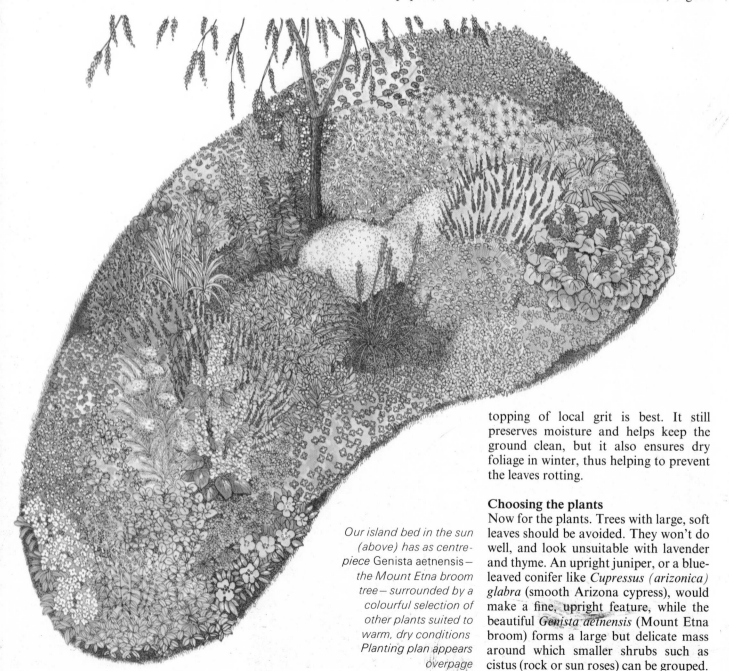

Our island bed in the sun (above) has as centre-piece Genista aetnensis – *the Mount Etna broom tree – surrounded by a colourful selection of other plants suited to warm, dry conditions Planting plan appears overpage*

topping of local grit is best. It still preserves moisture and helps keep the ground clean, but it also ensures dry foliage in winter, thus helping to prevent the leaves rotting.

Choosing the plants

Now for the plants. Trees with large, soft leaves should be avoided. They won't do well, and look unsuitable with lavender and thyme. An upright juniper, or a blue-leaved conifer like *Cupressus (arizonica) glabra* (smooth Arizona cypress), would make a fine, upright feature, while the beautiful *Genista aetnensis* (Mount Etna broom) forms a large but delicate mass around which smaller shrubs such as cistus (rock or sun roses) can be grouped.

Plants for Sun
Planting plan

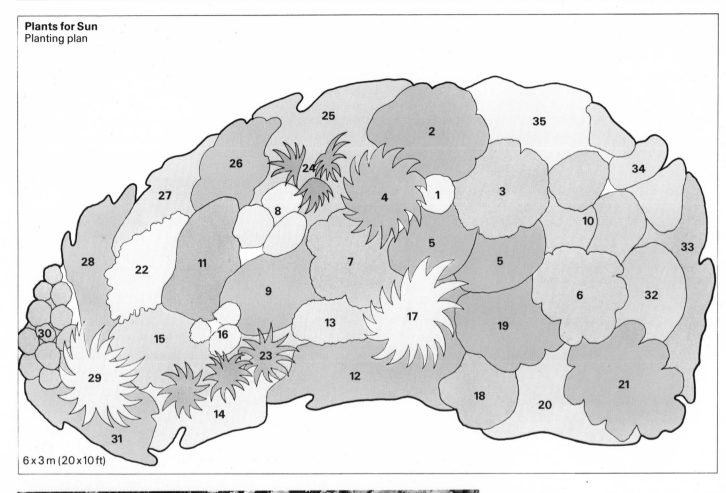

6 x 3 m (20 x 10 ft)

Ballota, blue rue, salvias and santolinas grow wild in countries bordering the Mediterranean. Their beautiful foliage is specially adapted to drought conditions, being either silky with soft hairs, felted with white 'wool', or wax-coated blue.

Other plants, like sedum and sempervivum (houseleek), have thick, fleshy leaves that are themselves built-in water storage units. Others still, such as cistus, lavender and thyme, contain aromatic oils that preserve the leaves from excessive dryness. Planted round the house, their perfume fills the air on still summer evenings. And all these plants remain in winter, covering the bare soil and maintaining a picture.

This picture becomes the background in summer to many vivid flowering plants that flourish in full sun. Euphorbias (spurges), with their acid yellow-greens; helianthemums (rock roses) making cushions of pink, apricot and yellow; saponaria and mat-forming phlox, both buried beneath their carpets of flowers – all these do well in open, sunny sites with the minimum of assistance. And when they have finished flowering, they will still contribute to the colour and design of the garden with their permanent foliage.

To keep this type of gardening controlled and fresh it is important to tidy up

Striking, woolly-textured foliage of Ballota pseudodictamnus *(above) is specially adapted to drought conditions*
Flower spikes of Salvia × superba *(below left) are much admired in late summer*
Eriophyllum lanatum *(right) makes useful ground cover for sun-parched soil*

and prune the plants once a year. A cutback, usually after flowering, will induce new growth that quickly covers bare stems, and makes a tidy cushion for the rest of the year. For other plants, among them ballota and blue rue, a trim in mid spring (March) will prevent an open, sprawling heap.

Extra colour from spring to autumn can be provided by bulbs. Iris and tulips are ideal, while crocus look delightful in flower though their long, grassy leaves can be a nuisance among smaller plants, smothering some of the mats, and so letting in weeds later in the year.

In the following list, numbers preceding plant names correspond with those on the accompanying planting plan.

1 *Genista aetnensis* (Mount Etna broom) forms a dainty tree up to 4½m (15 ft) tall, casting little shade, its dainty, leafless branches smothered in scented, golden yellow, pea-like flowers in mid summer (June).

2 *Cistus* × *corbariensis* has crinkled, leathery green leaves, bronze-tinted in winter, and pink buds that open to small white flowers in mid summer (June). It grows to a height of 45–75cm (18–30 in).

3 *Senecio laxifolius* is an excellent background shrub, with grey, white-backed leaves and sprays of pretty, silvery buds

that open to yellow daisies during mid and late summer (June and July). It needs to be pruned after it has flowered if plenty of young growth is to be ensured. Height is 1·2–1·8m (4–6 ft).

4 *Euphorbia (venata) wulfenii* makes a magnificent feature all the year round, and is made up of many strong stems clothed cylindrically with narrow, blue-grey foliage. The huge heads of lime-green flowers light up the garden for months from mid spring to mid summer (March to June). An established plant can be 1·2 × 1·2m (4 × 4 ft).

5 *Ruta graveolens* Jackman's Blue (rue) makes mounds of blue, filigree foliage 60–90cm (2–3 ft) high, and has yellow flowers from mid summer to early autumn (June to August). Prune it in mid spring (March) to keep it tidy.

6 *Salvia officinalis* Purpurascens (purple-leaved sage) has soft, greyish purple, velvet foliage when young, and spikes of blue flowers in summer. It can form a lax bush 1·2m (4 ft) across, and should be pruned in spring.

7 *Salvia officinalis* Icterina (golden sage) is a coloured form of cooking sage, and comes in shades of primrose, gold and sage-green. It flowers in summer and grows about 60cm (2 ft) tall.

8 *Salvia haematodes* is a tall-stemmed,

handsome-flowered sage that adds height and a soft lilac-blue colour to the garden. It flowers in early summer (May) and reaches a height of 1·2m (4 ft).

9 *Salvia* × *superba* (*S. virgata* Nemorosa) is shorter than *S. haematodes* and valued in late summer (July) for its stiff spikes of intense violet-purple flowers with crimson bracts. It reaches a height of some 60–90cm (2–3 ft).

10 *Eryngium tripartitum* is one of several sea hollies that could be used. Its graceful, branching stems are topped with metallic-blue flowers in summer. Height is about 90cm (3 ft).

11 *Achillea taygetea* Moonshine makes good clumps of silvery grey foliage, resembling soft plumes. 90cm (3 ft) branching stems carry many flat heads of clear yellow flowers in mid and late summer (June and July), and again in autumn.

12 *Geranium grandiflorum* Alpinum forms dense mats of pretty, finely-cut leaves that are covered with cupped, violet-blue flowers in mid summer (June). Grows to approximately 23cm (9 in).

13 *Othonnopsis cheiriifolia* has lax stems carrying paddle-shaped, blue-grey leaves of a waxy texture, that are topped in early summer (May) with fresh yellow daisies. Height is about 30cm (12 in).

light a sunny border for six months. It dies down in winter, to reappear in the following spring. Blue flowers appear in early and mid summer (May and June). Grows to approximately 60cm (2 ft).

25 *Phuopsis stylosa* has refreshingly green, ferny foliage that makes a spreading carpet. The flowers look like pink pin cushions stuck with pink pins. Height is about 15cm (6 in).

26 *Hebe* Carl Teschner forms low mounds of small, shiny, evergreen leaves on purple stems smothered with purple-blue flowers in mid and late summer (June and July). Height is around 23cm (9 in).

27 *Saponaria ocymoides* (rock soapwort) is a vigorous trailer completely smothered in bright pink, campion-like flowers between early and mid summer (May and June). Grows to approximately 15cm (6 in).

28 *Cerastium columnae* has irresistible white foliage that makes foraging mats covered with white-cupped flowers in early summer (May). Reaches only about 10cm (4 in) high.

29 *Artemisia purshiana* runs about sending up tall stems covered with grey, mealy, willow-like leaves, topped with spires of small, pale, mimosa-like yellow blossoms in autumn. It dries well. Grows up to 90–120cm (3–4 ft) high.

30 *Arabis albida* Flore Pleno forms spreading mats of green rosettes from which stand 25cm (10 in) stems clothed in clotted-cream double flowers resembling tiny stocks in early summer (May).

31 *Stachys lanata* Silver Carpet (lamb's tongue) makes unbeatable ground cover in full sun, creeping stems carrying silky silver foliage. This variety rarely flowers, so the neat effect is long lasting. Has a height of 30–45cm (12–18 in).

32 *Sedum maximum* (ice plant) has green, fleshy foliage touched with bronze. From mid to late autumn (September to the end of October) it sends up 45cm (18 in) stems of lime-green flowers with bronze buds.

33 *Thymus* Doone Valley (thyme) is exceptionally attractive, with close mats of dark green foliage heavily marked with gold, and large heads of mauve flowers in late summer (July). It has a lemon scent and a height of about 8cm (3 in).

34 *Helianthemum nummularium* Wisley Primrose (rock rose) has mounds of silvery grey leaves and large flowers of primrose yellow in summer. Reaches around 15–30cm (6–12 in) in height.

35 *Eriophyllum lanatum* never fails in sun-scorched ground, and quickly makes large patches of silvery white, finely-divided leaves. In summer there is a show of orange-yellow daisies. Height is approximately 15cm (6 in).

14 *Oenothera (macrocarpa) missouriensis* has large, yellow flowers that smother the foliage, and lax, sprawling red stems for weeks between summer and early autumn (June and August). Reaches a height of around 23cm (9 in).

15 *Ballota pseudodictamnus* is another superb foliage plant. From a woody base spring long, curving stems of round leaves, whitened in summer with 'felt'. Curious, white, purple-spotted flower bobbles appear in late summer (July), and these dry well. Grows to 60cm (2 ft).

16 *Verbascum chaixii* has 60cm (2 ft) stems that are tightly packed with yellow or white flowers, each of which has a mauve eye. Its upright form makes it useful as a contrast with the mound shape of other plants.

17 *Kniphofia galpinii* Slim Coral Red has fine, grassy foliage, and slender spikes of a deep coral red. Height is about 90cm (3 ft).

As an alternative to Slim Coral Red there is *K. galpinii* Little Maid, with dainty foliage and delicate ivory and green spikes. It flowers for about eight weeks, from mid to late autumn (September to October), and is ideal for the edge of the border, growing to a height of about 75cm (2½ ft).

18 *Helianthemum nummularium* Wisley Pink has soft pink flowers over silvery-grey mounds during mid summer (June), and grows 15–30cm (6–12 in) tall.

19 *Santolina virens* forms a neat, round bush of vivid green, aromatic foliage,

Mat-forming Phlox subulata *Benita is at home in rock garden and border alike*

making it a good contrast among silver-foliaged plants. Its yellow, button-like flowers appear in late summer (July). About 45–60cm (18–24 in) tall.

20 *Phlox subulata* Benita is one of many valuable carpeting phlox, with flowers of a pale lavender-blue with a dark eye in early summer (May). Height is only about 10–15cm (4–6 in).

21 *Bergenia cordifolia purpurea*, with its rosettes of large, green, wavy-edged leaves, that become burnished a purplish-red in winter, contrasts well with many small- or cut-leaved, drought-resisting plants grouped together. There are flowers of a bright magenta in early and mid summer (May and June). Height is approximately 30cm (12 in).

22 *Eryngium maritimum* (sea holly) is an English native from coastal sand dunes. It has beautiful, waxy, blue-grey leaves, and blue flower-heads and stems between late summer and mid autumn (July and September). The flowers dry well. Reaches a height of around 60cm (2 ft).

23 *Euphorbia niciciana* is a superb plant, in bloom for three months between mid summer and mid autumn (June and September) with brilliant lime-green flower-heads on 45cm (18 in) stems. Narrow, blue-grey leaves in winter.

24 *Iris pallida* Variegata, with boldly-striped, green-and-white leaves, will high-

PLANTS FOR SHADE

Shady areas in the garden can vary enormously: some are favourable to growth, others next to impossible. For example, a woodland garden with plenty of good leaf mould and in an area of ample rainfall is worlds away from the poor, dry conditions to be found at the base of a privet hedge, or beneath the shade of an immense horse chestnut tree. Here we describe a selection of plants that could be grown beneath a north- or east-facing wall, in a garden that doesn't get too much rain.

The shady area on the north- or east-facing side of a house or garden wall can be dry unless the soil is very good and there is adequate rainfall. You will probably need to add extra humus before planting, and also old muck, well-rotted garden refuse, old turfs, and well-wetted peat with a little bonemeal – any or all of which will help plants to grow well and cover the soil quickly.

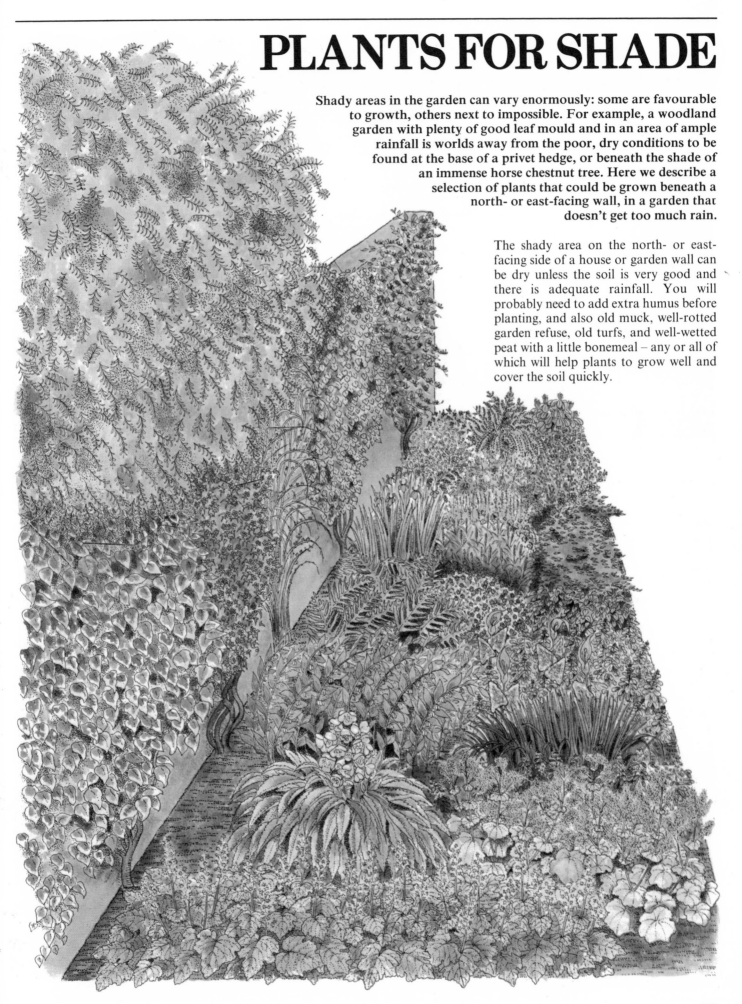

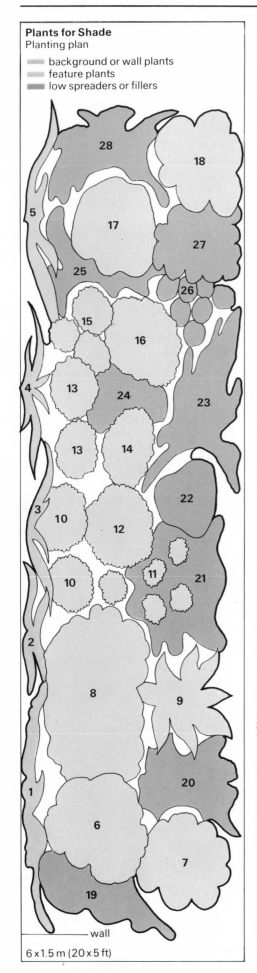

Plants for Shade
Planting plan

background or wall plants
feature plants
low spreaders or fillers

28
18
5
17
27
25
26
15
16
13
24
23
13
14
22
3
10
12
10
11
21
2
8
9
20
1
6
7
19

— wall

6 x 1.5 m (20 x 5 ft)

Above: decorative, ivory-veined leaves of
Arum italicum marmoratum
Above left: attractive, soft-leaved hop
Humulus lupulus *Aureus*
Left: seeds of Iris foetidissima *make an*
eye-catching display in autumn

It is pointless trying to grow conventional flowering plants like pelargonium or petunia in a shady border. However, if you begin to consider plants that have interesting foliage, many of which provide colour and interest for the greater part of the year, then such a border can become a most attractive part of the garden. A thick covering of peat or crushed bark put down after planting is completed is an added attraction that has the practical value of suppressing weeds and conserving moisture.

Provided the rainfall in your garden is reasonable, you could include hemerocallis (day lily), hosta (plantain lily), *Humulus lupulus* Aureus (golden hop), pulmonaria (lungwort) and tradescantia, in addition to the plants shown on our planting plan. Ornamental grasses can be grown for a change of texture and colour – among them *Milium effusum aureum* (Bowles' golden grass), that provides vivid bunches of pale golden ribbons in spring, and *Holcus mollis* Albovariegatus, that makes low carpets more white than green in autumn, and has new growth of running tuffets striped green and white.

Dry shade at the base of a hedge is not easy to contend with. Whenever possible, have a path alongside the hedge so that the border is at least a little way from the dense root system. If that is not possible, then you must do everything you can to enrich the soil before planting. In a narrow border composed mostly of ground coverers, try some of the following: *Euphorbia cyparissias* (cypress spurge), *E. robbiae*, *Hedera helix* (ivy) varieties, *Lamium maculatum* (spotted dead nettle), *Vinca minor* (lesser periwinkle) and *Viola labradorica*, with *Iris foetidissima* for contrast.

At the Royal Botanic Gardens, Kew, there are some enormous old trees underplanted with great circles of *Hedera hibernica* (Irish ivy), with its very large, dark green leaves – they look splendid. In fact, all hedera make good ground cover. A mixture of several coloured varieties of *H. helix* could look attractive under smaller trees. Cyclamen, too, thrive under trees where little else will flourish, and there is a very useful kind of bramble called *Rubus tricolor* that, when estab-

lished, sends out long, prostrate stems up to 3m (10 ft) long, furred with soft, reddish hairs, and closely set with beautiful, polished green leaves that are bronze-bordered in autumn. It will form a complete, weed-proof cover under trees.

Many spring bulbs enjoy a shady border. Eranthis (winter aconite), galanthus (snowdrop), *Hepatica triloba* (or *Anemone hepatica*), *A. blanda* and the species daffodils will all help to make this a favourite part of the garden.

The following selection will stand shade and a certain amount of drought, provided some humus is added to the soil. Lush conditions are not necessary – the plants will thrive along a north- or east-facing wall, or among small trees and shrubs. The background climbers could be on a wall, or trained over ugly stumps.

Plants are numbered as they appear on the planting plan.

Climbers

1 *Hedera canariensis* Variegata (variegated ivy) has large, grey-green leaves marbled with white, and pink-tinted in winter. It is not good in draughty places, but is quite hardy on a wall, and looks splendid draped over a stump.
2 *Clematis montana* Rubens is a glorious sight in early summer (May), smothered in deep pink flowers and purplish-tinted foliage.
3 *Jasminum nudiflorum* (winter-flowering jasmine) has bright yellow flowers for weeks in mid winter (December). The buds are undamaged by frost, but the plant needs regular pruning to keep it tidy and encourage long sprays of flowers.
4 *Hedera helix* Cristata has long sprays of pelargonium-shaped leaves that are heavily crimped at the edges. It is a very attractive plant, especially in autumn, when young, pale green leaves contrast with dark, mature ones.
5 *Lonicera periclymenum* Serotina (late Dutch honeysuckle) is sweetly scented and flowers well into autumn, setting trusses of currant-like red berries.

'Feature' plants

6 *Helleborus corsicus* (Corsican hellebore) has magnificent, jade-green foliage and stiff stems 90cm (3 ft) tall, that are topped with large clusters of pale, apple-green cups from late winter to mid summer (January to June). It will cover an area of approximately 1 sq m (3 × 3 ft).
7 *Alchemilla mollis* (lady's mantle) sprays out long stems of frothing, lime-green, starry flowers from a mound of velvety, rounded leaves in mid summer (June). It is invaluable for flower arrangers, and grows to a height of 60cm (24 in).

8 *Polygonatum multiflorum* (Solomon's seal) spreads slowly by underground rhizomes, and sends up arching stems 90cm (3 ft) long, set with pairs of dark green leaves. In early summer (May) white-and-green-flushed bells hang beneath the leaves.

9 *Hosta lancifolia* is not used as much as the variegated varieties, but is a very attractive and useful plant. Narrow, shining, dark green leaves form tidy mounds above which stand tall stems of dark lilac bells for weeks in autumn (August to October). It grows 45cm (18 in) tall.

10 *Dryopteris filix-mas* (male fern) survives in dry shade and is very useful. It reaches a height of 75cm (2½ ft).

11 *Arum italicum marmoratum* is a superb foliage plant with new leaves that begin to unroll from leaf-mouldy soil in late autumn (October), and continue to grow throughout the winter undamaged by bitter frost. By late spring (April) the elegant, spear-shaped leaves are poised on 45cm (18 in) stems of a dark glossy green, marvellously veined in ivory.

12 *Hypericum* × *moserianum* Tricolor is a slow-growing little bush prettily variegated in white, pink and green. It reaches a height of about 75cm (2½ ft).

13 *Iris foetidissima* is a splendid evergreen with strong, shining clumps of fresh green foliage that are invaluable as a feature for flower arranging. The small flowers are a soft ochre-yellow, and followed in autumn by great, bursting seed pods packed with vivid orange seeds. The height is 75cm (2½ ft).

14 *Liriope muscari* forms clumps of narrow, dark evergreen leaves that last the year round. The long spikes of curious violet-blue flowers on violet stems are a feature for weeks in autumn.

15 *Thalictrum aquilegiifolium* (meadow rue) is graceful and very compact. Its 1·2m (4 ft) purplish stems rise up from a base of delicate sprays of leaves, and are topped with large heads of fluffy lilac flowers in mid summer (June). The seedheads are attractive either green or dried.

16 *Valeriana phu* Aurea is an unusual plant that matures green but is topped with tall stems of small white flowers in mid summer (June). Its new spring foliage is a clear yellow, rivalling daffodils.

17 *Lonicera nitida* Baggessen's Gold is a bright golden variety of the familiar hedging honeysuckle that forms a beautiful specimen shrub and makes a delicate filigree accent among darker greens. It covers an area of around 1 sq m (3 × 3 ft).

18 *Bergenia cordifolia* Purpurea is not widely loved, although – with large, round, wavy-edged leaves that become

Bright spring flowers of Waldsteinia ternata *contrast with evergreen foliage*

burnished a purplish red with winter frost – it makes superb contrast to other plants in the border. In early summer (May) tall, rhubarb-red stalks carry vivid magenta flowers and reach about 45cm (18 in).

Ground cover

19 *Tiarella cordifolia* (foam flower) has running trails of pointed green leaves that make total cover. In spring, there is a mass of foaming, creamy-white flower spikes. Height about 23–30cm (9–12 in).

20 *Ajuga reptans* Atropurpurea (bugle) spreads rapidly with rosettes of very dark, chocolate-purplish brown, shining leaves.

21 *A. r.* Burgundy Glow has unusually beautiful foliage suffused rose, magenta and cream. Its 15cm (6 in) spikes of blue flowers provide strong contrast in spring, and often again in autumn.

22 *Epimedium* × *versicolor* Sulphureum (barrenwort) has heart-shaped leaves on wiry stems. The leaves are delicate shades of copper in early spring (February), turning to green for all of the summer, and becoming bronzed by the winter cold. Sprays of tiny yellow, columbine-like flowers appear in mid spring (March).

23 *Hedera helix* Manda's Crested (ivy) quickly makes excellent ground cover of very attractive, curling foliage. The pale, copper-tinted, new autumn leaves contrast with the mature summer foliage.

24 *Tellima grandiflora* Purpurea is an all-year-round foliage plant with spreading clumps of round, scalloped leaves that become bronze-tinted in winter, and are a rich carmine-red beneath. The stems of tiny green, pink-fringed bells are pretty in spring. The plant grows to a height of approximately 60cm (24 in).

25 *Viola labradorica* makes a creeping mass of small, dark purple leaves that set off quantities of lighter-coloured, scentless flowers. Height is around 10cm (4 in).

26 *Saxifraga umbrosa* Variegata (variegated London pride) makes excellent ground cover, its richly-mottled, gold and green rosettes being a feature all year. Pink flowers appear in early and mid summer (May and June), and the plant grows to a height of approximately 23cm (9 in).

27 *Waldsteinia ternata* is a useful carpeter, with spreading, dark-lobed leaves, evergreen and glossy, that contrast with bright yellow flowers in late spring and early summer (April and May).

28 *Vinca minor* Bowles' Variety is the best of all periwinkles, making close mats of small, dark green leaves, that in spring are lost beneath quantities of large blue flowers. It grows about 15cm (6 in) tall.

PLANTS FOR DAMP

A damp garden must remain moist for much of the growing season, for plants that don't flower until late autumn or early winter (October or November) – such as tricyrtis (toad lily) – will not put up with drought in late summer (July). As the soil will inevitably be heavy, probably like plasticine, it is vital that you do something to make life easier for both the plants and yourself before planting. A layer of mixed sand, peat, compost, well-rotted manure and leaf mould – as many of these as you can obtain – piled on top of the soil or lightly forked in, will help plants to establish quickly, before their roots penetrate the clay. Remember that weeds never stop growing in damp soil, so you must plant strong growers to cope with native competition.

When planting is done, a 5cm (2 in) layer of peat or crushed bark is much more than a luxury – it really will prevent that rash of germinating weed seeds that otherwise seem to appear overnight. Any knob of soil left exposed will grow a mat of water weed 90cm (3 ft) across, smothering your fine primulas in no time.

Where there is room, salix (willow) and cornus (dogwood) make a splendid effect planted *en masse*, while taxodium and metasequoia (dawn redwood or water fir) are both dramatic feature plants. For a small area where trees and shrubs would be unsuitable, phormiums are ideal, with their great sheaves of blade-like, evergreen leaves.

Blessed are those people who have a bit of ill-drained soil, especially if it is spring-fed. Soggy land is a haven for bog-loving plants, and with a little digging and damming a small – or large – pond can be created that will transform the site immediately.

Heavy, low-lying soil, with plenty of humus added – and possibly a little shade – can also provide a home for many lovely plants that prefer cool, damp conditions, and we describe some of these here.

Most plants suited to damp soil disappear in winter, so those few that do remain are very useful – without them, a bog garden in winter would be nothing but a patch of mud with a few withered remains. *Phormium tenax* (New Zealand flax) and its dwarf counterpart *P. colensoi* add form to the winter landscape, and there are several sedges that last. *Carex morrowii* Variegata provides welcome colour with its tuffets of brilliant gold leaves edged with a narrow green band, while *Luzula maxima* Marginata, another rushy plant, also keeps its dark green clumps. Try to have a few bergenias (pig squeak) nearby – but not too close to the water's edge, as they do not like bog conditions.

Polygonum affine (knotweed) makes a warm carpet of foxy brown foliage in its winter state, while the ajugas (bugle) provide colour unless the weather is exceptionally hard. Gunneras thrive magnificently in damp soil if there is room, but peltiphyllum (umbrella plant) would suit a smaller site, provided it is not allowed to spread its rhizomes too far. Rapid colonizers like myosotis (forget-me-not), *Lysimachia nummularia* (creeping Jenny), and the many forms of mimulus (musk) will run around the main feature plants and in only one season produce a lush effect.

Astilbe (false goat's beard), *Euphorbia palustris* (fen or bog spurge), ligularia and trollius (globe flower) will all grow without a pond present, but there must be ample moisture throughout the season.

Conditions around a pool are ideal for bog-loving plants and others liking cool, damp soil

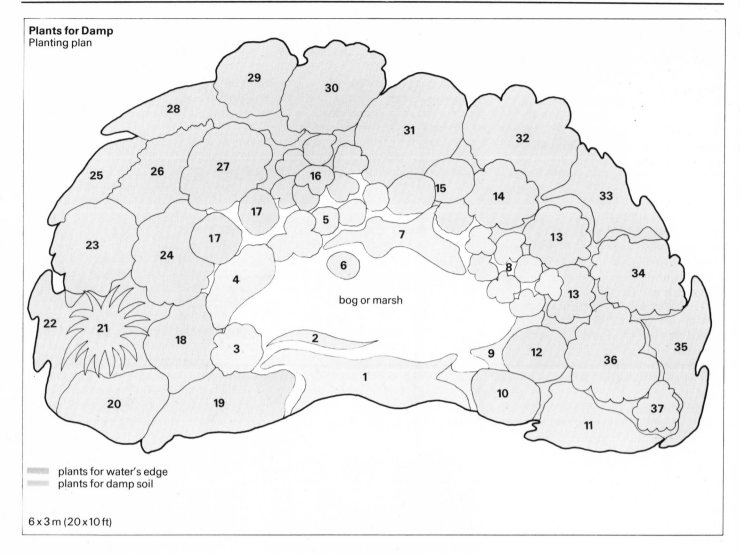

Plants for Damp
Planting plan

bog or marsh

plants for water's edge
plants for damp soil

6 x 3 m (20 x 10 ft)

Partial shade will sometimes retain the necessary coolness, but in dense shade the plants will be spindly and will probably not flower at all.

For damp woodland conditions there is a host of lovely things to grow, among them rhododendrons and other moist mountain shrubs. Some can be raised successfully in small gardens, but the controlling factor is always moisture. Being willing to cart the odd can of water is not enough. Among flowering plants that like partial shade and will thrive where there is enough rainfall are actaea, astrantia (masterwort), hardy geraniums (cranesbill), hosta (plantain lily), meconopsis and primula. Interesting foliage plants include *Filipendula ulmaria* Aurea, *Scrophularia nodosa* Variegata (variegated figwort) and rodgersia.

Many ferns add delicacy and charm to woodland plantings, *Polystichum setiferum* Acutilobum and *Matteuccia struthiopteris* for example, while by the waterside, *Osmunda regalis* (flowering royal fern) dies down in a glory of autumn shades.

The planting plan shows the different zones of planting around a pond or boggy area. Numbers preceding plant names in the following selection correspond with those on the plan.

The water's edge
Conveniently, some plants enjoy water-logged soil, and would not survive in dry conditions: these are the ones to put round the edge of a natural pond where they will push out into shallow water.

1 *Mimulus* Wisley Red spreads quickly, and has beautiful, ruby-red flowers that appear in mid summer (June). Height is about 30cm (12 in).

2 *Calla palustris* (bog arum) sends out long shoots that root into wet mud. Tiny, arum-like white flowers appear in spring, and the plant reaches a height of around 30cm (12 in).

3 *Mimulus ringens* (lavender water musk) is an unusual musk with branching stems of approximately 75cm (2½ ft) and, in summer, lilac flowers that last for weeks.

4 *Caltha palustris* Plena is the double-flowered form of *C. palustris*, and grows about 38cm (15 in) tall.

5 *Primula bulleyana* comes in shades of

orange, and is one of several possible bog primulas. Height is around 75cm (2½ ft).

6 *Scirpus palustris* Zebrinus is *the* striped rush, green and white in colour, and makes a handsome feature in water, but it needs plenty of room. Height is approximately 105cm (3½ ft).

7 *Myosotis palustris* (water forget-me-not) makes sheets of blue along the pond edge, flowering in early and mid summer (May and June). Height is about 15–30cm (6–12 in).

8 *Peltiphyllum peltatum* (umbrella plant) is a splendid feature plant, with each leaf resembling a scalloped parasol 30cm (12 in) across. The plant reaches a height of around 75cm (2½ ft).

9 *Lysimachia nummularia* Aurea (golden creeping Jenny) makes a bright carpet beneath water iris, flowering in the summer.

Damp soil
The following selection of plants prefer soil that is better drained than that by the water's edge, but which still has plenty of moisture and humus.

10 *Molinia caerulea* Variegata is one of

the loveliest grasses, with dainty tuffets variegated green and white. It grows to a height of approximately 45cm (18 in).

11 *Astilbe chinensis* Pumila pushes out spreading clumps of weed-smothering foliage, and slender spikes of rose-lilac flowers. Height is about 30cm (12 in).

12 *Iris laevigata* comes in several colour forms, and does not mind being in water. Height is around 60cm (2 ft).

13 Astilbe hybrids have beautiful foliage and feathery flower-heads in all shades from white to red in summer. Plants grow 30–90cm (1–3 ft) high.

14 *Lobelia cardinalis* Queen Victoria has chocolate-coloured leaves, and stems 75cm (2½ ft) long, that carry vivid scarlet flowers during mid and late autumn (September and October).

15 *Trollius europaeus* (globe flower) grows wild in wet mountain meadows. Bowl-shaped flowers of pale gold appear in early and mid summer (May and June). Height is approximately 75cm (2½ ft).

16 *Ligularia clivorum* Desdemona is a giant groundsel with large, heart-shaped, purple-bronze leaves, and orange-rayed daisies in early and mid autumn (August and September). It reaches a height of about 90cm (3 ft).

17 *Matteuccia struthiopteris* (ostrich feather fern) forms a perfect shuttlecock of lacy, pale green fern fronds.

18 *Scrophularia nodosa* Variegata (variegated figwort) has richly marbled leaves of cream and green, and grows to a height of around 90cm (3 ft).

19 *Astilbe simplicifolia* Sprite is charming: dark green, ferny foliage sends up wide sprays of shell-pink flowers in mid summer (June). Height is 25cm (10 in).

20 *Carex morrowii* Variegata is another foliage plant that is effective as a feature, especially in winter, radiating tuffets of narrow, gold-and-green leaves. Height is approximately 40cm (16 in).

21 *Phormium colensoi* (dwarf New Zealand flax) does not grow too large, and is useful for smaller pond sites. It flowers in summer and reaches a height of 90–120cm (3–4 ft).

22 *Prunella webbiana* Pink Loveliness is the raspberry-pink form of 'self heal', and makes a vivid carpet of colour between mid summer and mid autumn (June and September). It is good ground cover, and grows to a height of around 23cm (9 in).

23 *Campanula lactiflora* (milky bell-flower) makes a great show in rich soil, with milky blue, bell-shaped flowers in summer on 1.5m (5 ft) stems.

24 *Euphorbia palustris* (fen or bog spurge) grows into a large plant, 1.2 × 1.2m (4 × 4 ft), and is spectacular all summer with great heads of gold-green flowers.

Caltha palustris *Plena (above) grows in water of up to 15cm (6in) in depth, but does better with the crown submerged.* Calla palustris *(below) has exquisite spring flowers*

Top: Iris Laevigata *Atropurpurea. Above (left): inner, fertile fronds of* Matteuccia struthiopteris. *Above (right):* Gentiana asclepiadea, *a good choice for shade*

25 *Veronica gentianoides*, with its spreading rosettes of glossy green leaves, makes good ground cover. The 30cm (12 in) spikes of ice-blue flowers in early summer (May) are a bonus.

26 *Physostegia virginiana* Summer Spire provides colour in early and mid autumn (August and September) with rich lilac, trumpet-shaped flowers in spires. Height is about 38cm (15 in).

27 *Filipendula palmata* Elegans is a first-class meadow sweet with deep rose flowers throughout the summer, followed by showy, bronze-red seed-heads. It grows to a height of some 90cm (3 ft).

28 *Viola cornuta* has moundy mats of small, blue and white flowers all summer, and again in the autumn. Height is around 15cm (6 in).

29 *Gentiana asclepiadea* (willow gentian) has arching, 38cm (15 in) stems, wreathed in blue trumpet flowers in mid autumn (September).

30 *Eupatorium purpureum* has 1.8m (6 ft) purple stems carrying flat-domed heads of fluffy, cinnamon-pink flowers in mid autumn (September).

31 *Miscanthus sinensis* Zebrinus is a zebra-striped grass making good contrast in form. It can develop to a height of more than 1.5m (5 ft).

32 *Hosta sieboldiana* has crisp, robust, bluish grey leaves, heavily wrinkled and veined, that make a huge, overlapping mound. It is a spectacular feature when well grown, and reaches a height of 60–90cm (2–3 ft).

33 *Ajuga reptans* Burgundy Glow makes a vivid carpet all winter, with foliage suffused rose and magenta, and edged with cream. During summer, too, it is an eye-catching sight, with 15cm (6 in) spikes of blue flowers.

34 *Tricyrtis stolonifera* (toad lily) makes spreading clumps of 60–90cm (2–3 ft) stems topped, in late autumn (September), with small, white, lily-like flowers, so heavily spotted with purple that they appear lilac.

35 *Mentha rotundifolia* Variegata (apple mint) has green, woolly leaves heavily splashed with white, and – in summer – purplish white, flowers. Height is about 90cm (3 ft).

36 *Hosta fortunei* Albopicta has lilac flowers in late summer and early autumn (July and August), and large leaves magnificently marbled in shades of bright yellow, primrose, soft green and olive. It grows to approximately 45cm (18 in) in height.

37 *Geum* Lionel Cox forms clumps of soft green foliage with summer sprays of nodding cream cups, touched with apricot. Height is around 30cm (12 in).

BIBLIOGRAPHY

Beazley, Elizabeth *Design and detail of the space between buildings* (Architectural Press, London 1960)

Bloom, Alan *Perennials for trouble free gardening* (Faber & Faber, London 1960)

Brookes, John *Room Outside* (Thames and Hudson, London 1969)

Fox, Robin Lane *Variations on a garden* (Macmillan, London 1974)

Millar, S. Gault *The Dictionary of Plants in colour* (Michael Joseph, London 1976)

Hay, Roy and Synge, Patrick M. *The Dictionary of Shrubs in Colour* (Michael Joseph, London 1969)

Hellyer, A. G. L. *Shrubs in Colour* (Collingridge, Feltham 1965)

Hilliers manual of Trees and Shrubs (David and Charles, Newton Abbot 1972)

Huxley, A. (ed) *Financial Times Book of Garden Design* (David and Charles, Newton Abbot 1975)

Thomas, Graham Stuart *Plants for Ground Cover* (Dent, London 1971)

The Easy Path to Gardening (gardening for the disabled) (Readers Digest, 1972)

The Gardening Year (Readers Digest, 1968)

INDEX